If you want to automate your SharePoint 2010 environment, this book is for you.
—*Dr. Tobias Weltner, MVP PowerShell and PowerShellPlus Software Architect*

This book is a must for all SharePoint administrators!
—*Göran Husman, SharePoint MVP and author*

PowerShell should be at the top of every SharePoint IT pro and developer toolbox.
—*Jeremy Thake, SharePoint Server MVP*

A must-read, task-based guide to using PowerShell for SharePoint administration.
—*Ravikanth Chaganti, MVP PowerShell*

About the Authors

Niklas Goude is a technical consultant for Enfo Zipper in Sweden, who works with infrastructure and migration projects. Niklas specializes in the Microsoft environment, focusing on Active Directory, SQL Server, and SharePoint products and technologies. Most of his daily work is performed using Windows PowerShell. He is also a trainer, teaching Microsoft courses focused on Windows PowerShell, and has been a speaker at various conferences such as Microsoft Tech Days, SharePoint & Exchange Forum, and SharePoint conferences in Australia and New Zealand.

Niklas is active in the PowerShell community, acting as a moderator for Scripting Guy's official forum and an expert at SecretsOfSharePoint.com. He has also written an e-book about the fundamentals of Windows PowerShell (in Swedish), which can be downloaded for free from www.powershell.se. Niklas contributes to the PowerShell community by sharing scripts, guides, and ideas through his blog at www.powershell .nu. In 2010, Microsoft recognized Niklas for his technical knowledge and community activities by acknowledging him as a Microsoft Most Valued Professional (MVP).

Niklas lives in Stockholm, Sweden with his wife Anna, his collection of guitars, and a lot of computers.

Mattias Karlsson is a senior consultant for Enfo Zipper in Sweden. Mattias has a long history of working with SharePoint products and technologies, focusing mainly on solution architecting, implementation, administration, and configuration of SharePoint environments in midsize to large enterprise companies.

Mattias is active in the SharePoint community. He contributes his experience, lessons learned, and thoughts on SharePoint via his popular blog at www.mysharepointofview .com. He is also a moderator and expert in residence at SecretsOfSharePoint.com and has contributed to CodePlex projects. He is a frequent trainer and speaker at both national and international SharePoint events, and helps organize the Swedish usergroup meetings in Gothenburg.

Mattias lives in Gothenburg, Sweden together with his girlfriend Caroline, enjoys football, and is slightly addicted to *Seinfeld*.

About the Technical Editor

Sergey Zelenov is a Premier Field Engineer working for Microsoft in the United Kingdom. Most of the ten years of his IT career—which has spanned countries, as well as companies and roles—has been spent working with the Microsoft SharePoint products and technologies, beginning from the early days of SharePoint Team Services 1.0, back in 2001. Sergey is also an avid scripter. He started with Windows Scripting Host, VBScript, and Perl, and has recently developed a true addiction to Windows PowerShell. He uses Windows PowerShell on almost a daily basis to help Microsoft customers meet various challenges in their SharePoint environments. To share his exciting findings in the Windows PowerShell land with the wider world, Sergey contributes to the From The Field blog (http://sharepoint.microsoft.com/Blogs/fromthefield), the SharePoint Management PowerShell Scripts project on CodePlex (http://sharepointpsscripts .codeplex.com/), and the Microsoft TechNet Script Center.

Sergey lives in London with his wife and 2-year-old son.

PowerShell for Microsoft® SharePoint® 2010 Administrators

NIKLAS **GOUDE** AND MATTIAS **KARLSSON**

New York   Chicago   San Francisco
Lisbon   London   Madrid   Mexico City   Milan
New Delhi   San Juan   Seoul   Singapore   Sydney   Toronto

The McGraw·Hill Companies

Cataloging-in-Publication Data is on file with the Library of Congress

McGraw-Hill books are available at special quantity discounts to use as premiums and sales promotions, or for use in corporate training programs. To contact a representative, please e-mail us at bulksales@mcgraw-hill.com.

PowerShell for Microsoft® SharePoint® 2010 Administrators

1234567890   QFR QFR   109876543210

ISBN   978-0-07-174797-4
MHID   0-07-174797-4

Sponsoring Editor Roger Stewart	**Copy Editor** Marilyn Smith	**Illustration** Glyph International
Editorial Supervisor Janet Walden	**Proofreader** Debbie Liehs	**Art Director, Cover** Jeff Weeks
Project Manager Harleen Chopra	**Indexer** Karin Arrigoni	**Cover Designer** Jeff Weeks
Acquisitions Coordinator Joya Anthony	**Production Supervisor** James Kussow	
Technical Editor Sergey Zelenov	**Composition** Glyph International	

At a Glance

v

Contents

Part I
An Introduction to SharePoint 2010

Part II

An Introduction to PowerShell in SharePoint 2010

Part III

SharePoint 2010 and PowerShell: Real-World Solutions

Foreword

Windows SharePoint 2010 is a huge product. Believe it or not, it is also a complicated product. Sure, you can launch startup—click, click, click through the wizard—and come out on the other side with a SharePoint installation, but that is only scratching the surface.

Windows SharePoint is one of the fastest growing products in history, and it is quickly becoming mission-critical for numerous companies around the world. Whereas SharePoint 2007 was a really cool product, with an automation API, its use for automation purposes was a bit complicated for the average SharePoint administrator. This is why Windows PowerShell is included as a management tool for SharePoint 2010.

But guess what? When you attempt to automate a huge and complicated product, the automation tools quickly become unwieldy. Even when leveraging the Windows PowerShell intuitive automation model, and following the Windows PowerShell naming scheme using verbs like get to get things and set to set things, it can still become confusing.

With more than 500 Windows PowerShell cmdlets, administrators and consultants arriving at the steps of Windows SharePoint 2010 automation for the first time need a guide. That guide is *PowerShell for Microsoft SharePoint 2010 Administrators* by Niklas Goude and Mattias Karlsson.

Written in an easy-to-read manner, the book begins with a quick overview of the new features of SharePoint 2010. The major new features are highlighted, and it is an interesting read for someone who may not be familiar with SharePoint 2010. Next, the book provides an introduction to Windows PowerShell in SharePoint 2010. If you are already familiar with Windows PowerShell 2.0, the two chapters on SharePoint 2010 and Windows PowerShell 2.0 will be a quick but helpful read. If you are unfamiliar with Windows PowerShell, the four remaining chapters in this section will be worth careful perusal.

For me, the most exciting part of the book are the real-world solutions. This is where the combined experience of the two authors really shines through. Beginning with a nice chapter on scripted installations, these guys show you how to use the SharePoint 2010 cmdlets to quickly create reproducible and verifiable SharePoint installations. They really pack the detail into the pages. Install the help files, install the services, the features, the configuration database … it is all here in one easy-to-use chapter. This is just the beginning. Working with SharePoint lists, document management, content databases … I won't spoil the plot, but I will tell you the outcome: a well-written, action-packed volume that will quickly become one of your favorite SharePoint 2010 books.

Ed Wilson, MCSE, MCDBA, MCSD, MCT
Microsoft Scripting Guy
Author of *Windows PowerShell 2.0 Best Practices*, Microsoft Press

Acknowledgments

This book has been a tumbling journey with many long days and late nights of writing, and wouldn't have been possible without the help from people all over the world.

First of all, we would like to thank Neil Salkind at Studio B and Göran Husman who introduced us to the world of writing. Thanks to the group of people at McGraw-Hill who believed in our idea, especially Roger Stewart and Joya Anthony for their support and patience. We also want to thank Ed Wilson at Microsoft Scripting Guys for helping us out. Thanks to our colleagues at Enfo Zipper for their help and support, and especially to Erik Brügge for his support and sincere interest in our project. Thanks to Dr. Tobias Weltner, Jeremy Thake, Ravikanth Chaganti, Wictor Wilén, Jason Shirk, and Henrik Parkkinen for their contribution. The SharePoint and PowerShell community also deserves a big thank you for all your articles, blog posts, and twitter messages. You are all brilliant, talented, and helpful people who made the writing so much easier. Keep contributing—you are all heroes!

Finally, we want to give a very special thank you to a person who has worked with us along the way. He has provided us with ideas and recommendations that have improved the content and quality of the book significantly. Thank you, Sergey Zelenov!

I want to thank my wife, Anna Goude, for her love, patience, support, and understanding when I spent most of the nights of our vacation writing. I also want to thank my parents for their love and support, and my family and friends.

–Niklas Goude

I'd like to thank Niklas for not hesitating a second when the idea of writing a book came up. It has been a pleasure working with you, and I have had a lot of fun. Let's do this again sometime.

I also want to thank my family and friends who have stood by me during these six months, and especially my girlfriend Caroline for her tireless support and endless love. This has been so much easier with you by my side.

–Mattias Karlsson

Introduction

Welcome to *PowerShell for Microsoft SharePoint 2010 Administrators*. In SharePoint 2010, the use of Windows PowerShell has become fully integrated and is now providing SharePoint administrators with a revolutionary set of tools that will help automate and control their SharePoint 2010 environment. This book uses a hands-on approach to guide you through the basics of Windows PowerShell and demonstrates how to manage your SharePoint 2010 environment through real-world scenarios.

This book is intended for technicians, administrators, and anyone interested in using Windows PowerShell to automate the administration of SharePoint 2010. The typical reader is an administrator familiar with the concept of scripting; however, you do not need any prior knowledge of Windows PowerShell.

This book is organized into three parts:

Part I: An Introduction to SharePoint 2010 This part introduces the new, cool stuff in SharePoint 2010, not only from an administrator perspective, but from a product and end-user perspective as well. The first chapter gives you a holistic view of the six capability areas of SharePoint 2010 and describes the enhancements made for SharePoint administrators. Chapter 2 covers the different components of SharePoint 2010 to introduce the terminology you'll encounter in the rest of the book.

Part II: An Introduction to PowerShell in SharePoint 2010 This part gives a detailed tour through the Windows PowerShell language, including the syntax and built-in cmdlets. Many of the examples focus on using Windows PowerShell through a SharePoint 2010 administrator's perspective. Chapter 3 introduces Windows PowerShell and covers some of the fundamental features, such as cmdlets, pipelines, and aliases. Chapter 4 covers the SharePoint 2010 cmdlets in detail, showing examples on how to manage web applications, site collections, and more. Chapter 5 introduces variables, arrays, and hashtables. Chapter 6 covers the use of operators. Chapter 7 begins with an introduction of flow control, demonstrating how to perform conditional and looping statements, and also introduces object disposal. Chapter 8 covers the use of functions and scripts and demonstrates how you can use Windows PowerShell remotely.

Part III: SharePoint 2010 with PowerShell: Real-World Solutions   The third part, Chapters 9 to 21, is purposely the majority of this book. Each chapter covers one or more real-world solutions. We not only demonstrate how to solve common problems, but also explain how and why things need to be done in the way demonstrated. You'll find examples that you can relate to and put into your own context. The chapters also outline additional possibilities available using Central Administration, to show where tasks can be done using Central Administration and when Windows PowerShell is needed.

Since this is a book on Windows PowerShell, it includes a lot of code examples and scripts. Commands that are run interactively (as typed by the user) start with PS > followed by a command. Any output produced by a command is displayed after the command line. Here is a typical line of code:

```
PS > Get-SPSite -Identity http://nimaintra.net
Url
---
http://nimaintra.net
```

Some of the code examples span over multiple lines. These commands terminate either with a pipeline or with a backtick (`), which is the line-continuation character in Windows PowerShell. Subsequent lines will be preceded by >>, as shown here:

```
PS > Get-SPSite `
>> -Identity http://nimaintra.net |
>> Select-Object -Property Url
Url
---
http://nimaintra.net
```

Scripts and functions are written without any prefix.

Source code for all functions and scripts can be downloaded from **www.mhprofessional.com/computingdownload**.

In some cases, this book includes links to sites with additional information on a specific topic or sites where you can download tools or software. You can find a complete list of the links used at www.sharepointandpowershell.com.

We would like to keep in touch with the readers and hear your thoughts about this book. If you have any questions or comments, please visit www .sharepointandpowershell.com. There, you can get news, updates, and tips and find out how to contact us and share your feedback. You can also contact Niklas by e-mail at niklas.goude@zipper.se and Mattias at mattias.karlsson@zipper.se.

PART I | An Introduction to SharePoint 2010

CHAPTER 1 | Overview of SharePoint 2010

SharePoint 2010 is the business collaboration platform for the enterprise and the Internet. By offering a rich set of capabilities and enhanced functionality, SharePoint 2010 empowers users to connect, share, and work with information in new and much more efficient ways. For businesses of all types, it provides out-of-the-box solutions and tools to increase end users' productivity through effective collaboration. Tools are also available to streamline and enrich solutions, and to interact with other systems to fulfill extended requirements and meet special needs of a business.

SharePoint 2010 offers scalability and flexibility to enable consolidation of business solutions by integrating them into the SharePoint platform. This decreases maintenance costs and the total cost of ownership (TCO), and at the same time allows administrators and information technology (IT) departments to gain better control over the technical platform and improve manageability.

This chapter provides an overview of SharePoint 2010, outlining its capabilities and architectural components. This will not only set the context for the rest of the book, but also give you a technical understanding of what makes SharePoint 2010 *the* collaboration platform for the enterprise and the Internet.

Capability Areas of SharePoint 2010

SharePoint 2010 is not a single product, but rather a family of products and technologies. SharePoint Foundation 2010 is pretty much what it sounds like—the foundation, or enabling technology of SharePoint 2010. SharePoint Foundation 2010 includes a rich set of web-based collaboration features like document libraries, blogs, wikis, and team workspaces. SharePoint Server 2010 relies on SharePoint Foundation 2010 for its core functionality. SharePoint Server complements SharePoint Foundation with a rich set of features and capabilities, including those fit for full enterprise scenarios (in combination with the Enterprise Client Access License). Some of the features and capabilities described here are available only in SharePoint Server 2010.

SharePoint 2010 can be divided into six capability areas to better describe its versatile nature and its strengths as a platform: Sites, Communities, Content, Search, Insights, and Composites. In the following pages, we will briefly describe each of these six capability areas to give you an understanding of its meaning and what possibilities it offers.

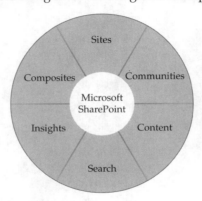

Sites

With SharePoint 2010, the experience when working with sites has been significantly improved compared to earlier versions of SharePoint. It offers support for a wider range of browsers and mobile clients, as well as enhanced integration with Office 2010 desktop applications.

New User Interface

To give a uniform end-user experience, the familiar Office Ribbon, which was introduced in the Microsoft Office 2007 application suite, has been implemented in SharePoint 2010, as shown in Figure 1-1. The contextual Ribbon menu gives you easier and faster access to the actions available in the context in which you are currently working.

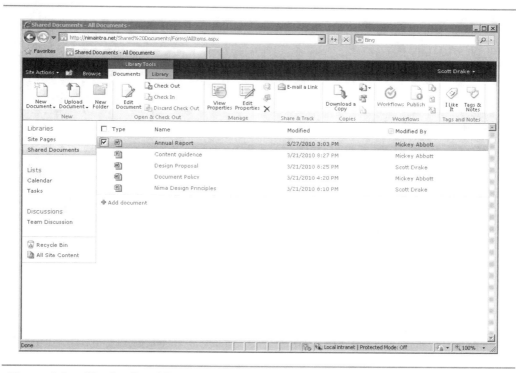

Figure 1-1.   The familiar Office Ribbon user interface in SharePoint 2010

AJAX offers richer navigation and interaction. In-place editing significantly decreases the amount of page reloads that need to be made each time something needs to be updated.

In addition, the multilingual support has been improved. Along with allowing different languages in navigation elements and menus within the same site, fields within SharePoint lists can be configured to use different languages.

Office Web Applications

The Office Web Applications feature enables Microsoft Office Word, PowerPoint, Excel, and OneNote documents to not only be rendered in the browser, but also offers the capability to edit the contents of documents without the locally installed client application. Figure 1-2 shows an example of this feature used with a PowerPoint document.

Figure 1-2. Office Web Applications enabling PowerPoint in the browser

In Microsoft Office SharePoint Server 2007, we had support for Excel and InfoPath through the Excel Calculation Services and Forms Services. In SharePoint 2010, these services have been updated. Visio and Access services are also available as service applications.

SharePoint Workspace 2010

The Microsoft Groove product that was introduced in the Office 2007 suite has been enhanced and renamed to SharePoint Workspace 2010, which is now part of the Microsoft Office 2010 suite. This application enables you to take SharePoint 2010 content offline, including whole sites with custom lists and line-of-business data, as shown in Figure 1-3.

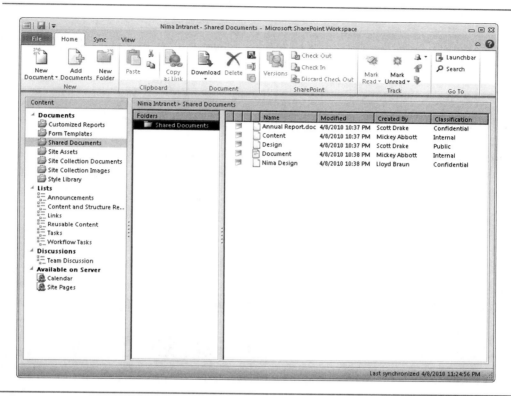

Figure 1-3.   SharePoint Workspace 2010 enabling offline content

Whenever you lose the connection to your SharePoint 2010 site, SharePoint Workspace will start caching any changes you make. As soon as the connection is restored, it uses a new intelligent synchronization mechanism to synchronize only the changes, rather than whole files.

Communities

SharePoint 2010 offers new and enhanced tools and functions to foster collaboration through social networking, making it easy for people to interact both within and across organizational boundaries. The main purpose is to increase productivity by facilitating sharing of information and knowledge. The time to find information and resources is dramatically decreased by the use of these tools.

Social Networking and Feedback

Most people are familiar with blogs, rating of content, and status updates from Internet applications, where these functions have been available for many years. SharePoint 2010 now offers this set of tools throughout the whole working experience. Users can rate and tag information, bookmark content, view status updates, and stay connected with colleagues through the activity feed that displays all relevant activities.

Collaboration

Together with the new user experience, SharePoint 2010 offers a "wikis everywhere" approach that makes it much easier to quickly create and update content as the information changes. This means that even team sites can be edited with live previews and links to other pages, as shown in Figure 1-4. Most types of content—blogs, calendars, task lists, contacts, and so on—have been improved to strengthen the collaboration and make it easier to work with the information.

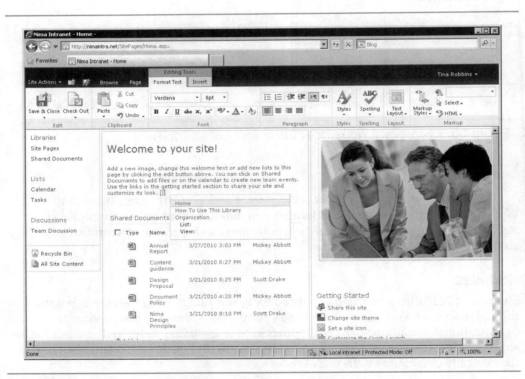

Figure 1-4.   Editing content with the wiki approach

My Sites and User Profiles

The new enhanced My Site acts as the hub in the new social networking experience within SharePoint 2010, as shown in Figure 1-5. From here, you can keep track of your social network in the organization and follow your news feed. Together with the updated user profile, the site focuses on your expertise and skills. This makes it easier for people within large companies to find the resources and information they need.

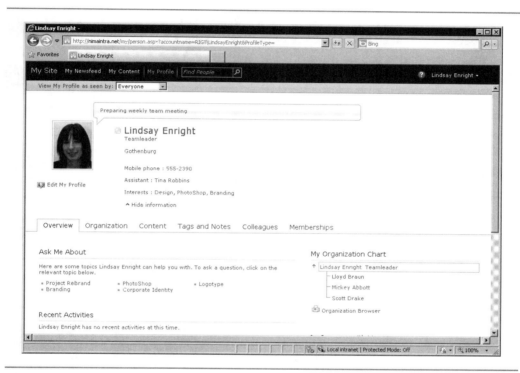

Figure 1-5.   My Site

Content

SharePoint 2010 takes document, record, and web content management to a new level by offering a robust enterprise content management (ECM) platform with tools to support the whole content life cycle, from creation to disposition. The new and improved features enable more people to participate in the ECM process and provide a much more controlled content management solution.

Large List Repositories

A lot of improvements have been made to lists and libraries in SharePoint 2010 to allow them to support tens of millions of items. Metadata-driven navigation, as shown in Figure 1-6, allows you to quickly locate the content you are looking for, no matter how many items a list or document library actually contains.

SharePoint 2010 can be configured to assign each document with a unique document ID. This enables users to find a specific document within a site collection using a special URL, even if the sites have been restructured or the document library has been moved.

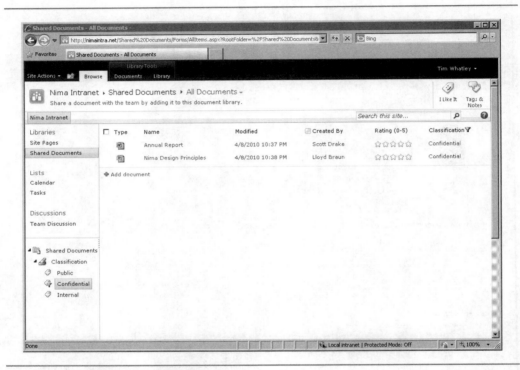

Figure 1-6.   Metadata-driven navigation

Metadata for the Enterprise

Metadata is now everywhere. It is possible to build enterprise taxonomy structures (as shown in Figure 1-7) that can be used not only within sites, but also throughout the whole environment or even between farms. The taxonomy structure can then easily be added to a list or library, and with autocomplete, metadata tagging for the end user is much easier than in previous versions. End users can also automatically extract metadata from new content.

Social tagging, also known as *folksonomy*, adds a new dimension to metadata, as it combines the controlled metadata with the unmanaged metadata tagging. Together, they help improve the search experience, making it easier to find the desired content in less time.

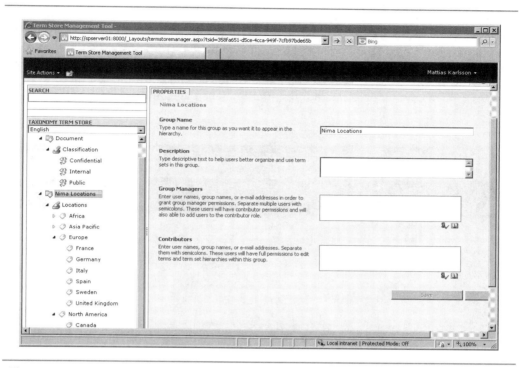

Figure 1-7.   Managed metadata

Web Content Management

A number of improvements have been made to encourage the use of SharePoint 2010 as a web content management platform for Internet and intranet sites. This is suitable for scenarios where most users are content consumers, rather than active contributors.

By introducing the Office Ribbon and minimizing the amount of page reloads when editing content, the experience for content owners has been significantly improved.

In addition, SharePoint 2010 now offers better support for rich media, such as images and videos. A built-in media asset library supports thumbnails, rating, and searching. An integrated media player enables streaming of video files directly from the browser.

Search

Whether or not you choose to use the built-in SharePoint Server 2010 Search tool or add the more complex Fast Search Server 2010 for SharePoint, you will see that a lot of effort has been made to improve the search capabilities. Everything from the end-user search experience to the flexibility and scaling at the back end has been completely remade, making it much easier to find the content you're seeking.

Improved Search Experience

SharePoint 2010 now offers faceted search—an easy way to refine a search query by using a navigator panel built from the metadata extracted from actual search results, as shown in Figure 1-8. You can drill down to the information you are looking for by refining the results by any metadata element, such as content author, last modified date, or type of content (document, presentation, web page, and so on).

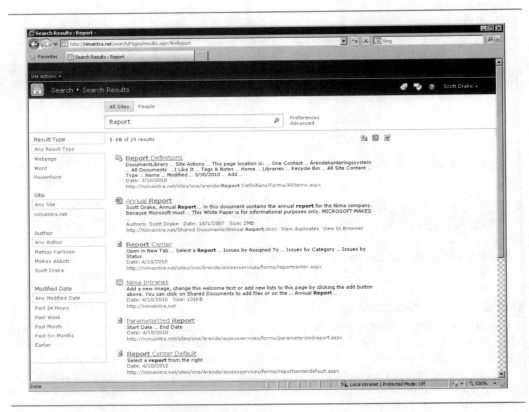

Figure 1-8.   Search result in SharePoint 2010

When you type your search query, suggestions (showing what others have searched for before) come up as you type. In addition, wildcard search and spell checks are now out-of-the-box features. Improved search relevance includes usage and social tagging in its calculations.

People Search

Significant updates have been made to the People Search function, to make it easier than ever before to find people and stay in touch with colleagues. By default, a person's expertise and participation in social networks are included in the search result. Another improvement is the ability to spell-check names and suggest variations for the name you are searching for.

Search Outside SharePoint

In a real-world enterprise environment, information is spread out across a wide range of different systems and line-of-business applications. In SharePoint 2010, it has become much easier to connect to these systems and applications in order to index this information and make it searchable from within SharePoint. With SharePoint Designer and the new Business Connectivity Services, these connections can often be made without writing a single line of code.

Insights

The Insights area in SharePoint 2010 is all about empowering users with business intelligence—not just a selected group of people armed with custom tools, but everyone within the organization. SharePoint 2010 offers a wide range of tools to analyze information from both structured and unstructured sources, and present it in a way that makes important business decisions easier.

PerformancePoint Services

What used to be available as a separate product (PerformancePoint Server 2007) is now fully integrated into the Enterprise Edition of SharePoint Server 2010 as a service application. This means that it uses the same security model, and its repository now consists solely of SharePoint document libraries and lists. In addition, a migration tool is available to move existing content from the previous version into the new repository. Enhancements have been made to objects such as key performance indicators, scorecards, and dashboards.

Visio Services

With SharePoint 2010, you are able to view Visio web diagrams directly in the browser using the new Visio Services. The diagrams are rendered in Silverlight or as image (PNG) files, making it easy to embed and share them in SharePoint 2010 pages. It is also possible to create and display data-connected diagrams, dynamically visualizing data from various sources.

Excel Services

Excel Services technology was first available in Microsoft Office SharePoint Server 2007 as a shared service that made it possible to work with Excel workbooks using only a browser. In SharePoint 2010, its capabilities have been improved with richer pivoting and slicing, and much better visualization.

Previously, an Excel workbook could not be loaded if it contained a feature that was unsupported by Excel Services, such as a Microsoft Visual Basic for Applications (VBA) macro. Now only the unsupported feature (like the macro) will be ignored, and the workbook will load.

Composites

One of the biggest efforts in improving SharePoint 2010 over its predecessors has been made in the area that Microsoft calls Composites. Composites is all about making it easy for business users to rapidly create SharePoint solutions tailored for a specific need or requirement. This is achieved by empowering them with a wide range of tools and building blocks, while at the same time giving the IT staff maximum control and the ability to isolate solutions to maintain stability in the environment.

Line-of-Business Data Connections

With the new Business Connectivity Services, previously known as Business Data Catalog (BDC), SharePoint 2010 offers an easier way to connect to line-of-business applications. You are now able to search, read, edit, create, and delete line-of-business data from within SharePoint, instead of having read-only access to the data, as was the case with BDC.

Connections can now be made from SharePoint Designer 2010 without any coding. This is a huge step forward when it comes to offering nontechnical information workers the ability to rapidly build customized SharePoint solutions in response to emerging business requirements.

SharePoint Designer 2010

SharePoint Designer 2010 has received more than just a facelift that enriches the user experience with features such as the Office Ribbon. It also offers better tools for managing site content, creating workflows, and connecting to external data.

SharePoint Designer has been a good tool for customizing SharePoint sites, but it was difficult for IT personnel to control modifications that could sometimes lead to serious performance implications. With SharePoint 2010, the IT staff is able to control the use of SharePoint Designer 2010 by locking out specific capabilities or restricting use to only specific sites within a SharePoint 2010 environment.

Sandboxed Solutions

Even though SharePoint 2010 offers a rich set of tools to create custom SharePoint solutions without needing to write any code, some coding may be required in order to meet specific business needs. However, if custom code is poorly written, it can be a threat to the overall performance and stability of your SharePoint environment. To address this issue, SharePoint 2010 introduces a new feature called *sandboxed solutions*.

Sandboxed solutions allow site collection administrators to deploy custom elements such as Web parts or event receivers within the context of their respective site collections. Such isolated solutions run with partial trust and do not have full access to the SharePoint object model. IT staff can limit the amount of resources that these solutions are allowed to consume in terms of CPU time, memory, and number of database queries. SharePoint disables the solution once the quota value has been reached, and prevents it from running again until action is taken.

Improvements for Administrators in SharePoint 2010

SharePoint 2010's advantages of flexibility and scalability also make it very comprehensive, and therefore complex to manage. To provide information workers with a stable platform, a lot of pressure is put on the infrastructure side of things, which is where we believe most of you work (as we do).

Fortunately, SharePoint 2010 does not only come with a lot of new exciting end-user features, but also includes many additions and enhancements for administrators. Here, we will summarize the improvements in SharePoint 2010 from an IT professional's perspective.

Flexible Deployments

A lot of effort has been put into making new deployments and upgrades to SharePoint 2010 easier and more manageable. One of the nicest features when performing the actual installation is the new prerequisites installer, which checks whether all software prerequisites are present in the system and will automatically download and install any that are missing.

When the installation of all prerequisites is done, you have the option to install SharePoint either by means of a step-by-step wizard with a graphical user interface or through a scripted installation using configuration files and PowerShell.

NOTE Using scripted installations is preferred, because this could also act as part of your disaster recovery plan. In case of a disaster, a server or the entire farm could easily be set up exactly as it was before. In addition, it can also be advantageous when installing different staging environments to make sure that your test, quality assurance, and production environments look the same.

Pre-Upgrade Checker

In Service Pack 2 for Microsoft Office SharePoint Server 2007 and Windows SharePoint Services 3.0, a new STSADM operation was introduced for the first time. The `preupgradecheck` operation is a tool that you run in your SharePoint Server 2007 or Windows SharePoint Services (WSS) 3.0 farm to generate an HTML report showing the state of your farm and the presence of any issues that need to be resolved before your environment is ready to be upgraded to SharePoint 2010.

Visual Upgrade

When upgrading from a previous version of SharePoint to SharePoint 2010, you have the option to keep the WSS 3.0 look and feel to minimize the initial impact on your end users. You are then able to switch on a per-site basis to the SharePoint 2010 preview mode to verify the content and looks of your site. Finally, you complete the upgrade by changing to the new SharePoint 2010 user experience, as shown in Figure 1-9.

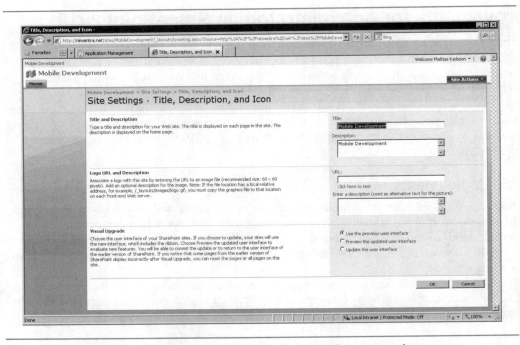

Figure 1-9. Changing the site to the new SharePoint 2010 user experience.

Managed Accounts

Managed accounts were introduced in SharePoint 2010 as a mechanism for keeping a centralized record of all service accounts. This feature will automatically change service account passwords according to domain policies, without requiring any administrator interaction or causing any downtime. It is also possible to be notified when a password is about to expire, if you prefer to control this process yourself. This should mitigate the risk of an outage due to expired passwords, and at the same time reduce administrative overload related to keeping track of service accounts and their expiration time.

Another highly acclaimed addition is the ability to use a Group Policy Object (GPO) to control on which servers SharePoint 2010 is allowed to be installed. This lets administrators prevent unapproved SharePoint installations and adhere to governance plans.

SharePoint 2010 Patching

A lot of enhancements have been made to improve the patching process of SharePoint 2010 to reduce downtime and provide better control over the patch level of your farm. With the new patch management user interface, administrators are able to get a view of each server's patch level and the status of the entire farm. A patch status health rule that is part of the new built-in monitoring infrastructure will inform administrators of any inconsistencies.

In addition, SharePoint 2010 offers a backward-compatibility mode, allowing administrators to apply the binaries of a patch to a front-end server but postpone changing the schema of the databases. This enables your SharePoint farm to run with different versions of binaries and database schema, and potentially reduces the downtime, as you can plan the upgrade in a much more controlled way. You also have the ability to reduce downtime even more by using the option to set databases to read-only, so users can access the data in read-only mode, or by using parallel upgrading of databases, which speeds up the process.

Productivity

To increase the productivity for administrators, the whole experience has been improved, including Central Administration, which now has the familiar Office Ribbon. New tools have been implemented to make monitoring of SharePoint farms much easier. And with the SharePoint Best Practices Analyzer, you can check the configuration and security settings of your farm, get recommendations, and in many cases, get help in resolving the issues within the same user interface.

Backup and Restore

Anyone who has been involved with backup and restore procedures in a SharePoint Server 2007 or WSS 3.0 environment knows that quite a few steps were required for recovery using just the out-of-the-box tools. You needed to restore a copy of the affected content database from a backup, attach it to a separate farm with the same patch level, export the site using STSADM, copy the export package onto a production server, and then import the site using STSADM again. Quite a time-consuming task!

In SharePoint 2010, the backup and restore procedure have been significantly improved by allowing content databases to be "mounted" to the farm, without actually being attached to any of the Web applications. This is referred to as an *unattached content database*, the contents of which can be browsed and exported down to list level. Using PowerShell, you can then restore the exported content back into one of the attached databases.

In Chapter 21, we will talk more about backup and restore in SharePoint 2010, including additional options available with Windows PowerShell.

Unified Logging

In SharePoint 2010, troubleshooting and finding root causes of problems in log files have become much easier thanks to the new logging database. Unified Logging Service (ULS) logs, Windows events, page requests, and so on are stored in an open schema database, so you can extract and work with the data in a much more efficient way. A number of predefined SQL views are available. And since the database has an open schema, it is possible to create new tools or use third-party tools to get views that better suit your needs.

Developer Dashboard

The Developer Dashboard, shown in Figure 1-10, is a per-page detailed report of latency across the SharePoint, ASP.NET, and SQL Srever layers. This makes it much easier to determine which components of a SharePoint page cause it to not perform as well as it should.

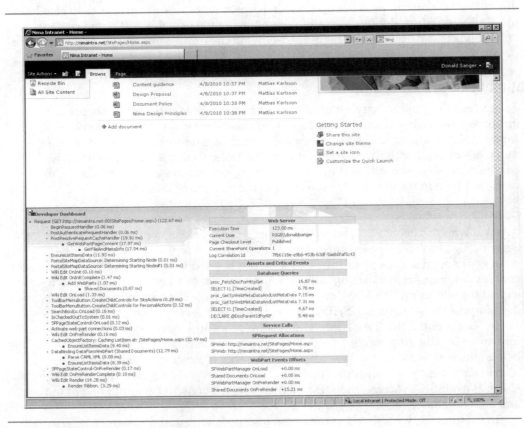

Figure 1-10. Developer Dashboard

PowerShell Cmdlets

As you will learn in this book, PowerShell is a huge asset to IT professionals managing SharePoint 2010 products. For now, we will just say that PowerShell is fully integrated into SharePoint 2010, with a huge number of predefined cmdlets.

Unified Infrastructure

The new unified infrastructure of SharePoint 2010 is now more scalable than ever before, increasing the performance and manageability of the environment, and empowering administrators to act proactively to maintain a stable SharePoint 2010 farm.

Shared Service Architecture

The new Shared Service architecture introduced in SharePoint 2010 allows a more flexible and scalable deployment of shared services. Shared services are now part of SharePoint Foundation 2010 and are also extensible, allowing third-party vendors to build services that can easily be deployed into a SharePoint 2010 farm. In addition, the new architecture allows sharing of services not only between Web applications, but also between farms.

Controlling Performance

SharePoint 2010 introduces new ways to control performance and protect server resources during peak hours. This is achieved by allowing administrators to configure threshold values per Web application. Then when the value of the relevant counter (such as CPU Time, Available Memory, or Requests in Queue) reaches the configured value, SharePoint can enter a throttling health state, denying new requests and preventing new timer jobs from running, to protect the SharePoint server.

Claims-Based Authentication

Claims-based authentication is a new flexible token-based authentication model. Its main principle is that a user can be authenticated by providing a minimum possible set of personal information (*claims*), as long as the target system trusts the authentication authority that can validate this information. Microsoft's implementation of this model is built on the Windows Identity Foundation framework, and it allows SharePoint Web applications to authenticate users with a variety of authentication methods, including Lightweight Directory Access Protocol (LDAP), relational databases, Active Directory Federation Services (ADFS), Windows Live ID, and different third-party providers.

An important aspect of claims-based authentication is that, in many scenarios, it provides an opportunity to personalize user experience based on the information contained in a user's token.

Multi-Tenancy

Multi-tenancy is a feature of SharePoint 2010 that makes it possible to isolate and secure service application resources between SharePoint sites. Service application data can be partitioned to allow different subsets of data to be accessible depending on each site's tenancy. This is managed by administrators assigning each tenant a subscription ID. This feature is ideal for hosting environments.

System Requirements

Table 1-1 lists the minimum hardware requirements for running SharePoint 2010 (and the minimum requirements to run the code examples provided in this book).

Component	Minimum Requirement
Processor	64-bit, four cores
RAM	4GB for developer or evaluation use 8GB for single server and multiple server farm installation for production use
Hard disk	80GB for installation

Table 1-1. SharePoint 2010 Hardware Requirements

For a database server used in a farm, either of the following Microsoft SQL Server editions is required for SharePoint 2010:

- 64-bit edition of SQL Server 2005 with Service Pack 3 (SP3) with Cumulative Update 3
- 64-bit edition of SQL Server 2008 with SP1 and Cumulative Update 2

The following are the minimum software requirements for a single server with a built-in database, web front end (WFE) server, or application server used in a farm:

- 64-bit edition of Windows Server 2008 Standard, Enterprise, Data Center, or Web Server with SP2
- Web Server (IIS) role
- Application Server role
- Microsoft .NET Framework version 3.5 SP1
- SQL Server 2008 Express with SP1
- Windows Identity Foundation (WIF)
- Microsoft Sync Framework Runtime v1.0 (x64)
- Microsoft Filter Pack 2.0
- Microsoft Chart Controls for the Microsoft .NET Framework 3.5
- Windows PowerShell 2.0
- SQL Server 2008 Native Client
- Microsoft SQL Server 2008 Analysis Services ADOMD.NET
- ADO.NET Data Services v1.5 CTP2

Architectural Components

SharePoint 2010 consists of the following architectural components:

- Server farm
- Service applications
- Application pools
- Web applications
- Content databases
- Site collections
- Sites
- My Site site

Here, we will provide a very high-level overview of these components and how they work together. We will highlight what is new to SharePoint 2010.

 NOTE   For a more in-depth discussion of the architectural components, we suggest that you review the number of available articles on Microsoft TechNet.

Server Farm

A *server farm* could be considered as the top-level element in a SharePoint implementation. It consists of one or many servers. When utilizing more than one server in a farm, SharePoint offers the flexibility to scale out each individual SharePoint Server role onto new dedicated servers, or simply move the services around on the already existing servers in your farm. This flexibility makes it easy to optimize the performance or align with new business requirements as your implementation grows over time.

Whether you have one or many servers in your farm, all the SharePoint 2010 services are bound together by a single configuration database in your SQL Server implementation.

Service Applications

The SharePoint 2010 products family has a new and more scalable service model than in Office SharePoint Server 2007. Shared Services is now a part of Microsoft SharePoint Foundation 2010, instead of SharePoint Server 2010, as in the previous version of the platform.

Instead of having a Shared Service Provider that provides all services available (Search Services, Forms Services, Excel Services, and so on) to the associated Web applications, you now have the ability to group and share service applications in a much more flexible way. This means that you can associate a specific set of service applications with one Web application and a different set of service applications with another Web application. If you need to have one service application used among all or many Web applications, that can be set up as well.

By publishing a service application, it is possible to share the service application so that other SharePoint 2010 farms can consume the actual service data from the service application and use it in the local farm. This kind of setup can be very useful in scenarios where you have a number of different farms within your company, but still want to use one common search service.

In addition to sharing a service application between Web applications, it is also possible to partition the actual service data. For instance, if you have a Search Service application used by two different Web applications, the search result, representing the service data in this case, would be different depending on the origin of the search request. This could be very useful in hosted environments and is called *partitioning*.

 NOTE Not all service applications have the capability of partitioning. Some service applications can be shared only within a single server farm.

Application Pools

Application pools can be seen as virtual containers, in which one or a group of Internet Information Services (IIS) web sites are running isolated from each other, with their own worker process (or processes).

Each time you create a new Web application from Central Administration, SharePoint will allow you to create a new application pool. All Web applications and service applications can have their own application pool for isolation, but you also can share application pools between Web applications and service applications if needed.

 NOTE In the design phase of your implementation, you should plan for application pools and how to consolidate and isolate your Web applications. Since each SharePoint environment is unique, it's difficult to give a general rule or guidance in how or when you should consolidate or isolate. However, if you have Web applications with a lot of homegrown custom code, you should probably think of isolating those within their own application pools to mitigate the risk of security flaws or memory leaks bringing down your entire SharePoint environment.

Web Applications

A *Web application* is a configuration object defined by SharePoint and mapped onto one or more IIS virtual servers. They are created from Central Administration or by script, through STSADM or PowerShell. (Chapter 10 discusses managing Web applications with PowerShell.)

With SharePoint 2010, we still have, as in its predecessor, the possibility to extend each Web application up to four times. Each time you extend a Web application, a new IIS Web site is created, and the Web application will be associated with a new zone. All zones, and thereby the corresponding virtual servers, are always pointing to the Web application that was originally created. This gives you the option to have different security settings, and even a different look and feel, for the same content, since you are able to use different authentication providers in different zones.

 NOTE   Zones are a way to have different logical paths to access the same Web application. For example, you may use zones in an intranet/extranet scenario, where you want to use Windows Integrated security when working on the company network and Forms-based authentication when accessing the content from the Internet.

In addition to being able to use different authentication providers in your zones, you also have the option to set a security policy for the Web application. You can then allow or deny security rights for specific users or groups, depending on from which zone they are accessing the Web application. For example, you might want to allow a service account like the crawl account to have access to all content, or you may want to limit the access for partners or vendors accessing your Web application through the extranet zone. A policy for Web applications overrules all security settings at the site collection level.

Content Databases

Content databases are where all content for a Web application is stored. Each Web application can have multiple content databases to be able to provide scalability when the amount of content increases. When you first create a Web application, you will need to specify a content database to use. If the content database does not exist in the specified database server, SharePoint will create a content database for you. Content databases can then be managed from Central Administration, as shown in Figure 1-11, or by using PowerShell.

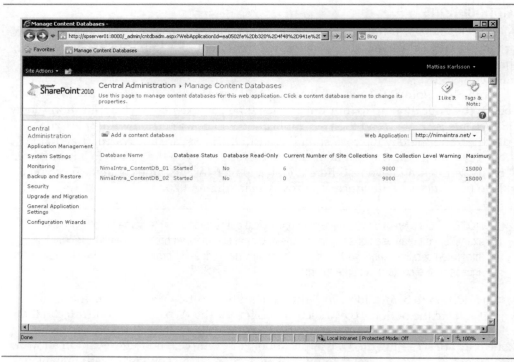

Figure 1-11. Content database management in Central Administration

When creating new content databases, you will need to specify how many sites should be allowed in the database and at what number of sites the warning level should be. You can have different content databases located on different SQL Server servers. This could be applicable in environments where you have a different service level agreement (SLA) for some sites and the requirement for the recovery time objective (RTO) makes it necessary to put content databases on a different SQL Server instance where you have more frequent backups and faster recovery tools.

When using SharePoint 2010 to store large binary files, you should consider using the new Remote Blob Storage (RBS) feature to minimize the size of your content databases. With RBS, you are able to store files outside your content databases, on local disks attached to the SQL Server server. For end users, there is no difference in how they work and interact with their files, as this will be handled automatically in the back end. In Chapter 20, we will look more at how to manage content databases and setting up RBS.

Site Collections

Site collections are collections of SharePoint sites. Each site collection has a top-level root site and can contain a hierarchy of subsites. Site collections are stored in a content database, and you can have thousands of site collections in each content database. You can control this amount using the threshold values at the content database level. SharePoint will then automatically create the next site collection in a new content database.

Site collections also enable sharing of items like master pages, page layouts, site templates, and so on. It's also common to use the same navigation and permissions throughout an entire site collection.

Site collections are usually created from Central Administration, as shown in Figure 1-12, but can also be scripted with PowerShell. When creating new site collections, you will need to assign a primary site collection administrator. This is

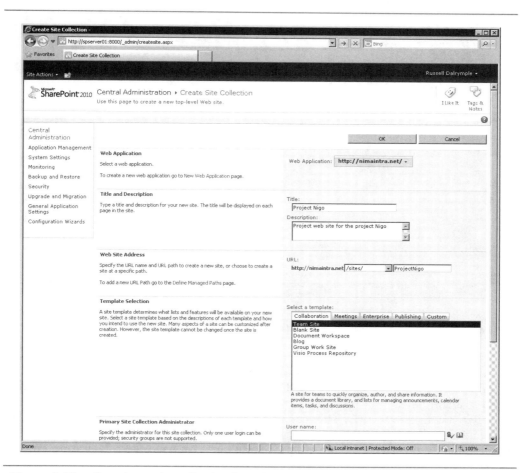

Figure 1-12.   Creating a site collection from Central Administration

the highest security role within the site collection and allows the user to manage settings like search, site hierarchy, content type publishing, features, and site collection policies. Chapter 11 discusses creating and managing site collections using PowerShell.

Sites

A *site* is hosted within a site collection and contains one or more web pages, lists, or libraries to store and present information. All sites are built on site templates. A number of predefined site templates are shipped with SharePoint 2010. As shown in Figure 1-13, the templates are designed to serve different purposes, such as for publishing sites, document centers, meeting workspaces, and team sites.

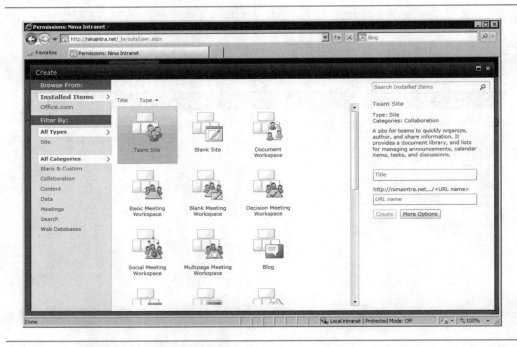

Figure 1-13.   Templates for creating a new site

You can also create custom site templates from scratch using tools like Microsoft Visual Studio 2010, or by using an existing template that you have customized and then saved as a template.

When it comes to security, sites can either inherit permissions from the above site or use unique permissions. In the latter case, you can grant users or groups permissions to the site directly, or you can create unique SharePoint groups for your users and groups. By doing this, you get better control of the permissions set on the site.

In SharePoint 2007, it was quite difficult to get a good view of which users actually had access to a site or what permission level they had, especially if you used unique permissions on different site levels and used Active Directory groups, either directly on the site or added through SharePoint groups. To verify that a user had access to a site, you needed to look in each Active Directory group you had added to the site. This way of working is now gone.

In SharePoint 2010, you have a Check Permissions tool, as shown in Figure 1-14, which is easily accessible from the Site Permissions tool. Here, you can enter the user ID to see a list of the permissions the user has on the site and how those permissions are set—directly through SharePoint groups or through an Active Directory group.

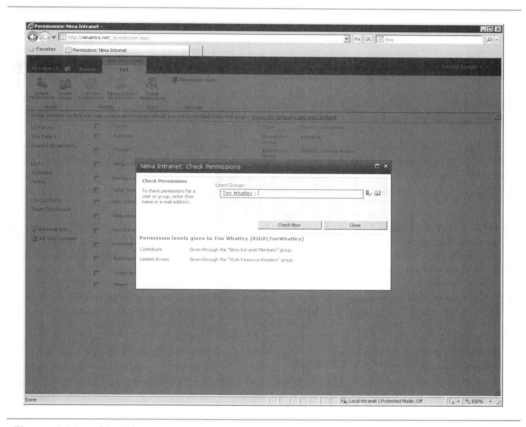

Figure 1-14.   Checking permissions

Lists and Libraries

Lists and libraries are where you store your data in SharePoint, as shown in Figure 1-15. It's important to know that libraries are actually lists as well, but customized in a way so that they are better suited for storing files.

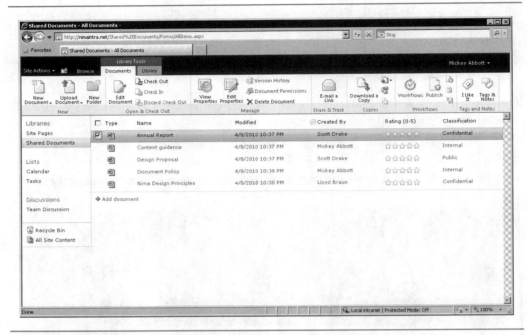

Figure 1-15. Document library with the new Ribbon interface

Many types of lists and libraries are already available in SharePoint out of the box. They can be used as they are or as a starting point to tailor them to fulfill your specific business requirements. Lists have a set of configurable settings that apply to all lists, as well as custom settings that apply only to the specific type of list used.

Among the many SharePoint 2010 improvements and new features for lists and libraries are ratings of documents and information, form validation settings, and the possibility to reuse custom list views so that you don't need to re-create your custom list view in all your document libraries.

Items

Items are always stored within a list or library and can be of any type: a document in a document library, a calendar booking in a calendar list, or simply an entry in a custom list. In SharePoint 2010, you can have as many as 50 million items in each list. When you have a large amount of items, you will need to be sure that it does not affect the performance of your environment. To support this, SharePoint 2010 has the ability to set limitations and rules for how large lists should be handled. We will cover how you can control your large lists in Chapter 2.

Web Parts

Web parts can be seen as small reusable applications presented on pages in sites. They are often used for a specific purpose, like displaying the content of a list or library. They can also be connected and used when filtering data in one Web part by selecting another type of data in another Web part.

To give you a better understanding of what role Web parts play in SharePoint, it is fair to say that most of the content displayed when using SharePoint is presented through Web parts—everything from announcements to search results.

My Sites

My Site (available only in Microsoft SharePoint Server 2010) is a special type of SharePoint site that is customizable for each user. It enables the users to customize the site for their own needs, and to create a profile specifying things like contact details, profile picture, colleagues, and memberships. The user profile is controlled by the user and exposes that user's details to colleagues. At the same time, the My Site web site offers a secure place to store files, lists, and libraries accessible only by the user or the persons who have been granted access.

SharePoint 2010 has taken a huge step toward social networking, and therefore the My Site feature has been dramatically improved. New concepts like status updates, activity feeds, and note boards—all well-known concepts from social networking applications—have been introduced.

As mentioned when discussing lists and libraries, rating of content is now included in SharePoint 2010 products. Together with social tagging and feedback, users can more easily discover new content that might be relevant to them by reviewing what others think of the content.

With the Knowledge Mining feature, users are able to add keywords and tags of what they are interested in, or subjects they can or are willing to answer questions about. To support users with the process of adding keywords, it's possible to extract keywords from the users' Outlook 2010 mailboxes when editing the user profile.

Summary

In this chapter, we have gone through the six capability areas (Sites, Community, Content, Search, Insights, and Composites) of SharePoint 2010 and highlighted some of the new features to give you an idea of the endless possibilities that the platform offers. We have also introduced you to the enhanced functionalities and tools that can be used by administrators to get better control, reduce downtime, increase productivity, and provide end users with a stable and highly available SharePoint environment.

In addition, we briefly explained the architectural components of the SharePoint 2010 products family to set the terminology for the coming chapters. It's important to at least have a holistic view of the components, as they come up frequently used in Part III of this book.

In the next chapter, we will take a look at the options and tools administrators have to manage SharePoint 2010.

CHAPTER 2 | Managing SharePoint 2010

I n this chapter, we will briefly walk through the options administrators have when it comes to managing SharePoint 2010. Those of you who have worked with SharePoint products will recognize many of these tools, but you will notice that a lot of effort has been put into improving them. Administrators now have more options to better control and manage their SharePoint 2010 environment.

Central Administration

In SharePoint 2010 Central Administration, an administrator of a SharePoint farm or a specific service can manage, configure, and monitor SharePoint 2010 and its components. Central Administration in SharePoint 2010 has been enriched with new and enhanced features. All tasks available in Central Administration are now grouped into functional areas, instead of being divided into Operations and Application Management categories, as in the previous version of SharePoint. The Central Administration Home page displays these groups with links to common tasks, as shown in Figure 2-1. By clicking a link or using the navigation panel on the left side of the page, you can access the items available within each functional group.

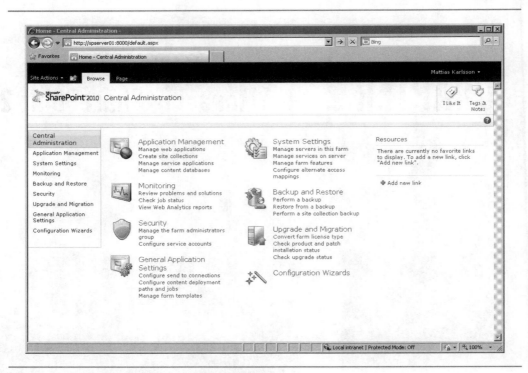

Figure 2-1. SharePoint 2010 Central Administration

Like other SharePoint 2010 sites, Central Administration makes full use of the Ribbon, providing quick access to all the currently available actions through a set of graphic contextual menus.

Besides the facelift of the user interface, there are a lot of other innovations in Central Administration. Here, we will highlight a few of these enhanced features.

Web Applications Management

The Web Applications Management page in Central Administration, shown in Figure 2-2, is a good example of how the Ribbon makes working with Web applications much easier, as it consolidates all related tasks for easy access from one single view.

Figure 2-2.   Managing Web applications through Central Administration

SharePoint 2010 offers a couple of new configurable items at the Web application level, giving you much more control over the content and performance of your Web applications. This includes the ability to set whether SharePoint Designer 2010 is allowed to be used against the sites in each Web application. In addition, you can restrict some of the SharePoint Designer 2010 functions; for example, you can specify that users are not allowed to modify master pages.

As mentioned in the previous chapter, large SharePoint lists (those with more than 2,000 items) potentially have serious performance implications. Although SharePoint is perfectly capable of maintaining lists with millions of items, trying to return more than 2,000 in a single query is a very resource-intensive operation. The most common example of this is rendering a default view of a list or document library. This could, in some cases, even affect the performance and stability of the whole farm.

To mitigate the risk of performance issues caused by large lists, SharePoint 2010 introduces a way to centrally control how these lists are handled. For each Web application, you can set rules and limitations on the queries allowed against lists. As shown in Figure 2-3, the default value for the amount of items returned in a query performed by a user is set to 5,000.

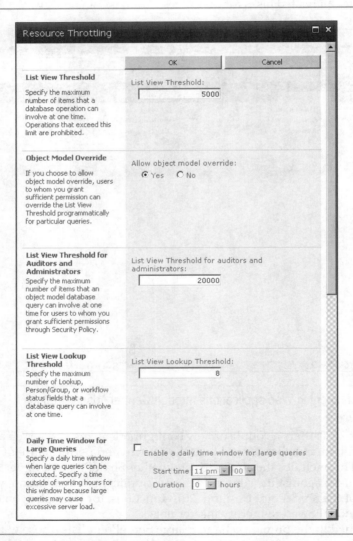

Figure 2-3. Resource Throttling settings in Central Administration

Other configurable items include the number of lookup fields that are allowed in a single query and the amount of unique permissions that a list can have at the same time. In addition, you can specify a time window when larger list queries are allowed for end users. If you use this kind of "happy hour," you should set this time to be outside normal business hours so the queries do not affect the overall performance of your SharePoint 2010 farm.

On the same page where you configure the threshold values for list queries, you are also able to turn HTTP request monitoring and throttling on or off. This provides a way to control requests and protect the SharePoint 2010 environment during peak loads. When HTTP request monitoring and throttling are enabled, a timer job monitors the front-end web servers, and if there is a request overload, low-priority tasks are put on hold.

NOTE   From Central Administration, HTTP request monitoring can only be turned on or off. To change the settings, you need to use PowerShell.

Service Application Management

Management of service applications is now done from Central Administration or through PowerShell, instead of a separate administration site as it was in Office SharePoint Server 2007 with its Shared Service Provider infrastructure. Figure 2-4 shows the Manage

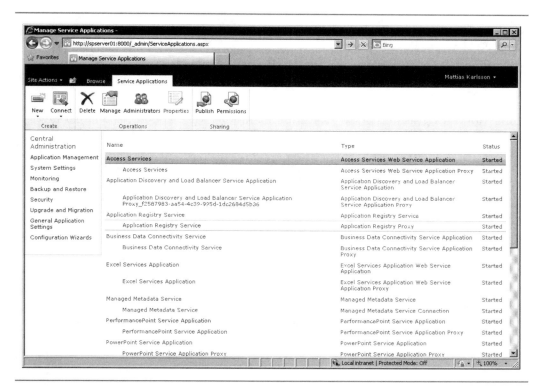

Figure 2-4.   Managing service applications through Central Administration

Service Applications page. To access the settings page for a particular service application, click its name in the list.

Each service application can have its own set of administrators, which is configurable using the Administrators button in the Ribbon on the Manage Service Applications page. This provides a new level of flexibility when it comes to granular delegation of control over various service applications.

As noted in Chapter 1, the SharePoint 2010 service application architecture is extremely flexible. You can have different sets of service applications for different Web applications and also share service applications between Web applications or even between farms. When sharing service applications between Web applications, the actual service application data can be partitioned, so that search results from different Web applications are separated from each other, for instance.

Each service application has its own application proxy, which is a logical object (a Windows Communication Foundation web service) used by the consumer of the service (a Web application or its component) for connecting to the service application. Proxies can be grouped into different proxy groups to make it easier to manage different sets of service applications. Managing new proxy groups can be done only with PowerShell cmdlets, and the same goes for managing site subscriptions, which are used for partitioning service data to separate it between site collections.

In Chapter 18, we will discuss how to manage service applications.

SharePoint 2010 also offers the option to isolate service applications by using different application pools. To change the properties of a service application select the service application in the Manage Service Applications list and click Properties in the Ribbon. The Service Application Properties page contains options for changing application pool or creating a new one, as shown in Figure 2-5.

Health and Monitoring

In the Monitoring section of Central Administration, you can find the SharePoint Health Analyzer. The Health Analyzer is a new feature that periodically or on demand checks for potential configuration and performance problems within your farm by matching the configuration against a set of health rules. SharePoint 2010 provides a number of predefined health rules, and you can also create custom health rules to extend the monitoring capabilities or to monitor custom solutions built on SharePoint products.

When problems are identified, they are shown in the Central Administration console. A status report describes the problems in more depth and tells you what actions are required to resolve them, as shown in the example in Figure 2-6. In some cases, the problems are fixed automatically or you can resolve the problem directly from within the status report.

Also available in the Monitoring section is the enhanced diagnostics logging configuration page. Here, you'll find all the configurable logging categories broken

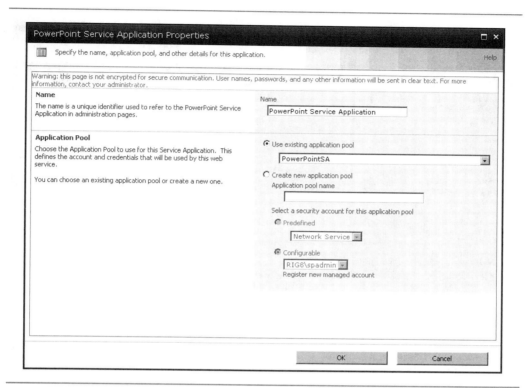

Figure 2-5.   Configuring a service application to use an application pool

down into subcategories in a much more detailed view than in previous versions. Each of the logging categories can be configured either individually or by inheriting settings from the parent category, as shown in Figure 2-7.

In addition, SharePoint 2010 introduces something called *event log flood protection*. This detects repeating log events and suppresses them until the problem is fixed or conditions return to normal. This helps administrators reviewing the application event log, as it will not be flooded with multiple iterations of the same event.

In SharePoint 2010, you not only have the option to set the number of days the trace log files should be retained, but you can also specify the maximum amount of disk space the log files can use. SharePoint will restrict the log files from growing larger than the configured value.

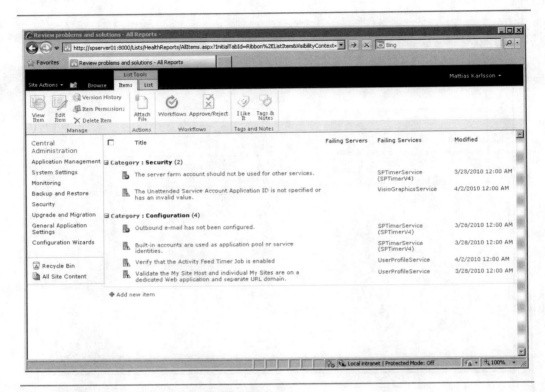

Figure 2-6.   SharePoint Health Analyzer report

NOTE   SharePoint 2010 uses NTFS file system compression to reduce the size of trace log files by more than 50%.

Another improvement made in SharePoint 2010 that will significantly help administrators with troubleshooting is the use of correlation IDs. Each request in SharePoint is associated with a correlation ID that will follow the request all the way down to the database layer and back. This makes it much easier to track down the root cause of a problem. In addition, a correlation ID is shown in the browser whenever a error is raised, so that administrators can actually find the specific request that caused the problem for the end user.

With the Usage and Health Data Collection service application that is provisioned and started by default, SharePoint 2010 can log useful information about page requests,

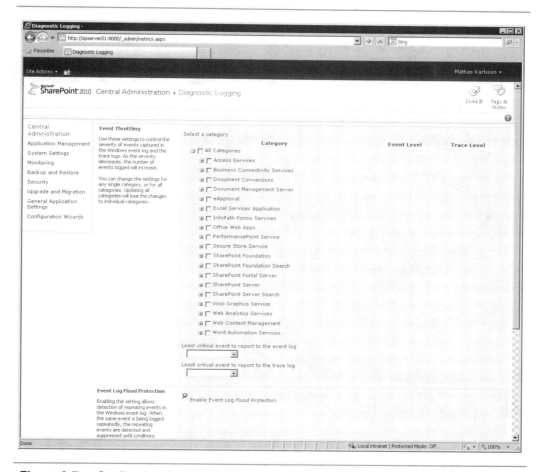

Figure 2-7. Configuring diagnostics logging

search query usage, feature usage, and so on. Figure 2-8 shows an example of a built-in web analytics report. The data is stored in a special logging database that has an open schema, so third-party vendors can build additional reports to complement those supplied with SharePoint.

TIP Even though there have been a lot of improvements made to the trace logging feature of SharePoint, troubleshooting can still be difficult. ULSViewer is a free tool that provides a user-friendly way to view log files. It also offers advanced features like sorting, filtering, highlighting, and appending logs to make troubleshooting much easier. You find the tool at http://code.msdn.microsoft.com/ULSViewer.

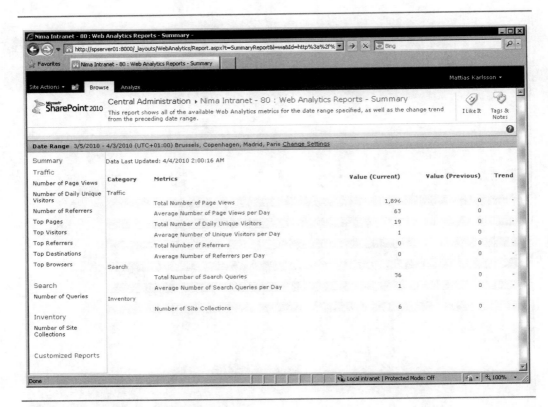

Figure 2-8. A web analytics report

Backup and Restore

As noted in Chapter 1, backup of SharePoint content has been significantly improved in SharePoint 2010. With the new concept of unattached content databases, you are able to connect a content database to the farm without having it attached to a specific Web application. This makes it possible to browse the content database through all the site collections, all the way down to the list level, and export data to a .bak (site collections) or .cmp (sites and lists) file. The exported file can be imported into a Web application or site through a simple PowerShell cmdlet. (It is also possible to export a site or list directly from a "live" environment using the same PowerShell cmdlets.)

In addition to this new level of granular backups, SharePoint 2010 has improved functionality when it comes to farm backup and restore. Farm backups can be done either from Central Administration or through PowerShell. New in SharePoint 2010 is the option to create a backup that contains only the farm configuration—an XML file with just the SharePoint configuration. This makes it possible for administrators to perform a restore or to build a separate farm on different hardware with these configuration settings. This is very useful when setting up new staging environments.

Chapter 21 covers the details of backup and restore operations in SharePoint 2010.

Configuration Wizard

When you first set up SharePoint 2010, you will not have any Web applications or service applications. To help you create and configure these applications, SharePoint 2010 introduces the Farm Configuration Wizard. The Initial Farm Configuration Wizard will start up the first time you go to your Central Administration page, as shown in Figure 2-9. It can also be accessed from the navigation panel in Central Administration.

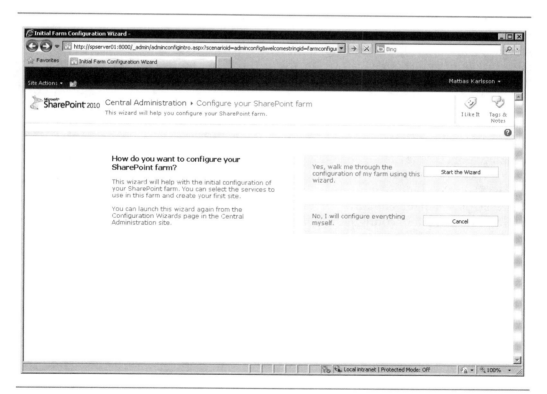

Figure 2-9. The Farm Configuration Wizard

The wizard walks you through a number of steps where you can select which service applications you want to create and which service accounts to use for them. SharePoint will apply all the settings and get the services working for you.

The Farm Configuration Wizard is very convenient, but it may not be the best route for setting up enterprise environments. You cannot apply corporate naming standards to the service application databases. The wizard will create each of these databases with a globally unique identifier (GUID) in the name, which could create confusion for both SharePoint and Database administrators. In addition, all service applications will be set up to run under the same service account, but you can change this later from the Manage Service Applications page in Central Administration.

NOTE   To get full control over your environment from the beginning, we recommend that you use the Farm Configuration Wizard only in proof-of-concept stages or when setting up test environments.

In chapter 9, we will discuss how to create a scripted installation using PowerShell.

Managed Accounts

When setting up a SharePoint 2010 environment with different Web applications and services, you can easily end up with quite a lot of service accounts. To keep track of these accounts, and change their passwords before they expire, is an important and time-consuming task. To mitigate the risk of having your SharePoint environment malfunctioning or even have an outage due to expired passwords, SharePoint 2010 introduces managed accounts.

Managed accounts makes it possible to let SharePoint manage your service accounts, and even to change their passwords automatically in accordance with your company policy. This can be done transparently in the background, without any interference or downtime of your SharePoint 2010 farm. In addition, it is also possible to have SharePoint notify you when a password is about to expire, so you can handle the password change manually.

You can set up and configure managed accounts throught the Managed Accounts page in Central Administration, as shown in Figure 2-10. You can also handle them through PowerShell.

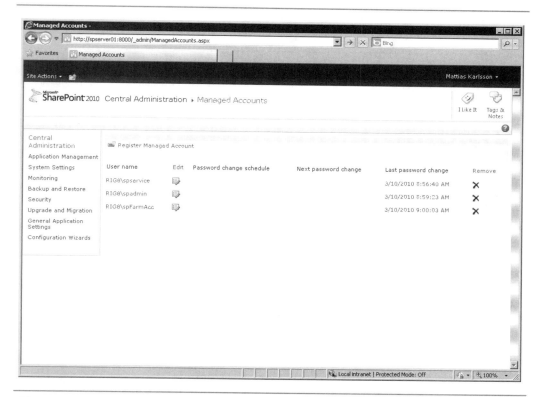

Figure 2-10.   Configuring managed accounts

STSADM

STSADM is a tool for command-line administration of SharePoint. In previous versions, it has been the administrator's best friend, allowing you to perform many of the administrative tasks that were not available through the Central Administration user interface.

STSADM is still available in SharePoint 2010. However, with the broad introduction of PowerShell, the tool has not been further developed. Since everything that can be done with STSADM can be done with PowerShell (but not the other way around), the main reason it is still available is to provide the opportunity to transfer scripts and batch files over to SharePoint 2010 without needing to rewrite them.

If you need to use STSADM, the tool can be found at the following location: %COMMONPROGRAMFILES%\Microsoft Shared\Web Server Extensions\14\BIN.

 NOTE Since SharePoint 2010 has a different Shared Service model than previous versions, all the STSADM commands that were used for configuring Shared Service Providers (SSPs) are now removed.

SharePoint Designer

Together with the release of SharePoint 2010, Microsoft released a new version of SharePoint Designer. SharePoint Designer 2010 has been significantly updated and is now a tool that can be used in the enterprise environment. Figure 2-11 shows the start page of this new version.

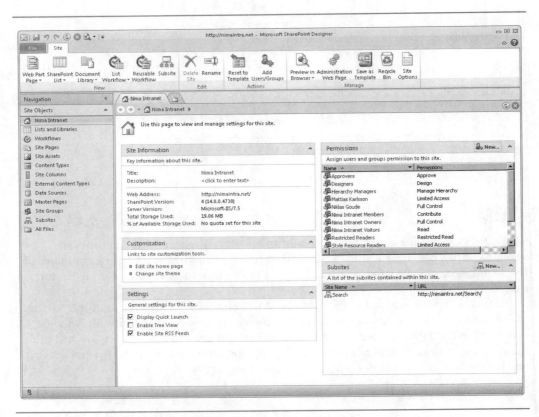

Figure 2-11. The start page of SharePoint Designer 2010

Those of you who worked with SharePoint Designer 2007 know that there were very limited options for building solutions that could be reused in sites other than the one in which they were created. SharePoint Designer 2010 addresses this by changing the focus from page editing to allowing users to build reusable solutions like lists, workflows, content types, site columns, and data source connections.

One of the most anticipated enhancements is the ability to build advanced and reusable workflows without needing to write any code. With SharePoint Designer 2010, you can package a workflow into a .wsp file, which can be used throughout the whole SharePoint environment or imported into Microsoft Visual Studio for further development. In addition, you can use Microsoft Visio to design workflows and then import them into SharePoint Designer 2010, or you can export SharePoint workflows to Visio, which is useful when documenting the solution.

As mentioned in Chapter 1, the addition of Business Connectivity Services makes it much easier to connect to external databases or line-of-business applications. With SharePoint Designer 2010, you can connect to these data sources through a wizard and without needing to write any code.

TIP   SharePoint Designer 2010 is a free tool. It can be downloaded from http://www.microsoft.com/downloads.

Summary

This chapter introduced the various tools available to SharePoint 2010 administrators. The SharePoint Central Administration site still plays a central role, offering a graphical user interface from which you can configure and manage most of the available settings.

We looked at some of the options for mitigating performance problems through resource throttling. These options allow you to control queries of large lists and protect the environment from overload during peak hours by monitoring HTTP requests.

Service applications can easily be managed from Central Administration. You can delegate administrative tasks by assigned dedicated administrators for each service application.

Next, we briefly discussed some backup and restore options. Administrators now have a more granular level of backup, thanks to the unattached content database feature.

Management of service accounts has also been significantly improved. SharePoint 2010 now can manage all service accounts and handle changing passwords for you, without affecting the environment.

Finally, we took a quck look at the new version of SharePoint Designer, another tool that is available for managing SharePoint 2010.

In this chapter, we often referred to PowerShell as an alternative for configuring options and additional settings. In fact, some items can be configured only through PowerShell, and are just not available through the graphical user interface. In the next part of this book, we will focus on how to use PowerShell in SharePoint 2010.

PART II | An Introduction to PowerShell in SharePoint 2010

CHAPTER 3

Getting Started with PowerShell in SharePoint 2010

Welcome to the world of Windows PowerShell, where everything can be automated with a single line of code! Well, that's not completely true, but thanks to the cmdlets, many administrative tasks can be accomplished with just a few lines of code.

Before we dig into the automated world of SharePoint, we will take a tour of Windows PowerShell and go through some of its concepts, so that you understand how it can help you in your daily work. First on the menu is starting up Windows PowerShell.

Starting Up Windows PowerShell

In Windows 7 and Windows Server 2008 R2, Windows PowerShell is installed by default. You'll find the Windows PowerShell icon on the Start menu in the Accessories folder named Windows PowerShell. In Windows 7, the folder contains two different icons pointing to Windows PowerShell: one labeled Windows PowerShell and one labeled Windows PowerShell ISE. Windows PowerShell ISE offers additional features, such as a graphical user interface and multiline editing. In this book, we'll focus on the standard Windows PowerShell console.

Click the Windows PowerShell icon to start the Windows PowerShell console. One thing to keep in mind is that programs run in Windows Server 2008 R2 start without administrative privileges by default. This also applies to Windows PowerShell. In order to run Windows PowerShell with administrative privileges, you need to right-click the icon and choose Run as administrator.

In SharePoint 2010, you can also start Windows PowerShell through the SharePoint 2010 Management Shell. You'll find the SharePoint 2010 Management Shell in the Microsoft SharePoint 2010 Products folder located under All Programs in the Start menu. When you start PowerShell this way, the shell loads all SharePoint cmdlets included in SharePoint 2010.

As you've seen, it's easy to get Windows PowerShell up and running. Now let's review some PowerShell basics before diving into scripting.

Windows PowerShell Basics

Over the years, Microsoft's command line has been relatively weak compared to that offered by some other operating systems. This was mainly because Microsoft developers made a tactical decision and put most of their resources into optimizing the graphical interface, which allowed Microsoft to reach a leading position in the personal computing market. One of the downsides of this is that the command line and scripting capabilities were a little underdeveloped.

In 2003, Microsoft started to develop a new shell that would cover the command line and scripting functionality in the Windows environment. The codename for the shell was Monad, which became Windows PowerShell, Microsoft's new command line and scripting environment.

Windows PowerShell is based on the .NET Framework, which has deep ties to almost every aspect of the Windows operating system. By using .NET, Windows PowerShell gets quick and simple access to various components of Windows.

Why Use Windows PowerShell?

Let's consider the typical administrative task of creating SharePoint team sites. You can create a new team site in Microsoft SharePoint 2010 through the web interface by clicking Site Actions, New Site, Collaboration, and finally Team Site. After that, you can add the title and the site's URL. You can also add other options, such as a description, permissions, and navigation.

Adding one site through the web interface is quite simple and does not take that much time. But what if you want to add ten new team sites? You could repeat the same process ten times in the web interface, or you could start the SharePoint 2010 Management Shell and run the following command:

```
PS > 1..10 | ForEach-Object {
>> New-SPWeb -Url "http://SPServer01/Web$_" -Description "Web $_" -Template STS#0
>> }
>>


Url
---
http://spserver01/Web1
http://spserver01/Web2
http://spserver01/Web3
http://spserver01/Web4
http://spserver01/Web5
http://spserver01/Web6
http://spserver01/Web7
http://spserver01/Web8
http://spserver01/Web9
http://spserver01/Web10
```

This creates ten new web sites with just a couple of lines of code.

Windows PowerShell is a very powerful asset to SharePoint administrators. By learning the Windows PowerShell language, you can save hours of work.

What Are Objects in Windows PowerShell?

One of Windows PowerShell's biggest differences from classic shells is that it works with objects instead of traditional strings. An *object* is a package containing both data and information describing how to use the object. The information about how to use the object is stored in methods. The data that you can retrieve and sometimes modify is stored in properties.

Let's check out an example of an object in PowerShell.

```
PS > $string = "My first String"
```

This example writes a bit of text enclosed within double quotation marks and assigns the text to the variable $string. In traditional languages, the variable would simply hold a string (nothing more than an encoded sequence of characters). But since Windows PowerShell works with objects containing rich data, $string is actually an instance of the .NET System.String class containing the various methods and properties available from the class.

Let's say we want to find out the length of the string. We can do that by simply calling the Length property:

```
PS > $string.Length
15
```

When we call the Length property, Windows PowerShell returns the number 15, since "My first String" contains 15 characters. Note that Windows PowerShell does not contain a library of string routines but uses .NET to leverage the object containing methods and properties.

Let's compare the preceding example to VBScript. When getting the length of a string in VBScript, we first need to create a variable holding the string, and then use the Len function on the string to retrieve its length.

```
strString = "My first String"
Wscript.echo Len(strString)
```

Even though both examples retrieve the same information, Windows PowerShell doesn't need to call an extra function, since the object itself contains the information.

Objects also contain methods that you can use. If we want to present our string in uppercase, we could simply use the uppercase method that is available on the object:

```
PS > $string.ToUpper()
MY FIRST STRING
```

If we want to achieve the same result with VBScript, we would need to use the UCase function:

```
strString = "My first String"
Wscript.echo UCase(strString)
```

Note that different types of objects contain different methods and properties, as you'll see in upcoming examples.

What Are Windows PowerShell Cmdlets?

Windows PowerShell offers many built-in cmdlets to help you in your daily work. A *cmdlet* (pronounced "command-let") is a single-feature command that manipulates objects in Windows PowerShell. You can easily recognize cmdlets by their `verb-noun` name, such as `Get-ChildItem`.

> **NOTE**   You can find a full list of the built-in cmdlets in your local Windows PowerShell help or its online version, at http://technet.microsoft.com/en-us/library/dd315281.aspx.

The Windows PowerShell product team publishes a set of guidelines for cmdlet designers, to make the process of finding and using the right cmdlet easier and more comprehensible. Probably the most important of those is that a cmdlet's name should always be a verb-noun pair, and that it should start with an approved (vetted by Microsoft) verb.

Windows PowerShell V2 (released with Windows 7 and Windows Server 2008 R2) introduced a new guideline, which recommends prefixing nouns with a short unique technology-specific moniker, such as `SP` for SharePoint and `AD` for Active Directory. Adding a prefix to the noun makes it easier to find cmdlets relating to a specific technology.

SharePoint 2010 Cmdlets

The set of cmdlets shipped with Windows PowerShell is restricted to generic cmdlets and those designed for managing different aspects of the Windows operating system. To ensure extensibility and allow other technologies such as SharePoint to make full use of its advantages, Windows PowerShell uses snap-ins—Microsoft .NET Framework assemblies that may contain custom Windows PowerShell cmdlets.

The SharePoint 2010 snap-in for Windows PowerShell contains more than 500 cmdlets that you can use to perform a large variety of administrative tasks. This snap-in is loaded automatically when you run the SharePoint 2010 Management Shell. If you start a standard PowerShell console, you need to load this snap-in manually in order to access the SharePoint 2010 cmdlets. Two native Windows PowerShell cmdlets can help with this: `Get-PSSnapin` to retrieve information about all the snap-ins registered in the system, and `Add-PSSnapin` to actually load the snap-in into the current Windows PowerShell session.

The following example uses the `Get-PSSnapin` cmdlet with the switch parameter `Registered` to find the name of the SharePoint 2010 snap-in:

```
PS > Get-PSSnapin -Registered


Name        : Microsoft.SharePoint.PowerShell
PSVersion   : 1.0
Description : Register all administration Cmdlets for Microsoft Share-
Point Server
```

And here's how to add the snap-in with the `Add-PSSnapin` cmdlet:

```
PS > Add-PSSnapin Microsoft.SharePoint.PowerShell
```

After you've added the SharePoint 2010 snap-in, you can access all the cmdlets included in SharePoint 2010.

The standard PowerShell console and the SharePoint 2010 Management Shell also differ in how threads are created and used. The PowerShell console runs each pipeline (as marked by a hit of the "Enter" button), function, or script on its own thread, while the SharePoint 2010 Management Shell runs each line, function, or script on the same thread. When working with the SharePoint object model using PowerShell, running code on separate threads can cause memory leaks, while commands running on the same thread have a smaller chance of doing so. This is because some SharePoint objects still use unmanaged code and the way memory is allocated to those objects.

The threading model used is determined by the value of the ThreadOptions property of each PowerShell runspace (each PowerShell console window is a runspace). The SharePoint 2010 Management Shell uses the ReuseThread option set in the SharePoint.ps1 file that is executed every time you start the shell from the SharePoint 2010 menu group. The standard PowerShell console, however, does not have this option configured out of the box and thus uses the default, which is UseNewThread. A good practice is to set the ThreadOption property to ReuseThread when working with SharePoint 2010 using the standard PowerShell console. The example below demonstrates how you set the ThreadOption property.

```
PS > $Host.Runspace.ThreadOptions = "ReuseThread"
```

Finding the SharePoint 2010 Cmdlets

Windows PowerShell includes a great cmdlet called `Get-Command`. This cmdlet returns basic information about cmdlets and other elements of Windows PowerShell commands, such as functions, aliases, filters, scripts, and applications. Figure 3-1 shows the output from `Get-Command`.

As mentioned earlier, all nouns of the SharePoint 2010 cmdlets start with SP. Knowing this, you can retrieve all SharePoint cmdlets. Just use `Get-Command`'s –Noun parameter followed by SP*:

```
PS > Get-Command -Noun SP*
```

The asterisk (*) is used to perform a wildcard match, meaning that you want to retrieve all cmdlets, aliases, functions, and so on where the noun starts with SP. As shown in Figure 3-2, the list is pretty long.

You can find out exactly how many SharePoint 2010 cmdlets are available by counting them and specifying that you want only cmdlets returned using the `CommandType` parameter:

```
PS > (Get-Command -Name *-SP* -CommandType cmdlet).Count
531
```

```
PS > Get-Command

CommandType   Name                                           Definition
-----------   ----                                           ----------
Alias         %                                              ForEach-Object
Alias         ?                                              Where-Object
Function      A:                                             Set-Location A:
Alias         ac                                             Add-Content
Cmdlet        Add-Computer                                   Add-Computer [-DomainName] <String> [-Credential...
Cmdlet        Add-Content                                    Add-Content [-Path] <String[]> [-Value] <Object[...
Cmdlet        Add-History                                    Add-History [[-InputObject] <PSObject[]>] [-Pass...
Cmdlet        Add-Member                                     Add-Member [-MemberType] <PSMemberTypes> [-Name]...
Cmdlet        Add-PluggableSecurityTrimmer                   Add-PluggableSecurityTrimmer [-UserProfileApplic...
Cmdlet        Add-PSSnapin                                   Add-PSSnapin [-Name] <String[]> [-PassThru] [-Ve...
Cmdlet        Add-SPClaimTypeMapping                         Add-SPClaimTypeMapping [-Identity] <SPClaimMappi...
Cmdlet        Add-SPDiagnosticsPerformanceCounter            Add-SPDiagnosticsPerformanceCounter [-Category] ...
Cmdlet        Add-SPInfoPathUserAgent                        Add-SPInfoPathUserAgent [-Name] <String> [-Assig...
Cmdlet        Add-SPServiceApplicationProxyGroupMember       Add-SPServiceApplicationProxyGroupMember [-Ident...
Cmdlet        Add-SPShellAdmin                               Add-SPShellAdmin [-UserName] <String> [-database...
Cmdlet        Add-SPSiteSubscriptionFeaturePackMember        Add-SPSiteSubscriptionFeaturePackMember [-Identi...
Cmdlet        Add-SPSiteSubscriptionProfileConfig            Add-SPSiteSubscriptionProfileConfig [-Identity] ...
Cmdlet        Add-SPSolution                                 Add-SPSolution [-LiteralPath] <String> [-Languag...
Cmdlet        Add-SPUserSolution                             Add-SPUserSolution [-LiteralPath] <String> -Site...
Cmdlet        Add-Type                                       Add-Type [-TypeDefinition] <String> [-Language <...
Alias         asnp                                           Add-PSSnapin
Function      B:                                             Set-Location B:
Cmdlet        Backup-SPConfigurationDatabase                 Backup-SPConfigurationDatabase [-DatabaseName <S...
Cmdlet        Backup-SPFarm                                  Backup-SPFarm -Directory <String> -BackupMethod ...
Cmdlet        Backup-SPSite                                  Backup-SPSite [-Identity] <SPSitePipeBind> -Path...
Function      C:                                             Set-Location C:
Alias         cat                                            Get-Content
Alias         cd                                             Set-Location
Function      cd..                                           Set-Location ..
Function      cd\                                            Set-Location \
Alias         chdir                                          Set-Location
Cmdlet        Checkpoint-Computer                            Checkpoint-Computer [-Description] <String> [[-R...
Alias         clc                                            Clear-Content
Alias         clear                                          Clear-Host
Cmdlet        Clear-Content                                  Clear-Content [-Path] <String[]> [-Filter <Strin...
Cmdlet        Clear-EventLog                                 Clear-EventLog [-LogName] <String[]> [[-Computer...
Cmdlet        Clear-History                                  Clear-History [[-Id] <Int32[]>] [[-Count] <Int32...
Function      Clear-Host                                     $space = New-Object System.Management.Automation...
Cmdlet        Clear-Item                                     Clear-Item [-Path] <String[]> [-Force] [-Filter ...
Cmdlet        Clear-ItemProperty                             Clear-ItemProperty [-Path] <String[]> [-Name] <S...
Cmdlet        Clear-SPLogLevel                               Clear-SPLogLevel [-Identity <String[]>] [-InputO...
Cmdlet        Clear-SPMetadataWebServicePartitionData        Clear-SPMetadataWebServicePartitionData [-Servic...
Cmdlet        Clear-SPPerformancePointServiceApplicationTruste... Clear-SPPerformancePointServiceApplicationTruste...
Cmdlet        Clear-SPSecureStoreCredentialMapping           Clear-SPSecureStoreCredentialMapping -Identity <...
Cmdlet        Clear-SPSecureStoreDefaultProvider             Clear-SPSecureStoreDefaultProvider [-AssignmentC...
Cmdlet        Clear-SPSiteSubscriptionBusinessDataCatalogConfig  Clear-SPSiteSubscriptionBusinessDataCatalogConfi...
```

Figure 3-1.   Using the Get-Command cmdlet

Here, you place the command within parentheses and use the `Count` property on the resulting `System.Array` object to retrieve the actual number of cmdlets where the noun starts with SP.

Placing commands or code within parentheses forces Windows PowerShell into expression mode, meaning that the contents of the parentheses are evaluated (and in this case executed) first. The result is returned as an object, and then that object's methods and properties are available for you to use. It's also possible to count the number of cmdlets using the `Measure-Object` cmdlet, as you will see in the "Measuring Objects in Windows PowerShell" section later in this chapter.

You can use `Get-Command` to find specific SharePoint 2010 cmdlets. Say you want to retrieve all SharePoint 2010 cmdlets that are used to manage site collections. You can achieve this by specifying that the noun should include SPSite:

```
PS > Get-Command -Noun SPSite


CommandType Name           Definition
----------- ----           ----------
Cmdlet      Backup-SPSite  Backup-SPSite [-Identity] <SPSitePipeBind> -Path <
Cmdlet      Get-SPSite     Get-SPSite [-Limit <String>] [-WebApplication <SPW
Cmdlet      Move-SPSite    Move-SPSite [-Identity] <SPSitePipeBind> -Destinat
```

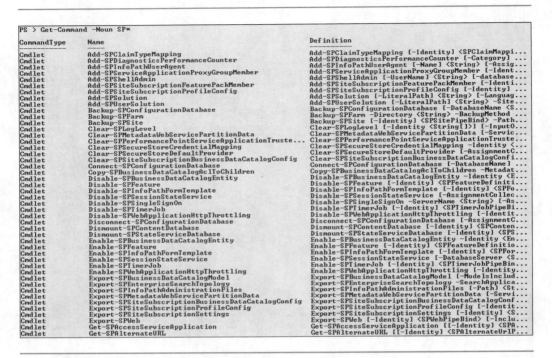

Figure 3-2. Using Get-Command with the -Noun parameter

```
Cmdlet     New-SPSite      New-SPSite [-Url] <String> [-Language <UInt32>] [-
Cmdlet     Remove-SPSite   Remove-SPSite [-Identity] <SPSitePipeBind> [-Delet
Cmdlet     Restore-SPSite  Restore-SPSite [-Identity] <String> -Path <String>
Cmdlet     Set-SPSite      Set-SPSite [-Identity] <SPSitePipeBind> [-OwnerAli
```

The output from the command shows seven different cmdlets that you can use when working with site collections. If you take a closer look at the verbs in the cmdlets, you'll see that they are self-describing. `Get` is used for getting information, `Set` is used for modifying site collections, and so on.

You can go even further and get information on a specific cmdlet. Here is how you can use `Get-Command` to retrieve information on the `Get-SPSite` cmdlet:

```
PS > Get-Command Get-SPSite

CommandType Name       Definition
----------- ----       ----------
Cmdlet      Get-SPSite Get-SPSite [-Limit <String>] [-WebApplication
```

You can see the command type, its name, and its definition.

Next, let's see how to get information about how to use a cmdlet in SharePoint 2010.

Getting Help

The `Get-Help` cmdlet returns information about concepts and commands in Windows PowerShell, including cmdlets, providers, aliases, functions, and scripts. Using `Get-Help` is a great way to find out more about how to use the various cmdlets in Windows PowerShell. Not only do you get detailed information about when and how to use the cmdlets, you also get great examples that show you how to perform administrative tasks.

Here's how to get help on the `Get-SPSite` cmdlet:

```
PS > Get-Help Get-SPSite
```

As shown in Figure 3-3, the command returns information that helps you understand the `Get-SPSite` cmdlet. It displays a synopsis that summarizes the purpose of the cmdlet, a syntax statement that shows how to run the cmdlet, a description that explains the cmdlet in detail, and related links to find out more about other cmdlets and resources. At the bottom of the returned text, you see that you can use the `Get-Help` cmdlet with additional parameters to get even more information.

If you want to see examples on how to use the cmdlet, add the `Examples` parameter:

```
Get-Help Get-SPSite -Examples
```

```
PS > Get-Help Get-SPSite

NAME
    Get-SPSite

SYNOPSIS
    Returns all site collections that match the given criteria.


SYNTAX
    Get-SPSite [-AssignmentCollection <SPAssignmentCollection>] [-Confirm [<SwitchParameter>]] [-Filter <ScriptBlock>]
    [-Limit <String>] [-WebApplication <SPWebApplicationPipeBind>] [-WhatIf [<SwitchParameter>]] [<CommonParameters>]

    Get-SPSite -Identity <SPSitePipeBind> [-AssignmentCollection <SPAssignmentCollection>] [-Confirm [<SwitchParameter>
    ]] [-Filter <ScriptBlock>] [-Limit <String>] [-Regex <SwitchParameter>] [-WhatIf [<SwitchParameter>]] [<CommonParam
    eters>]

    Get-SPSite -ContentDatabase <SPContentDatabasePipeBind> [-AssignmentCollection <SPAssignmentCollection>] [-Confirm
    [<SwitchParameter>]] [-Filter <ScriptBlock>] [-Limit <String>] [-WhatIf [<SwitchParameter>]] [<CommonParameters>]

    Get-SPSite -SiteSubscription <SPSiteSubscriptionPipeBind> [-AssignmentCollection <SPAssignmentCollection>] [-Confir
    m [<SwitchParameter>]] [-Filter <ScriptBlock>] [-Limit <String>] [-WhatIf [<SwitchParameter>]] [<CommonParameters>]


DESCRIPTION
    The Get-SPSite cmdlet returns either a single site that matches the Identity parameter, or all the sites that match
    the Filter parameter for the specified scope. The scopes are the WebApplication , ContentDatabase , and SiteSubscr
    iption parameters. If none of these scopes is provided, the scope is the farm. If the scope is specified with no Fi
    lter parameter, all sites in that scope are returned.

    The Identity parameter supports providing a partial URL that ends in a wildcard character (*). All site collections
    that match this partial URL for the specified scope are returned. Additionally, if the Regex parameter is provided
    , the Identity parameter is treated as a regular expression and any site collection with a URL provided in the give
    n scope that matches the expression is returned.

    The Filter parameter is a server-side filter for certain site collection properties that are stored in the content
    database; without the Filter parameter, filtering on these properties is a slow process. These site collection prop
    erties are Owner, SecondaryOwner, and LockState. The Filter parameter is a script block that uses the same syntax a
    s a Where-Object statement, but is run server-side for faster results.

    It is important to note that every site collection returned by the Get-SPSite cmdlet is automatically disposed of a
    t the end of the pipeline. To store the results of Get-SPSite in a local variable, the Start-SPAssignment and Stop-
    SPAssignment cmdlets must be used to avoid memory leaks. See Get-Help About_SPAssignment for more information.


RELATED LINKS
REMARKS
```

Figure 3-3.   Getting help with the Get-SPSite cmdlet

As shown in Figure 3-4, this command shows examples of how a cmdlet works in action.

```
PS > Get-Help Get-SPSite -Examples
NAME
    Get-SPSite
SYNOPSIS
    Returns all site collections that match the given criteria.

    -----------------EXAMPLE 1-----------------
    C:\PS>Get-SPSite 'http://sitename' | Get-SPWeb -Limit All | Select Title

    The preceding example gets the collection of subweb titles in site collection at http://sitename.
    -----------------EXAMPLE 2-----------------
    C:\PS>Get-SPSite -ContentDatabase "b399a366-d899-4cff-8a9b-8c0594ee755f" | Format-Table -Property Url, Owner, Secon
    daryOwner

    The preceding example gets a subset of data from all of the sites in the content database b399a366-d899-4cff-8a9b-8
    c0594ee755f.
    -----------------EXAMPLE 3-----------------
    C:\PS>Start-SPAssignment -Global C:\PS>$s = Get-SPSite -Identity http://MyApp/Sites/Site1 C:\PS>$s.Url C:\PS>Stop-S
    PAssignment -Global

    The preceding example gets the sites specified by the Identity parameter and inserts the results in the variable s
    The previous example uses the Global method of assignment collection. The Global method is easier to use but the co
    ntents of this object grows quickly. Be careful not to run a Get-SPSite command that returns many results while glo
    bal assignment is enabled.
    -----------------EXAMPLE 4-----------------
    C:\PS>$GC = Start-SPAssignment C:\PS>$Sites = $GC | Get-SPSite -Filter {$_.Owner -eq "DOMAIN\JDoe"} -Limit 50 C:\PS
    >Stop-SPAssignment $GC

    The preceding example gets the first 50 sites owned by user DOMAIN\JDoe by using a server-side query, and assigns t
    hem to a local variable.
    This example uses advanced Assignment Collection methods.
    -----------------EXAMPLE 5-----------------
```

Figure 3-4. Using the Get-Help –Examples parameter

Other `Get-Help` parameters are `Detailed`, which adds parameter descriptions and examples to the basic help display, and `Full`, which displays the entire help file for a cmdlet.

`Get-Help` also supports wildcards when searching for information about cmdlets and concepts in Windows PowerShell. Using wildcards in combination with verbs or nouns is a quick way to find out more about the many cmdlets included in SharePoint 2010. For example, you can get help on all cmdlets using the noun `SPSite` as follows:

```
PS > Get-Help *-SPSite
```

This displays each cmdlet's synopsis, instead of the complete definition, as shown in Figure 3-5.

It's also possible to access help for a particular cmdlet by typing the cmdlet's name followed by `-?`:

```
PS > Get-SPSite -?
```

Windows PowerShell also includes conceptual help topics stored in help files. Help topics in Windows PowerShell start with `about_` and contain detailed information

```
PS > Get-Help *-SPSite

Name                    Category  Synopsis
----                    --------  --------
New-SPSite              Cmdlet    Creates a new site collection at the specified URL.
Get-SPSite             Cmdlet    Returns all site collections that match the given criteria.
Set-SPSite             Cmdlet    Configures the specified sites.
Remove-SPSite          Cmdlet    Completely deletes an existing site collection and all subsites.
Move-SPSite            Cmdlet    Move-SPSite [-Identity] <SPSitePipeBind> -DestinationDatabase <SPContent...
Backup-SPSite          Cmdlet    Performs a backup of a site collection.
Restore-SPSite         Cmdlet    Restores a site collection.


PS > _
```

Figure 3-5.   Using Get-Help to retrieve information about multiple cmdlets

about functions, providers, scripts, operators, and so on. To get a list of all help topics available, use this command:

```
PS > Get-Help about_
```

As shown in Figure 3-6, this command displays a long list containing all available help files in Windows PowerShell. If you want to retrieve information from a specific help topic, simply type Get-Help followed by the topic's name.

The help for both the core Windows PowerShell and the SharePoint 2010 snap-in cmdlets are also available in the CHM format.

```
PS > Get-Help about_

Name                                  Category  Synopsis
----                                  --------  --------
about_aliases                         HelpFile  Describes how to use alternate names for cmdlets and commands in Windows
about_Arithmetic_Operators            HelpFile  Describes the operators that perform arithmetic in Windows PowerShell.
about_arrays                          HelpFile  Describes a compact data structure for storing data elements.
about_Assignment_Operators            HelpFile  Describes how to use operators to assign values to variables.
about_Automatic_Variables             HelpFile  Describes variables that store state information for Windows PowerShell.
about_Break                           HelpFile  Describes a statement you can use to immediately exit Foreach, For, While,
about_command_precedence              HelpFile  Describes how Windows PowerShell determines which command to run.
about_Command_Syntax                  HelpFile  Describes the notation used for Windows PowerShell syntax in Help.
about_Comment_Based_Help              HelpFile  Describes how to write comment-based Help topics for functions and scripts.
about_CommonParameters                HelpFile  Describes the parameters that can be used with any cmdlet.
about_Comparison_Operators            HelpFile  Describes the operators that compare values in Windows PowerShell.
about_Continue                        HelpFile  Describes how the Continue statement immediately returns the program flow
about_Core_Commands                   HelpFile  Lists the cmdlets that are designed for use with Windows PowerShell
about_data_sections                   HelpFile  Explains Data sections, which isolate text strings and other read-only
about_debuggers                       HelpFile  Describes the Windows PowerShell debugger.
about_do                              HelpFile  Runs a statement list one or more times, subject to a While or Until
about_environment_variables           HelpFile  Describes how to access Windows environment variables in Windows
about_escape_characters               HelpFile  Introduces the escape character in Windows PowerShell and explains
about_eventlogs                       HelpFile  Windows PowerShell creates a Windows event log that is
about_execution_policies              HelpFile  Describes the Windows PowerShell execution policies and explains
about_For                             HelpFile  Describes a language command you can use to run statements based on a
about_Foreach                         HelpFile  Describes a language command you can use to traverse all the items in a
about_format.ps1xml                   HelpFile  The Format.ps1xml files in Windows PowerShell define the default display
about_functions                       HelpFile  Describes how to create and use functions in Windows PowerShell.
about_functions_advanced              HelpFile  Introduces advanced functions that act similar to cmdlets.
about_functions_advanced_methods      HelpFile  Describes how functions that specify the CmdletBinding attribute can use
about_functions_advanced_param...     HelpFile  Explains how to add static and dynamic parameters to functions that declare
about_functions_cmdletbindinga...     HelpFile  Describes an attribute that declares a function that acts similar to a
about_hash_tables                     HelpFile  Describes how to create, use, and sort hash tables in Windows PowerShell.
about_History                         HelpFile  Describes how to retrieve and run commands in the command history.
about_If                              HelpFile  Describes a language command you can use to run statement lists based
about_jobs                            HelpFile  Provides information about how Windows PowerShell background jobs run a
about_job_details                     HelpFile  Provides details about background jobs on local and remote computers .
about_join                            HelpFile  Describes how the join operator (-join) combines multiple strings into a
about_Language_Keywords               HelpFile  Describes the keywords in the Windows PowerShell scripting language.
about_Line_Editing                    HelpFile  Describes how to edit commands at the Windows PowerShell command prompt.
about_locations                       HelpFile  Describes how to access items from the working location in Windows
about_logical_operators               HelpFile  Describes the operators that connect statements in Windows PowerShell.
about_methods                         HelpFile  Describes how to use methods to perform actions on objects in Windows
about_modules                         HelpFile  Explains how to install, import, and use Windows PowerShell modules.
about_objects                         HelpFile  Provides essential information about objects in Windows PowerShell.
about_operators                       HelpFile  Describes the operators that are supported by Windows PowerShell.
about_parameters                      HelpFile  Describes how to work with cmdlet parameters in Windows PowerShell.
about_Parsing                         HelpFile  Describes how Windows PowerShell parses commands.
about_Path_Syntax                     HelpFile  Describes the full and relative path name formats in Windows PowerShell.
about_pipelines                       HelpFile  Combining commands into pipelines in the Windows PowerShell
```

Figure 3-6.   Using Get-Help about_ to get a list of help topics

Aliases

Aliases are nicknames for cmdlets in Windows PowerShell that we can use instead of typing the cmdlets name. An example of an alias is dir, which is actually an alias for the Get-ChildItem cmdlet. To retrieve a list of all available aliases in Windows PowerShell, we can use the Get-Alias cmdlet and to retrieve a specific alias we can type

```
PS > Get-Alias dir
CommandType Name Definition
----------- ---- ----------
Alias       dir  Get-ChildItem
```

If we want to find out which aliases a cmdlet supports, we can use the -definition parameter and specify the cmdlets name.

```
PS > Get-Alias -Definition Get-ChildItem

CommandType Name Definition
----------- ---- ----------
Alias       dir  Get-ChildItem
Alias       gci  Get-ChildItem
Alias       ls   Get-ChildItem
```

We see that the Get-ChildItem cmdlet supports three different aliases, dir, gci, and ls. We can create our own aliases through the Set-Alias cmdlet. If we want to create an alias for a SharePoint 2010 cmdlet, we can type

```
PS > Set-Alias -Name site -Value Get-SPSite
PS > Get-Alias site
CommandType Name    Definition
----------- ----    ----------
Alias       site    Get-SPSite
```

When we type Get-Alias and specify our new alias as input to the command, we see that our new alias is created in the current session. We can now use this alias to run the cmdlet as shown in the example below.

```
PS > site
Url
---
http://spserver01
```

NOTE   The aliases created exist only in the current session. To make the aliases available in different Windows PowerShell sessions, add the alias to a profile script.

Using Parameters with Cmdlets

Most cmdlets in Windows PowerShell accept parameters that allow you to provide input and select options that tell the cmdlet how to behave. Parameters vary between different cmdlets, so it's a good idea to use the `Get-Help` cmdlet to see which parameters a specific cmdlet supports.

Let's continue looking at the `Get-SPSite` cmdlet. You can get information about all supported parameters with the `Get-Help` cmdlet by using the `Parameter` parameter with an asterisk:

```
PS > Get-Help Get-SPSite -Parameter *
```

Figure 3-7 shows the result. Let's take a closer look at how to use the different parameters.

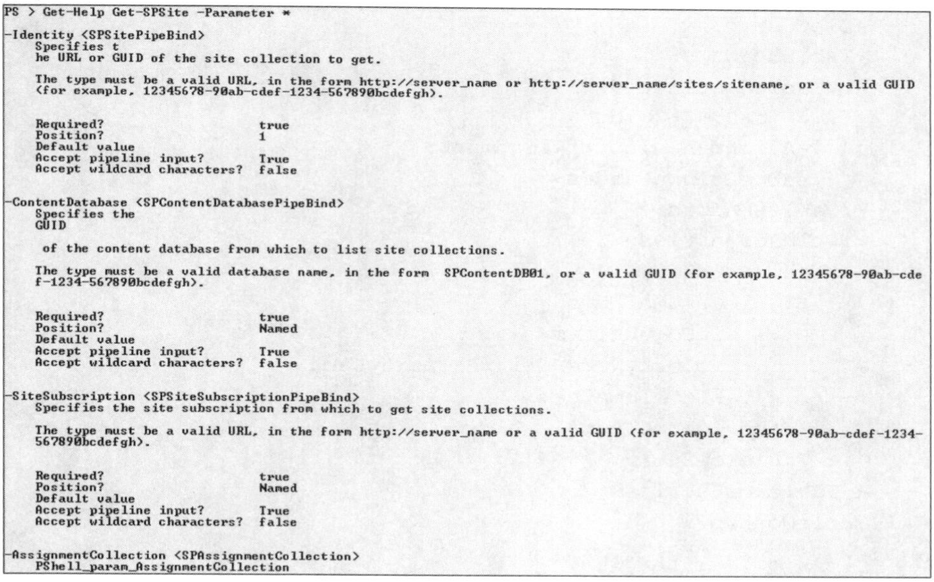

```
PS > Get-Help Get-SPSite -Parameter *

-Identity <SPSitePipeBind>
    Specifies t
    he URL or GUID of the site collection to get.

    The type must be a valid URL, in the form http://server_name or http://server_name/sites/sitename, or a valid GUID
    (for example, 12345678-90ab-cdef-1234-567890bcdefgh).


    Required?                    true
    Position?                    1
    Default value
    Accept pipeline input?       True
    Accept wildcard characters?  false

-ContentDatabase <SPContentDatabasePipeBind>
    Specifies the
    GUID

     of the content database from which to list site collections.

    The type must be a valid database name, in the form  SPContentDB01, or a valid GUID (for example, 12345678-90ab-cde
    f-1234-567890bcdefgh).


    Required?                    true
    Position?                    Named
    Default value
    Accept pipeline input?       True
    Accept wildcard characters?  false

-SiteSubscription <SPSiteSubscriptionPipeBind>
    Specifies the site subscription from which to get site collections.

    The type must be a valid URL, in the form http://server_name or a valid GUID (for example, 12345678-90ab-cdef-1234-
    567890bcdefgh).


    Required?                    true
    Position?                    Named
    Default value
    Accept pipeline input?       True
    Accept wildcard characters?  false

-AssignmentCollection <SPAssignmentCollection>
    PShell_param_AssignmentCollection
```

Figure 3-7. View Get-SPSite parameters

The `Identity` parameter is used to specify the URL or the GUID of the site collection. For example, if you have a site with the URL http://SPServer01, you can use the `Identity` parameter followed by this URL to retrieve the site collection in Windows PowerShell:

```
PS > Get-SPSite -identity http://SPServer01


Url
---
http://spserver01
```

Notice how the cmdlet displays only the URL of the site collection, although the returned object has a lot more properties. To generate this default display of various .NET objects, Windows PowerShell uses formatting files, which are specially constructed XML files whose names end in .format.ps1xml.

Windows PowerShell includes ten formatting files stored in the PowerShell install directory, and SharePoint 2010 comes with 13 additional formatting files stored in the SharePoint application directory (the 14 hive). The display of the Microsoft .SharePoint.SPSite object, which represents a site collection, is defined in the largest of these files, SharepointPowershell.Format.ps1xml, using the following code:

```
<View>
  <Name>SPSite</Name>
  <ViewSelectedBy>
    <TypeName>Microsoft.SharePoint.SPSite</TypeName>
  </ViewSelectedBy>
  <TableControl>
    <TableHeaders>
      <TableColumnHeader>
        <Width>55</Width>
        <Alignment>left</Alignment>
      </TableColumnHeader>
    </TableHeaders>
    <TableRowEntries>
      <TableRowEntry>
        <TableColumnItems>
          <TableColumnItem>
            <PropertyName>Url</PropertyName>
          </TableColumnItem>
        </TableColumnItems>
      </TableRowEntry>
    </TableRowEntries>
  </TableControl>
</View>
```

The formatting affects the display only, and not the functionality of objects or the way they are passed along the pipeline.

NOTE It is also possible to create your own custom formatting files in Windows PowerShell if required.

To see additional properties of the object, you can pipe the object to the Format-List cmdlet and display additional properties:

```
PS > Get-SPSite -identity http://SPServer01 | Format-List
```

Figure 3-8 shows the result of this example. Using pipelines is a simple but powerful way of combining cmdlets, as discussed in the next section.

```
PS > Get-SPSite -Identity http://SPServer01 | Format-List

ApplicationRightsMask               : FullMask
ID                                  : f8691b03-af19-478c-b06b-e71b0c74d0d0
SystemAccount                       : SHAREPOINT\system
Owner                               : POWERSHELL\administrator
SecondaryContact                    :
GlobalPermMask                      : FullMask
IISAllowsAnonymous                  : False
Protocol                            : http:
HostHeaderIsSiteName                : False
HostName                            : spserver01
Port                                : 80
ServerRelativeUrl                   : /
UpgradeRedirectUri                  : http://spserver01/
Zone                                : Default
Url                                 : http://spserver01
UserCodeEnabled                     : False
Impersonating                       : True
Audit                               : Microsoft.SharePoint.SPAudit
TrimAuditLog                        : False
AuditLogTrimmingCallout             :
AuditLogTrimmingRetention           : 0
AllWebs                             : {Home}
Features                            : {0c8a9a47-22a9-4798-82f1-00e62a96006e, 068bc832-4951-11dc-8314-0800200c9a66, 91
                                      5c240e-a6cc-49b8-8b2c-0bff8b553ed3, 2ed1c45e-a73b-4779-ae81-1524e4de467a...}
UserCustomActions                   : {}
PortalUrl                           :
PortalName                          :
LastContentModifiedDate             : 4/10/2010 9:21:35 PM
LastSecurityModifiedDate            : 3/28/2010 11:44:42 PM
CurrentResourceUsage                : 0
AverageResourceUsage                : 0
Cache                               : Microsoft.SharePoint.Administration.SPSiteCollectionPropertyCache
BrowserDocumentsEnabled             : True
CatchAccessDeniedException          : False
AllowUnsafeUpdates                  : True
UserToken                           : Microsoft.SharePoint.SPUserToken
IsPaired                            : False
SearchServiceInstance               :
WebApplication                      : SPWebApplication Name=SharePoint - 80
SiteSubscription                    :
ContentDatabase                     : SPContentDatabase Name=WSS_Content
Quota                               : Microsoft.SharePoint.Administration.SPQuota
RootWeb                             : Home
LockIssue                           :
Usage                               : Microsoft.SharePoint.SPSite+UsageInfo
UIVersionConfigurationEnabled       : False
ReadLocked                          : False
```

Figure 3-8.   Combining cmdlets in a pipeline

You can also place the command within parentheses and call a specific property. The following example retrieves the Id property of the object:

```
PS > (Get-SPSite -identity http://SPServer01).Id

Guid
----
f8691b03-af19-478c-b06b-e71b0c74d0d0
```

The object's Id is of the type System.Guid. Remember how the Identity parameter accepts a URL or a GUID as input? If you know the Id of a site collection, you can use it to retrieve a site collection with the Get-SPSite cmdlet. The following example stores the Id in a variable and uses it with the Get-SPSite cmdlet to retrieve the site collection.

```
PS > $id = (Get-SPSite -identity http://SPServer01).Id
PS > Get-SPSite $id

Url
---
http://spserver01
```

If you want to find out which site collections are available in a content database, you can use the `-ContentDatabase` parameter followed by the name or GUID of the content database. This example lists all site collections within the `WSS_Content` database.

```
PS > Get-SPSite -ContentDatabase WSS_Content

Url
---
http://spserver01
http://spserver01/my
```

The `Get-SPSite` cmdlet also supports the `Limit` parameter, which allows you to limit the number of site collections that are listed. By default, the limit is set to 200. You can specify a different number or set the limit to `ALL`, which lists all site collections. Let's see what happens if we set the limit to 1.

```
PS > Get-SPSite -ContentDatabase WSS_Content -Limit 1

Url
---
http://spserver01
WARNING: More results were found in Get-SPSite but were not returned.
Use '-Limit ALL' to return all possible results.
```

Since the content database contains more than one site collection, a warning message is displayed.

Another parameter supported by `Get-SPSite` is `Filter`. This parameter allows you to list all site collections that match a filter. The following example uses the `Filter` parameter to list all site collections where the owner equals PowerShell\administrator:

```
PS > Get-SPSite -Filter {$_.Owner -eq "PowerShell\administrator"}

Url
---
http://spserver01/my
http://spserver01
```

You can use different operators within the filter, such as `-match` and `-like`.

One parameter to keep in mind is the `WhatIf` switch. This is a risk-management parameter that forces a command to report what would happen if you executed it. When you use the `WhatIf` parameter, the command is not executed; instead, a message is returned that describes what would happen if you performed the command. The following example demonstrates using the `WhatIf` parameter with the `Remove-SPSite` cmdlet, which is used to delete site collections.

```
PS > Remove-SPSite http://SPServer01 -WhatIf
What if: Performing operation "Remove-SPSite" on Target "http://spserver01".
```

Pipelines

The pipeline is one of the most important operators in Windows PowerShell. It's used to combine a series of commands, sending the result of one command to the next. Each command in the pipeline receives its input from the previous command. Remember how Windows PowerShell works with objects instead of strings? When you combine commands with a pipeline, you do not just send a simple string down the pipeline— you send a rich object containing methods and properties.

Let's look at an example that shows how an object is passed from one command to another using a pipeline:

```
PS > Get-SPSite -Identity http://SPServer01 | Get-SPWeb
```

This example uses the Get-SPSite and Get-SPWeb cmdlets. It binds to a site collection with the Get-SPSite cmdlet, and then sends the object through a pipeline to the Get-SPWeb cmdlet, which is used to return all subsites of the specified site, as shown in Figure 3-9.

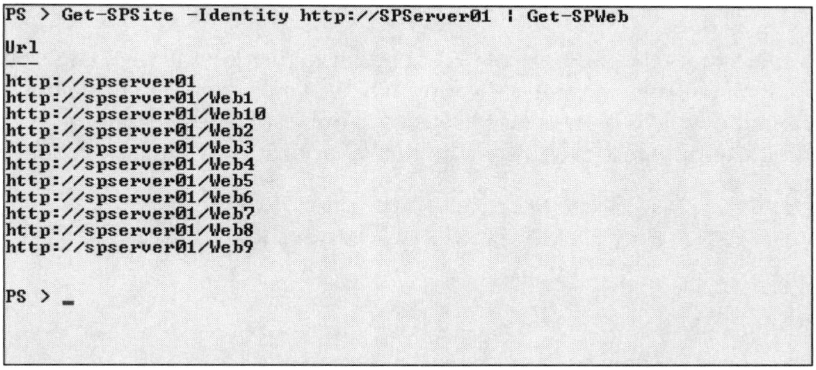

```
PS > Get-SPSite -Identity http://SPServer01 | Get-SPWeb

Url
---
http://spserver01
http://spserver01/Web1
http://spserver01/Web10
http://spserver01/Web2
http://spserver01/Web3
http://spserver01/Web4
http://spserver01/Web5
http://spserver01/Web6
http://spserver01/Web7
http://spserver01/Web8
http://spserver01/Web9


PS > _
```

Figure 3-9.   Combining cmdlets with a pipeline

The Get-SPWeb cmdlet supports the Identity parameter, which can take the URL of the target site as input. But if you look at the help file for Get-SPWeb, you may notice that the type of this parameter is SPWebPipeBind, meaning that the value for it can also be obtained from the pipeline.

Using Select-Object in a Pipeline

The Select-Object cmdlet offers a quick and easy way of gathering information from objects in Windows PowerShell. Notice how the command in the previous example displayed only the URLs of the sites listed in a table, although the object has a lot more properties. This is actually controlled by the formatting file stored in the SharePoint application directory (the 14 hive). Let's see how to list more properties using the `Select-Object` cmdlet.

```
PS > Get-SPSite -Identity http://SPServer01 | Get-SPWeb |
>> Select-Object -Property Title, Url, Description


Title          Url                       Description
-----          ---                       -----------
Home           http://spserver01         Home
Team Site      http://spserver01/Web1    Web 1
Team Site      http://spserver01/Web10   Web 10
Team Site      http://spserver01/Web2    Web 2
Team Site      http://spserver01/Web3    Web 3
Team Site      http://spserver01/Web4    Web 4
Team Site      http://spserver01/Web5    Web 5
Team Site      http://spserver01/Web6    Web 6
Team Site      http://spserver01/Web7    Web 7
Team Site      http://spserver01/Web8    Web 8
Team Site      http://spserver01/Web9    Web 9
```

This example uses the `Select-Object` cmdlet to display the title, URL, and description of all subsites in a site collection. The `Select-Object` cmdlet includes the `First` parameter, which allows you to select a number of objects from the beginning. The following example retrieves a specified number of subsites in a site collection.

```
PS > Get-SPSite -Identity http://SPServer01 | Get-SPWeb |
>> Select-Object -Property Title, Url, Description -First 2


Title          Url                       Description
-----          ---                       -----------
Home           http://spserver01         Home
Team Site      http://spserver01/Web1    Web 1
```

If you want to select objects from the end, use the `Last` parameter.

The `Select-Object` cmdlet contains a great feature that allows you to create constructed (hash table-based) properties. You can add constructed properties using a hash table with name and expression keys. One thing that might seem a little odd is the `$_` variable used in the constructed property.

The `$_` variable is an automatic variable in Windows PowerShell. It represents the current object in the pipeline. In other words, it represents each object that goes through the pipeline and performs the calculation on each object. To access the properties on an object with the `$_` variable, you need to add a dot followed by the property you want to access. The following example demonstrates how to access the `Groups` and `SiteUsers` properties.

```
PS > Get-SPWeb http://SPServer01 |
>> Select -Property Title, Description,
```

```
>> @{Name="Groups";Expression={$_.Groups.Count}},
>> @{Name="SiteUsers";Expression={$_.SiteUsers.Count}}

Title           Description   Groups   SiteUsers
-----           -----------   ------   ---------
Home            Home          9        17
```

This example uses the `Count` property to calculate the actual number of site users and groups in the subsite.

If you want to select all properties from an object in Windows PowerShell, you can use `Select-Object` followed by an asterisk:

```
PS > Get-SPWeb -Identity http://SPServer01 | Select-Object -Property *
```

Figure 3-10 shows the result of this command.

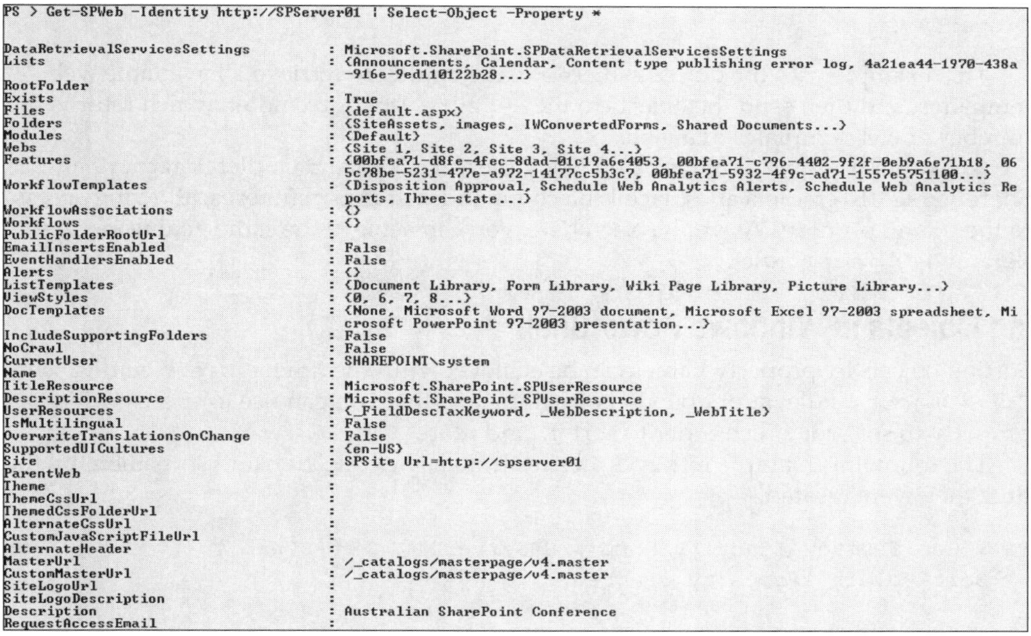

```
PS > Get-SPWeb -Identity http://SPServer01 | Select-Object -Property *


DataRetrievalServicesSettings        : Microsoft.SharePoint.SPDataRetrievalServicesSettings
Lists                                : {Announcements, Calendar, Content type publishing error log, 4a21ea44-1970-438a
                                       -916e-9ed110122b28...}
RootFolder                           :
Exists                               : True
Files                                : {default.aspx}
Folders                              : {SiteAssets, images, IWConvertedForms, Shared Documents...}
Modules                              : {Default}
Webs                                 : {Site 1, Site 2, Site 3, Site 4...}
Features                             : {00bfea71-d8fe-4fec-8dad-01c19a6e4053, 00bfea71-c796-4402-9f2f-0eb9a6e71b18, 06
                                       5c78be-5231-477e-a972-14177cc5b3c7, 00bfea71-5932-4f9c-ad71-1557e5751100...}
WorkflowTemplates                    : {Disposition Approval, Schedule Web Analytics Alerts, Schedule Web Analytics Re
                                       ports, Three-state...}
WorkflowAssociations                 : {}
Workflows                            : {}
PublicFolderRootUrl                  :
EmailInsertsEnabled                  : False
EventHandlersEnabled                 : False
Alerts                               : {}
ListTemplates                        : {Document Library, Form Library, Wiki Page Library, Picture Library...}
ViewStyles                           : {0, 6, 7, 8...}
DocTemplates                         : {None, Microsoft Word 97-2003 document, Microsoft Excel 97-2003 spreadsheet, Mi
                                       crosoft PowerPoint 97-2003 presentation...}
IncludeSupportingFolders             : False
NoCrawl                              : False
CurrentUser                          : SHAREPOINT\system
Name                                 :
TitleResource                        : Microsoft.SharePoint.SPUserResource
DescriptionResource                  : Microsoft.SharePoint.SPUserResource
UserResources                        : {_FieldDescTaxKeyword, _WebDescription, _WebTitle}
IsMultilingual                       : False
OverwriteTranslationsOnChange        : False
SupportedUICultures                  : {en-US}
Site                                 : SPSite Url=http://spserver01
ParentWeb                            :
Theme                                :
ThemeCssUrl                          :
ThemedCssFolderUrl                   :
AlternateCssUrl                      :
CustomJavaScriptFileUrl              :
AlternateHeader                      :
MasterUrl                            : /_catalogs/masterpage/v4.master
CustomMasterUrl                      : /_catalogs/masterpage/v4.master
SiteLogoUrl                          :
SiteLogoDescription                  :
Description                          : Australian SharePoint Conference
RequestAccessEmail                   :
```

Figure 3-10. Using Select-Object to list all properties

You can go further with a pipeline and combine it with other cmdlets to perform additional tasks. For example, to save the properties in a CSV file, add the `Export-Csv` cmdlet to the pipeline.

```
PS > Get-SPWeb -Identity http://SPServer01 | Select-Object -Property * |
>> Export-Csv C:\SiteInformation.csv
>>
```

Now you can retrieve the information from the CSV file with the `Import-Csv` cmdlet and select specified properties using the `Select-Object` cmdlet.

Measuring Objects in Windows PowerShell

Windows PowerShell includes a lot of cmdlets that help us in our daily work. Combining cmdlets through a pipeline is a great way to solve complex administrative tasks with a one-liner in Windows PowerShell. Here is another example that uses a pipeline to measure the number of web templates available in SharePoint 2010:

```
PS > Get-SPWebTemplate | Measure-Object


Count     : 50
Average   :
Sum       :
Maximum   :
Minimum   :
Property  :
```

This example uses the `Get-SPWebTemplate` cmdlet to retrieve all available web templates, and then send the objects to the `Measure-Object` cmdlet, which returns the number of web templates available.

An earlier example demonstrated using the `Get-Command` cmdlet to retrieve all SharePoint 2010 cmdlets and placed the command within parentheses, allowing access to the `Count` property. As you've seen here, you can achieve the same goal using the `Measure-Object` cmdlet.

Sorting Objects in Windows PowerShell

Sorting objects by property values can be achieved with the `Sort-Object` cmdlet. The `Sort-Object` cmdlet supports a set of parameters that you can use to specify which property to sort on, which order to sort in, and more.

The following example retrieves all sites from a site collection and sorts them by the time they were created.

```
PS > Get-SPSite -Identity http://SPServer01 | Get-SPWeb |
>> Sort-Object -Property Created

Url
---
http://spserver01
http://spserver01/Web1
http://spserver01/Web2
http://spserver01/Web3
http://spserver01/Web4
http://spserver01/Web5
http://spserver01/Web6
```

```
http://spserver01/Web7
http://spserver01/Web8
http://spserver01/Web9
http://spserver01/Web10
```

Summary

This chapter introduced Windows PowerShell, including how to start it. You learned how to call the SharePoint 2010 cmdlets and get additional information about cmdlets explaining how and when to use them. We looked at cmdlet parameters and how to use them to provide information and set options that tell the cmdlet how to behave. The last part of the chapter showed how to send commands through a pipeline to solve advanced administrative tasks with a simple one-liner in Windows PowerShell.

The next chapter describes how to manage SharePoint 2010 through Windows PowerShell using the SharePoint 2010 cmdlets.

CHAPTER 4 | Managing SharePoint 2010 with Windows PowerShell

A s you learned in Chapter 3, the SharePoint 2010 snap-in for Windows PowerShell includes more than 500 cmdlets, and some of these are designed to retrieve information from SharePoint. This chapter focuses on the cmdlets for configuring the SharePoint 2010 environment—that is, creating and deleting objects and modifying their properties.

Managing Permissions in SharePoint 2010

Running the SharePoint 2010 cmdlets in Windows PowerShell requires the user to be a member of the SharePoint Shell Access role in the configuration database, and the WSS_ADMIN_WPG local security group on the SharePoint 2010 server.

The Add-SPShellAdmin cmdlet is used to add users to the SharePoint Shell Access role and to the WSS_ADMIN_WPG local security group on all servers that have the SharePoint Foundation 2010 Web Application role. To add a user to the SharePoint Shell Access role for a specific database, you can type:

```
PS > Add-SPShellAdmin -UserName powershell\nigo `
>> -database (Get-SPContentDatabase -Identity WSS_Content)
PS > Get-SPShellAdmin
UserName
--------
POWERSHELL\nigo
```

In this example, we use the Add-SPShellAdmin cmdlet to add the user "powershell\nigo" to the SharePoint Shell Access role in the WSS_Content database and the farm configuration database. Notice how we also use the Get-SPContentDatabase cmdlet to retrieve a specific content database. If you do not specify a database, the user will be added only to the SharePoint Shell Access role in the farm configuration database.

The Get-SPShellAdmin cmdlet returns the login names of users who have the SharePoint Shell Access role in a specific database. You can use the cmdlet by typing:

```
PS > Get-SPShellAdmin (Get-SPContentDatabase -Identity WSS_Content)

UserName
--------
POWERSHELL\nigo
```

It is also possible to remove users from the SharePoint Shell Access role using the Remove-SPShellAdmin cmdlet as demonstrated in the example below.

```
PS > Remove-SPShellAdmin -UserName powershell\nigo `
>> -database (Get-SPContentDatabase -Identity WSS_Content)
```

Managing Content Databases in SharePoint 2010

Windows PowerShell includes eight cmdlets that you can use when working with the SharePoint 2010 content database. To retrieve a list of all content database cmdlets available, use `Get-Command` with the `Noun` parameter to list all cmdlets where the noun is `SPContentDatabase`:

```
PS > Get-Command -Noun SPContentDatabase

CommandType     Name                            Definition
-----------     ----                            ----------
Cmdlet          Dismount-SPContentDatabase      Dismount-SPContentDatabase
Cmdlet          Get-SPContentDatabase           Get-SPContentDatabase [[-Id
Cmdlet          Mount-SPContentDatabase         Mount-SPContentDatabase [-N
Cmdlet          New-SPContentDatabase           New-SPContentDatabase [-Nam
Cmdlet          Remove-SPContentDatabase        Remove-SPContentDatabase [-
Cmdlet          Set-SPContentDatabase           Set-SPContentDatabase [-Ide
Cmdlet          Test-SPContentDatabase          Test-SPContentDatabase [-Id
Cmdlet          Upgrade-SPContentDatabase       Upgrade-SPContentDatabase [
```

We'll explore how to use the first six cmdlets here.

Getting a SharePoint 2010 Content Database

The `Get-SPContentDatabase` cmdlet is used to return one or more content databases in SharePoint 2010. You can retrieve a specific content database, a content database based on a site collection, or a content database from a specified web application.

Let's start by retrieving all available content databases:

```
PS > Get-SPContentDatabase

Id                : 96dfa348-42df-4e9b-bbc5-1f4e8ee1051e
Name              : WSS_Content
WebApplication    : SPWebApplication Name=SharePoint - 80
Server            : SPServer01
CurrentSiteCount  : 2
```

To retrieve content databases for a specific site collection, use the `Site` parameter:

```
PS > Get-SPContentDatabase -Site http://SPServer01

Id                : 96dfa348-42df-4e9b-bbc5-1f4e8ee1051e
Name              : WSS_Content
WebApplication    : SPWebApplication Name=SharePoint - 80
Server            : SPServer01
CurrentSiteCount  : 2
```

It is even possible to specify a web application and retrieve the content databases attached to it. If the web application is associated with more than one content database, all are returned.

```
PS > Get-SPContentDatabase -WebApplication "SharePoint - 80"

Id                 : 96dfa348-42df-4e9b-bbc5-1f4e8ee1051e
Name               : WSS_Content
WebApplication     : SPWebApplication Name=SharePoint - 80
Server             : SPServer01
CurrentSiteCount   : 2
```

Like `SPSite` and `SPWeb`, the `SPContentDatabase` class has a large number of properties containing rich information, which you can retrieve through the appropriate cmdlet. As you saw in Chapter 3, the `Format-List` cmdlet displays the information as a list. Used with the asterisk wildcard, it retrieves all properties:

```
PS > Get-SPContentDatabase | Format-List *
```

Figure 4-1 shows the output from this command.

```
PS > Get-SPContentDatabase | Format-List *


Type                           : Content Database
IsAttachedToFarm               : True
ExistsInFarm                   : True
Server                         : SPServer01
SearchServiceInstance          :
PreferredTimerServiceInstance  :
TypeName                       : Content Database
CurrentSiteCount               : 2
WarningSiteCount               : 9000
MaximumSiteCount               : 15000
WebApplication                 : SPWebApplication Name=SharePoint - 80
CurrentChangeToken             : 1;0;96dfa348-42df-4e9b-bbc5-1f4e8ee1051e;634065897063000000;3987
Sites                          : {SPSite Url=http://spserver01, SPSite Url=http://spserver01/my}
IsPaired                       : False
CanMigrate                     : False
RemoteBlobStorageSettings      : Microsoft.SharePoint.Administration.SPRemoteBlobStorageSettings
SiteSubscriptions              : {}
NormalizedDataSource           : SPServer01
ServiceInstance                : SPDatabaseServiceInstance
FailoverServer                 :
FailoverServiceInstance        :
DatabaseConnectionString       : Server=SPServer01;Database=WSS_Content;Trusted_Connection=yes;App=Windows SharePoint Se
                                 rvices;Timeout=15
SqlConnectionString            : Data Source=SPServer01;Initial Catalog=WSS_Content;Integrated Security=True;Enlist=Fals
                                 e;Connect Timeout=15
Username                       :
Password                       :
Exists                         : True
Snapshots                      : {}
IsReadOnly                     : False
IncludeInVssBackup             : True
DiskSizeRequired               : 31457280
CanSelectForBackup             : True
CanSelectForRestore            : True
CanRenameOnRestore             : True
SchemaVersionXml               : <SchemaVersions><SchemaVersion Current="4.0.137.0" Target="4.0.137.0" Sequence="Microso
                                 ft.SharePoint.Upgrade.SPContentDatabaseSequence"/><SchemaVersion Current="4.0.8.0" Targ
                                 et="4.0.8.0" Sequence="Microsoft.SharePoint.Upgrade.SPContentDatabaseSequence2"/><Schem
                                 aVersion Current="14.0.4536.1000" Target="14.0.4536.1000" Sequence="Microsoft.SharePoin
                                 t.Upgrade.SPContentDatabaseStoreProcedureSequence"/><SchemaVersion Current="14.0.4536.1
                                 000" Target="14.0.4536.1000" Sequence="Microsoft.SharePoint.Administration.SPContentDat
                                 abase"/><SchemaVersions>
CanUpgrade                     : True
IsBackwardsCompatible          : True
NeedsUpgradeIncludeChildren    : False
NeedsUpgrade                   : False
UpgradeContext                 : Microsoft.SharePoint.Upgrade.SPUpgradeContext
```

Figure 4-1. Using Format-List to display all properties

Configuring the SharePoint 2010 Content Database

The `Set-SPContentDatabase` cmdlet is used to change the properties of a content database. This cmdlet allows you to change the maximum number of site collections that a content database can host, change the status of the content database, and specify the number of sites that can be created before a warning event is generated.

We'll start with modifying the maximum number of site collections allowed. First, let's get the current value of the `MaximumSiteCount` property:

```
PS > (Get-SPContentDatabase -Site http://SPServer01).MaximumSiteCount
15000
```

Here's how to change the value using the `Set-SPContentDatabase` cmdlet:

```
PS > Get-SPContentDatabase -Site http://SPServer01 |
>> Set-SPContentDatabase -MaxSiteCount 20000
PS > (Get-SPContentDatabase -Site http://SPServer01).MaximumSiteCount
20000
```

This example uses `Get-SPContentDatabase` to retrieve a content database, and then uses a pipeline to send the object to the `Set-SPContentDatabase` cmdlet. We then use the `MaxSiteCount` parameter and change the value to `20000`, increasing it by 5,000 sites. When we check the `MaximumSiteCount` property, we can see that the value has been updated.

Next, let's change the status of the content database to `Offline`:

```
PS > (Get-SPContentDatabase -Site http://SPServer01).Status
Online
PS > Get-SPContentDatabase -Site http://SPServer01 |
>> Set-SPContentDatabase -Status Offline
PS > (Get-SPContentDatabase -Site http://SPServer01).Status
Offline
```

In this example, we use the `-Status` parameter to change the status of the content database from `Online` to `Offline`. We verify that the change was made using the `Get-SPContentDatabase` cmdlet. It is just as simple to set the status to `Online`, as follows:

```
PS > Get-SPContentDatabase -Site http://SPServer01 |
>> Set-SPContentDatabase -Status Online
```

Attaching and Detaching a Content Database in SharePoint 2010

The SharePoint 2010 snap-in for Windows PowerShell offers two cmdlets that allow you to attach and detach content databases to a SharePoint 2010 farm.

To detach a content database, use the `Dismount-SPContentDatabase` cmdlet:

```
PS > Get-SPContentDatabase -Site http://SPServer01 | Dismount-SPContentDatabase

Confirm
Are you sure you want to perform this action?
Performing operation "Dismount-SPContentDatabase" on Target "WSS_Content".
[Y] Yes  [A] Yes to All  [N] No  [L] No to All  [S] Suspend  [?] Help
(default is "Y"): Y
```

As you can see, Windows PowerShell displays a confirmation prompt asking if you are sure that you want to perform the action. Cmdlets that perform actions that involve a risk to the system or to user data often require a confirmation. When you type Y or just press ENTER, the action is performed. If you now try to access your content database with the `Get-SPContentDatabase` cmdlet, nothing will be returned, since the content database is detached from the farm.

To attach a content database to a farm in SharePoint 2010, use the `Mount-SPContentDatabase` cmdlet:

```
PS > Mount-SPContentDatabase "WSS_Content" -DatabaseServer SPServer01 `
>> -WebApplication http://SPServer01


Id               : 96dfa348-42df-4e9b-bbc5-1f4e8ee1051e
Name             : WSS_Content
WebApplication   : SPWebApplication Name=SharePoint - 80
Server           : SPServer01
CurrentSiteCount : 2
```

Creating a New Content Database

Windows PowerShell lets you create new content databases with the `New-SPContentDatabase` cmdlet. The cmdlet has two required parameters:

■ The `Name` parameter sets the name of the content database.

■ The `WebApplication` parameter specifies to which web application in SharePoint 2010 the new content database should be attached.

The following example creates a new content database called `MyContentDB` and attaches it to a web application.

```
PS > New-SPContentDatabase -Name "MyContentDB" `
>> -WebApplication http://SPServer01:5077


Id               : 8975393a-cc0a-4d68-ab69-078b1b870904
Name             : MyContentDB
WebApplication   : SPWebApplication Name=My WebApplication
Server           : SPServer01
CurrentSiteCount : 0
```

Removing a Content Database in SharePoint 2010

To remove a content database with Windows PowerShell, use the Remove-
SPContentDatabase cmdlet:

```
PS > Get-SPContentDatabase -Identity "MyContentDB" | Remove-SPContentDatabase

Confirm
Are you sure you want to perform this action?
Performing operation "Remove-SPContentDatabase" on Target "MyContentDB".
[Y] Yes  [A] Yes to All  [N] No  [L] No to All  [S] Suspend  [?] Help
(default is "Y"): Y

Confirm
Removing 'MyContentDB' will permananetly delete the SQL database,
permanently deleting all content stored within it.
Use Dismount-SPContentDatabase if you do not want to delete the SQL database.
[Y] Yes  [A] Yes to All  [N] No  [L] No to All  [S] Suspend  [?] Help
(default is "Y"): Y
```

In this example, we use Get-SPContentDatabase to retrieve a content database
and a pipeline to send the current object to the Remove-SPContentDatabase cmdlet.
As with the Dismount-SPContentDatabase cmdlet, when you use Remove-
SPContentDatabase, Windows PowerShell asks for confirmation before performing
the operation.

Managing SharePoint 2010 Web Applications

Four Windows PowerShell cmdlets are available for working with web applications
in SharePoint 2010. You can retrieve a list of all the web application cmdlets using the
Get-Command cmdlet with the noun SPWebApplication:

```
PS > Get-Command -Noun SPWebApplication

CommandType Name                    Definition
----------- ----                    ----------
Cmdlet      Get-SPWebApplication    Get-SPWebApplication [[-Identity] <
Cmdlet      New-SPWebApplication    New-SPWebApplication -Name <String>
Cmdlet      Remove-SPWebApplication Remove-SPWebApplication [-Identity]
Cmdlet      Set-SPWebApplication    Set-SPWebApplication [-Identity] <S
```

We'll look at each of these cmdlets, starting with Get-SPWebApplication.

Getting Web Applications in SharePoint 2010

The `Get-SPWebApplication` cmdlet returns the web applications in SharePoint 2010. You can use the `Identity` parameter to return a specific web application. If you don't specify a web application, all web applications are returned:

```
PS > Get-SPWebApplication

DisplayName                    Url
-----------                    ---
SharePoint - 80                http://spserver01/
```

By default, Central Administration is excluded from the set of returned web applications. Using the `IncludeCentralAdministration` switch parameter forces the Central Administration web application to be included:

```
PS > Get-SPWebApplication -IncludeCentralAdministration

DisplayName                    Url
-----------                    ---
SharePoint - 80                http://spserver01/
SharePoint Central Administ... http://spserver01:23815/
```

Modifying Web Applications in SharePoint 2010

To configure web applications in SharePoint 2010, use the `Set-SPWebApplication` cmdlet. This cmdlet supports a variety of parameters corresponding to different configuration settings of web applications, such as e-mail addresses, SMTP server, and time zone.

First, let's look at how to configure the From and Reply-to e-mail addresses. When configuring the e-mail addresses used by the web application, you must specify an SMTP server to use.

```
PS > Get-SPWebApplication -Identity http://SPServer01 |
>> Set-SPWebApplication -OutgoingEmailAddress from@nima.com `
>> -ReplyToEmailAddress reply@nima.com -SMTPServer ExcServer01
```

In this example, we use `Get-SPWebApplication` to retrieve a specific web application, and then pipe the object to the `Set-SPWebApplication` cmdlet, where we use the `SMTPServer` parameter to specify which SMTP server to use. We also specify the From and Reply-to e-mail addresses that should be used by the web application. Figure 4-2 shows what the configuration looks like in Central Administration.

It is also possible to allow anonymous access with the `Set-WebApplication` cmdlet. Allowing anonymous access at the web application level enables individual site collection administrators to turn on anonymous access.

```
PS > Get-SPWebApplication -Identity http://SPServer01 |
>> Set-SPWebApplication -AllowAnonymousAccess -Zone Default
```

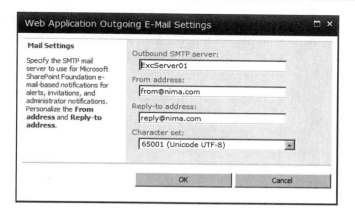

Figure 4-2. Setting the From e-mail address, Reply-to e-mail address, and SMTP mail server through PowerShell

To disable anonymous access, use the same switch parameter followed by `:$False`:

```
PS > Get-SPWebApplication -Identity http://SPServer01 |
>> Set-SPWebApplication -AllowAnonymousAccess:$False -Zone Default
```

CAUTION   If anonymous access is turned off when using Forms-based authentication, Forms-aware client applications may fail to authenticate correctly.

Use the `Set-SPWebApplication` cmdlet's `DefaultTimeZone` parameter to set the time zone that should be used for new site collections:

```
PS > Get-SPWebApplication -Identity http://SPServer01 |
>> Set-SPWebApplication -DefaultTimeZone 4
```

In this example, we use the `DefaultTimeZone` parameter to set the time zone used by new site collections to 4, which corresponds to Western Europe Standard Time. You can list the other values for time zones using the SPRegionalSettings class as demonstrated below.

```
PS > [Microsoft.SharePoint.SPregionalSettings]::Globaltimezones
```

Creating a New Web Application in SharePoint 2010

You can create new web applications in SharePoint 2010 with the `New-SPWebApplication` cmdlet. This cmdlet has several parameters for configuring the new web application, including the following:

- The `Name` parameter specifies the name of the new web application.
- The `Port` parameter sets the port from which the web application can be accessed.

■ The `ApplicationPool` parameter specifies the application pool to use. If the application pool does not exist, a new application pool will be created.

■ When creating new application pools with the `New-SPWebApplication` cmdlet, an application pool account must be specified. You can specify the account through the `ApplicationPoolAccount` parameter.

Here is a basic example showing how to create a web application through Windows PowerShell:

```
PS > New-SPWebApplication -Name "My WebApplication" -Port 5077 `
>> -ApplicationPool "MyAppPool" `
>> -ApplicationPoolAccount (Get-SPManagedAccount powershell\managedaccount)


DisplayName                     Url
-----------                     ---
My WebApplication               http://spserver01:5077/
```

In this example, we use the `Get-SPManagedAccount` cmdlet to retrieve an account that is registered in the configuration database.

When the command is run, a content database is also created. Since we didn't specify a name for the content database in this example, a name will be autogenerated in the format `WSS_Content_<GUID>`. Alternatively, you can specify a custom name through the `DatabaseName` parameter.

Removing a Web Application in SharePoint 2010

The `Remove-SPWebApplication` cmdlet removes an existing web application. You can use the `Zone` parameter to remove a specific zone. If the zone is not specified, all zones are removed. The cmdlet also supports switch parameters that allow you to delete the IIS web site associated with the target zone (or all zones) and the content database associated with the web application. Here's an example:

```
PS > Remove-SPWebApplication -Identity http://SPServer01:5077 `
>> -DeleteIISSite -RemoveContentDatabases

Confirm
Are you sure you want to perform this action?
Performing operation "Remove-SPWebApplication" on Target "My WebApplication".
[Y] Yes  [A] Yes to All  [N] No  [L] No to All  [S] Suspend  [?] Help
(default is "Y"): Y
```

In this example, we remove the web application that we previously created. We also add the `DeleteIISSite` and `RemoveContentDatabase` switch parameters to remove the IIS web site and content database associated with the web application. As with the other removal cmdlets, Windows PowerShell prompts for a confirmation before the command is executed.

Managing SharePoint 2010 Sites

Let's see which cmdlets are provided for handling site collections:

```
PS > Get-Command -Noun SPSite

CommandType    Name            Definition
-----------    ----            ----------
Cmdlet         Backup-SPSite   Backup-SPSite [-Identity] <SPSitePipeBind>
Cmdlet         Get-SPSite      Get-SPSite [-Limit <String>] [-WebApplicat
Cmdlet         Move-SPSite     Move-SPSite [-Identity] <SPSitePipeBind> -
Cmdlet         New-SPSite      New-SPSite [-Url] <String> [-Language <UIn
Cmdlet         Remove-SPSite   Remove-SPSite [-Identity] <SPSitePipeBind>
Cmdlet         Restore-SPSite  Restore-SPSite [-Identity] <String> -Path
Cmdlet         Set-SPSite      Set-SPSite [-Identity] <SPSitePipeBind> [-
```

We'll start with the `Set-SPSite` cmdlet.

Configuring a Site Collection in SharePoint 2010

The `Set-SPSite` cmdlet is used to configure a site collection. This cmdlet supports
a few interesting parameters that you can use to change a site collection. Here's how to
add a secondary owner to a site collection:

```
PS > Set-SPSite -Identity http://SPServer01 -SecondaryOwnerAlias powershell\nigo
```

In this example, we use the `SecondaryOwnerAlias` parameter and set the domain
user `powershell\nigo` as the secondary owner of the site collection.

Another nice feature is the `UserAcountDirectoryPath` parameter, which defines
a scope for user accounts, meaning that only accounts within the organizational unit
can be added as members of the site collection. People pickers will also be limited
to this scope. The following example limits the scope to the Company/Site/Users
organizational unit.

```
PS > Set-SPSite -Identity http://SPServer01 `
>> -UserAccountDirectoryPath "OU=Users,OU=Site,OU=Company,DC=Powershell,DC=nu"
```

If we now try searching for users through the people picker in SharePoint, we
will be able to find users only within the scope and users already added to the site
collection.

NOTE   Users added before the scope change is committed will still be able to access the site
collection.

Backing Up and Restoring Site Collections in SharePoint 2010

You can take a backup of a site collection with the `Backup-SPSite` cmdlet and restore a site collection from a backup file using the `Restore-SPSite` cmdlet. The use of these cmdlets is pretty straightforward.

Here is an example of taking a backup of a site collection:

```
PS > Backup-SPSite -Identity http://SPServer01 -Path C:\Backup\siteCollection.bak
```

By default, the site collection is temporarily set to read-only, so that no changes can be made while the backup is performed. The `Backup-SPSite` cmdlet also supports the `NoSiteLock` switch parameter, which specifies that the site collection not be locked during the backup, however, this parameter is not recommended using if users are writing to the site collection while a backup is performed. Using the `UseSqlSnapshot` parameter is recommended if the database server hosting the content database supports database snapshots.

After you have a backup file of the site collection, you can use the `Restore-SPSite` cmdlet to restore the site collection:

```
PS > Restore-SPSite -Identity http://SPServer01 -Path C:\Backup\siteCollection.bak

Confirm
Are you sure you want to perform this action?
Performing operation "Restore-SPSite" on Target "http://SPServer01".
[Y] Yes  [A] Yes to All  [N] No  [L] No to All  [S] Suspend  [?] Help
(default is "Y"): Y
```

Typing **Y** or pressing ENTER at the confirmation prompt performs the action and restores the site collection.

Creating a New Site Collection

To create new site collection, use the `New-SPSite` cmdlet. This cmdlet has two required parameters: `Url` and `OwnerAlias`. You can specify a template with the `Template` parameter. It is also possible to specify a content database to use with the `ContentDatabase` parameter.

Here is an example of creating a new site collection:

```
PS > New-SPSite -Url http://SPServer01:5077 `
>> -OwnerAlias powershell\administrator -Template "STS#0"

Url
---
http://spserver01:5077
```

Here, we point the URL to the root of an existing web application, set the owner for the site collection, and specify a template. The template name might look a little strange, but if you take a quick peek with the `Get-SPWebTemplate` cmdlet, you will see which template we are using.

Removing Site Collections in SharePoint 2010

The `Remove-SPSite` cmdlet completely deletes an existing site collection and all sites. The cmdlet supports the `GradualDelete` switch parameter, which removes the site collection gradually, reducing system load. This parameter is recommended for deleting large sites.

```
PS > Remove-SPSite -Identity http://SPServer01:5077 -GradualDelete -Confirm:$False
```

In this example, we delete the new site collection that we previously created. We also add the `GradualDelete` switch parameter and set the `Confirm` switch parameter to `$False` so that no confirmation is required.

Managing SharePoint 2010 Sites

Finally, let's take a look at the cmdlets used to manage sites in SharePoint 2010. All the cmdlets for managing sites in SharePoint 2010 use the `SPWeb` noun.

```
PS > Get-Command -Noun SPWeb

CommandType    Name           Definition
-----------    ----           ----------
Cmdlet         Export-SPWeb   Export-SPWeb [-Identity] <SPWebPipeBi
Cmdlet         Get-SPWeb      Get-SPWeb [[-Identity] <SPWebPipeBind
Cmdlet         Import-SPWeb   Import-SPWeb [-Identity] <SPWebPipeBi
Cmdlet         New-SPWeb      New-SPWeb [-Url] <String> [-Language
Cmdlet         Remove-SPWeb   Remove-SPWeb [-Identity] <SPWebPipeBi
Cmdlet         Set-SPWeb      Set-SPWeb [-Identity] <SPWebPipeBind>
```

Let's look at how to use each of these, starting with `New-SPWeb`.

Creating Sites in SharePoint 2010

The `New-SPWeb` cmdlet creates a new site in an existing site collection. The only parameter that is required is the URL, which must be in an existing site collection and unique. You can also specify the language, site template, name, and description, as well as set unique permissions, add the site to the parent site's Quick Launch bar, and set the top navigation bar options.

Here's an example of creating a new site:

```
PS > New-SPWeb -Url http://SPServer01/NewSite -Template "STS#0" `
>> -Name "New Site" -Description "My New Site" -AddToTopNav -UseParentTopNav

Url
---
http://spserver01/NewSite
```

In this example, we set the template to use. Next, we specify the name and description of the site. Finally, we use the `AddToTopNav` switch parameter to add the site to the top-level navigation bar and the `UseParentTopNav` switch parameter to specify that the site uses the same top-level navigation bar as the parent site.

 NOTE   If you do not set a template when creating the new site, you can add it later, either in the browser or with the `Set-SPWeb` cmdlet.

Configuring Sites in SharePoint 2010

The `Set-SPWeb` cmdlet lets you configure existing sites in SharePoint 2010. The following example changes the description of an existing site.

```
PS > Get-SPWeb http://SPServer01/NewSite | Select-Object -Property Description

Description
-----------
My New Site

PS > Get-SPWeb http://SPServer01/NewSite |
>> Set-SPWeb -Description "A New Description"

PS > Get-SPWeb http://SPServer01/NewSite | Select-Object -Property Description

Description
-----------
A New Description
```

First, we use `Get-SPWeb` and pipe the object to the `Select-Object` cmdlet to retrieve the current value of the `Description` property. We then use the `Set-SPWeb` cmdlet to change the site's description. Finally, we verify that the change occurred by retrieving the site's description again.

Exporting and Importing Sites in SharePoint 2010

With the `Export-SPWeb` cmdlet, you can export a site, as follows:

```
PS > Export-SPWeb -Identity http://SPServer01/NewSite `
>> -Path C:\Backup\spWebBackup.bak
```

This example exports an entire site to a backup file. It is also possible to export specific content from a site, such as lists, document libraries, and even list items. You use the `ItemUrl` parameter to export lists or list items from a site. Here is an example of exporting a list called `Calendar` from a site:

```
PS > Export-SPWeb -Identity http://SPServer01/NewSite `
>> -ItemUrl "Lists/Calendar" -Path C:\Backup\spWebCalendar.bak
```

The `Export-SPWeb` cmdlet also supports the `IncludeUserSecurity` switch parameter, which allows you to include access control lists for all items.

By default, `Export-SPWeb` exports the last major version of a list item, but you can change this by setting the `IncludeVersions` parameter to include the current version, last major and minor version, or all versions of each item.

Once you have an export file, you can use the `Import-SPWeb` cmdlet to import it into a site. Importing a site works as long as you specify a site collection that contains a matching template; otherwise, an error occurs.

In the following example, we will delete the Calendar list in SharePoint 2010 and perform an import with the `Import-SPWeb` cmdlet. Figure 4-3 shows how to delete a list in SharePoint 2010.

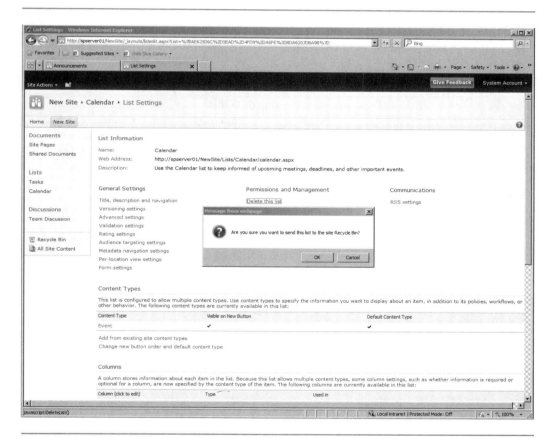

Figure 4-3.   Deleting the Calendar list

Now that the list is removed, we can go ahead and run `Import-SPWeb`:

```
PS > Import-SPWeb -Identity http://SPServer01/NewSite `
>> -Path C:\Backup\spWebCalendar.bak
```

The `Import-SPWeb` cmdlet also supports the `UpdateVersions` parameter, which allows you to specify how to handle items that already exist in a list. The possible values are `Append`, `Overwrite`, and `Ignore`.

Removing Sites in SharePoint 2010

The `Remove-SPWeb` cmdlet removes a specific site from SharePoint 2010. If the top-level site is deleted, the site collection is also removed. Here is an example of running this cmdlet:

```
PS > Remove-SPWeb -Identity http://SPServer01/NewSite -Confirm:$false
```

Summary

This chapter covered how to use the cmdlets in Windows PowerShell to manage the SharePoint 2010 environment. We began with content database and web application management. As you saw, you can use cmdlets to create, manage, and remove content databases and web applications with Windows PowerShell. Then we covered the basics of site collection and site management with Windows PowerShell. We included examples of creating, configuring, removing, and backing up sites and site collections.

In the next chapter, we will dig deeper into the core functionality of Windows PowerShell. We'll look at items such as variables, functions, operators, scripts, and remoting.

CHAPTER 5 | Variables, Arrays, and Hashtables

This chapter covers the use of variables, arrays, and hashtables. First, we will demonstrate how to work with variables in Windows PowerShell, including creating, setting, and removing variables. We will also take a brief look at different data types. Then we will move on to using arrays and hashtables in Windows PowerShell.

Variables in Windows PowerShell

Windows PowerShell, like most other scripting languages, stores values in variables. Variables are represented by single-word text strings that begin with the dollar sign ($). Windows PowerShell supports four types of variables: user-created, automatic, preference, and environment variables.

Working with Variables

The simplest way to create a variable is by using the assignment operator = to set a variable to a specific value. The following example creates the variable $string and assigns it the value My String.

```
PS > $string = "My String"
```

You can also use the New-Variable cmdlet to create variables. This cmdlet offers some additional functionality, such as adding a description, setting the variable to read-only or constant, and setting a specific scope for a variable. Here is an example:

```
PS > New-Variable -Name string -Value "My String" `
>> -Description "Created using New-Variable" -Option ReadOnly -Force
```

This creates the variable $string and sets the value to My String. We also specify a description, use the Option parameter to set the variable to ReadOnly, and use the -Force switch parameter since the variable already exists.

If we try to assign a new value to the variable using the assignment operator, an error occurs since the variable is set to read-only.

```
PS > $string = "New Value"
Cannot overwrite variable string because it is read-only or constant.
At line:1 char:8
+ $string <<<<  = "New Value"
    + CategoryInfo          : WriteError: (string:String) [],
SessionStateUnauthorizedAccessException
    + FullyQualifiedErrorId : VariableNotWritable
```

Instead, we can use the Set-Variable cmdlet with the -Force switch parameter to set a new value. We also change the Option parameter from ReadOnly to None.

```
PS > Set-Variable -Name string -Value "New Value" -Option None -Force
```

The Get-Variable cmdlet is used to retrieve variables, as follows:

```
PS > Get-Variable -Name string

Name                Value
----                -----
string              New Value
```

This example returns an object of the type System.Management.Automation
.PSVariable, which contains properties that describe the variable. If you want to
display only the variable's value, use the -ValueOnly switch parameter.

```
PS > Get-Variable -Name string -ValueOnly
New Value
```

This example returns an object of the type System.String. This corresponds to
just typing a dollar sign ($) followed by the variable's name:

```
PS > $string
New Value
```

You can display additional information about a variable by using the Get-Variable
cmdlet and sending the object to the Format-List cmdlet.

```
PS > Get-Variable -Name string | Format-List
Name        : string
Description : Created using New-Variable
Value       : New Value
Visibility  : Public
Module      :
ModuleName  :
Options     : None
Attributes  : {}
```

To clear the value of a variable, use the Clear-Variable cmdlet.

```
PS > Clear-Variable -Name string
```

When using the Clear-Variable cmdlet, the variable's value is set to null. You can
also set a variable to null using the assignment operator.

```
PS > $string = $null
```

To delete a variable, use the Remove-Variable cmdlet.

```
PS > Remove-Variable -Name string
```

 NOTE   You cannot delete variables set as constants or variables owned by the system.

Data Types

When you use the assignment operator = to set a variable to a specified value, Windows PowerShell automatically assigns the best-suited data type for the given value. In our first example, we used a simple string as input, which stored an object of the type System.String in a variable. In this example, we set a variable to a numeric value:

```
PS > $int = 10
```

We can use the GetType() method with the FullName property to find out the variable's data type.

```
PS > $int.GetType().FullName
System.Int32
```

This shows that the variable $int is of the type System.Int32, which represents a 32-bit integer.

If we use a number that is too large for a 32-bit integer, a different data type will be used.

```
PS > $int64 = 10000000000000
PS > $int64.GetType().FullName
System.Int64
```

If the value is a decimal number, the System.Double data type will be used.

```
PS > $decimal = 1.2
PS > $decimal.GetType().FullName
System.Double
```

Rather than letting Windows PowerShell assign the data type, you can specify the type for a variable. To assign a specific data type to a variable, enclose the data type's name in square brackets before the variable name. If the data type is not at the root of the System namespace, you must type the data type's full name; otherwise, you can omit the System part of the name, as shown in this example:

```
PS > [uri]$url = "http://SPServer01"
PS > $url.GetType().FullName
System.Uri
```

Here, we use an URL as value, but rather than letting Windows PowerShell assign a data type we assigned it a specific data type, giving us a completely different type of object. The type System.Uri is an object representation of a uniform resource identifier (URI), which, according to Microsoft Developer Network (MSDN), is "a compact representation of a resource available to your application on the intranet or Internet."

The next example demonstrates how to assign the type System.Int32 to a variable.

```
PS > [int32]$val = 32
PS > $val
32
```

Since we assigned a fixed type to the variable, only values within the permitted range for the type are allowed. If we try to add a string value to the typed variable, an error occurs.

```
PS > [int32]$val = "http://SPServer01"
Cannot convert value "http://SPServer01" to type "System.Int32". Error: "Input
string was not in a correct format."
At line:1 char:12
+ [int32]$val <<<<  = "http://SPServer01"
    + CategoryInfo          : MetadataError: (:) [],
ArgumentTransformationMetadataException
    + FullyQualifiedErrorId : RuntimeException
```

Windows PowerShell also supports a number of *type accelerators* (also known as *type shortcuts*). The type accelerators allow you to use short name syntax for commonly used .NET types. For instance, instead of typing [System.Xml.XmlDocument], you can simply type [xml]. Table 5-1 shows some of the most common type accelerators.

Type	Description	Example
[string]	String of Unicode characters	[string]"Hi"
[int]	32-bit integer	[int32]12
[long]	64-bit integer	[int64]1200000
[char]	Unicode character	[char]34
[bool]	True or false value	[bool]$false
[byte]	8-bit integer	[byte]255
[decimal]	Decimal number	[decimal]12.44
[double]	Double-precision decimal number	[double]12.44
[float]	Single-precision floating number	[float]12.44
[array]	An array	[array]1,2,3
[hashtable]	Hashtable	[hashtable]@{"Name"="Value"}
[xml]	XML document	[xml]"<name>Sergey</name>"
[adsi]	Active Directory service interface	[adsi] "LDAP://DC=PowerShell,DC=nu"
[wmi]	Type accelerator for ManagementObject	[wmi]("Win32_ComputerSystem.Name='SPServer01'")

Table 5-1.   Common Windows PowerShell Type Accelerators

To find out the type accelerator's corresponding .NET type, use the `FullName` property.

```
PS > ([string]).FullName
System.String
PS > ([xml]).FullName
System.Xml.XmlDocument
PS > ([adsi]).FullName
System.DirectoryServices.DirectoryEntry
```

NOTE   Type accelerators are considered before regular type lookup. Regular type lookup searches for the name typed within square brackets without prepending `System`. If that fails, `System` is prepended. For accelerated types in the `System` namespace, the accelerator ensures that you won't pick up some global (not in any namespace) type.

Properties and Methods

Since what is actually stored in a variable is a .NET object, you can use all of its methods and properties. You can use the Windows PowerShell `Get-Member` cmdlet to retrieve all members of an object. Let's store an object of the type `System.String` in a variable and explore its methods and properties.

```
PS > [string]$url = "http://SPServer01"
PS > $url | Get-Member
```

The `Get-Member` cmdlet returns information about the properties and methods of the object, as well as its type, as shown in Figure 5-1.

Now that we know which methods and properties the object supports, we can use them to retrieve information and manipulate the object. For example, to find out how many characters the string contains, type the following:

```
PS > $url.Length
17
```

The output tells us that the string's length is 17 characters. We can manipulate the string through the various methods available. For example, we could change all the characters to uppercase, like this:

```
PS > $url.ToUpper()
HTTP://SPSERVER01
```

Notice that method calls in Windows PowerShell end with parentheses, as is common syntax for method invocation in many scripting and programming languages. If a method accepts parameters, those need to be specified within the parentheses. Let's look at the `Replace()` method of the `System.String` type as an example:

```
PS > $url.Replace("http://","https://")
https://SPServer01
```

```
PS > $url | Get-Member


   TypeName: System.String

Name                 MemberType            Definition
Clone                Method                System.Object Clone()
CompareTo            Method                int CompareTo(System.Object value), int CompareTo(string strB)
Contains             Method                bool Contains(string value)
CopyTo               Method                System.Void CopyTo(int sourceIndex, char[] destination, int destinationIndex,...
EndsWith             Method                bool EndsWith(string value), bool EndsWith(string value, System.StringCompari...
Equals               Method                bool Equals(System.Object obj), bool Equals(string value), bool Equals(string...
GetEnumerator        Method                System.CharEnumerator GetEnumerator()
GetHashCode          Method                int GetHashCode()
GetType              Method                type GetType()
GetTypeCode          Method                System.TypeCode GetTypeCode()
IndexOf              Method                int IndexOf(char value), int IndexOf(char value, int startIndex), int IndexOf...
IndexOfAny           Method                int IndexOfAny(char[] anyOf), int IndexOfAny(char[] anyOf, int startIndex), i...
Insert               Method                string Insert(int startIndex, string value)
IsNormalized         Method                bool IsNormalized(), bool IsNormalized(System.Text.NormalizationForm normaliz...
LastIndexOf          Method                int LastIndexOf(char value), int LastIndexOf(char value, int startIndex), int...
LastIndexOfAny       Method                int LastIndexOfAny(char[] anyOf), int LastIndexOfAny(char[] anyOf, int startI...
Normalize            Method                string Normalize(), string Normalize(System.Text.NormalizationForm normalizat...
PadLeft              Method                string PadLeft(int totalWidth), string PadLeft(int totalWidth, char paddingChar)
PadRight             Method                string PadRight(int totalWidth), string PadRight(int totalWidth, char padding...
Remove               Method                string Remove(int startIndex, int count), string Remove(int startIndex)
Replace              Method                string Replace(char oldChar, char newChar), string Replace(string oldValue, s...
Split                Method                string[] Split(Params char[] separator), string[] Split(char[] separator, s...
StartsWith           Method                bool StartsWith(string value), bool StartsWith(string value, System.StringCom...
Substring            Method                string Substring(int startIndex), string Substring(int startIndex, int length)
ToCharArray          Method                char[] ToCharArray(), char[] ToCharArray(int startIndex, int length)
ToLower              Method                string ToLower(), string ToLower(System.Globalization.CultureInfo culture)
ToLowerInvariant     Method                string ToLowerInvariant()
ToString             Method                string ToString(), string ToString(System.IFormatProvider provider)
ToUpper              Method                string ToUpper(), string ToUpper(System.Globalization.CultureInfo culture)
ToUpperInvariant     Method                string ToUpperInvariant()
Trim                 Method                string Trim(Params char[] trimChars), string Trim()
TrimEnd              Method                string TrimEnd(Params char[] trimChars)
TrimStart            Method                string TrimStart(Params char[] trimChars)
Chars                ParameterizedProperty char Chars(int index) {get;}
Length               Property              System.Int32 Length {get;}

PS > _
```

Figure 5-1.   Using the Get-Member cmdlet to retrieve methods and properties

When you use the `Replace()` method, you need to provide additional information to the method telling it what to replace and what to replace it with. A simple way of finding information about a method is by calling the method without the parentheses.

```
PS > $url.Replace
```

Figure 5-2 shows the information returned for the `Replace()` method.

```
PS > $url.Replace

MemberType          : Method
OverloadDefinitions : {string Replace(char oldChar, char newChar), string Replace(string oldValue, string newValue)}
TypeNameOfValue     : System.Management.Automation.PSMethod
Value               : string Replace(char oldChar, char newChar), string Replace(string oldValue, string newValue)
Name                : Replace
IsInstance          : True

PS > _
```

Figure 5-2.   Getting the Replace() method definition

Another resource is the MSDN library (http://msdn.microsoft.com), which provides information about the classes in .NET, including the methods and properties they support. To get information about the `Replace()` method, search for "`System.String Replace.`"

In the following example, we store the output from the `Get-SPWeb` cmdlet in a variable and use the various methods and properties to work with the stored object. We also use the value stored in the `$url` variable as input.

```
PS > $url = "http://SPServer01"
PS > $spWeb = Get-SPWeb -Identity $url
```

When we type the variable's name, the default properties of the object are displayed in the console, as shown here:

```
PS > $spWeb

Url
---
http://spserver01
```

To display all of the object's properties, pipe the object to the `Format-List` cmdlet, as shown in this example:

```
PS > $spWeb | Format-List
```

Let's take a closer look at the methods and properties available on the `SPWeb` object.

```
PS > $spWeb | Get-Member
```

Figure 5-3 shows the available methods and properties.

You can retrieve values of specific properties by using standard property notation—appending a property's name to the object-containing variable with a dot.

```
PS > $spWeb.Url
http://spserver01
PS > $spWeb.Title
Home
PS > $spWeb.Created

Sunday, March 28, 2010 11:44:11 PM
```

You can also use a pipeline and the `Select-Object` cmdlet to retrieve specific properties from a site.

```
PS > $spWeb | Select-Object -property IsRootWeb, WebTemplate, WebTemplateID

IsRootWeb   WebTemplate   WebTemplateId
---------   -----------   -------------
     True   STS                       1
```

```
PS > $SPWeb | Get-Member


   TypeName: Microsoft.SharePoint.SPWeb

Name                                    MemberType  Definition
----                                    ----------  ----------
AddApplicationPrincipal                 Method      Microsoft.SharePoint.SPUser AddApplicationPrincipal(string logonNam...
AddSupportedUICulture                   Method      System.Void AddSupportedUICulture(System.Globalization.CultureInfo ...
AllowAllWebTemplates                    Method      System.Void AllowAllWebTemplates()
ApplyTheme                              Method      System.Void ApplyTheme(string strNewTheme)
ApplyWebTemplate                        Method      System.Void ApplyWebTemplate(Microsoft.SharePoint.SPWebTemplate web...
BreakRoleInheritance                    Method      System.Void BreakRoleInheritance(bool copyRoleAssignments, bool cle...
BypassUseRemoteApis                     Method      System.Void BypassUseRemoteApis()
CheckPermissions                        Method      System.Void CheckPermissions(Microsoft.SharePoint.SPBasePermissions...
Close                                   Method      System.Void Close()
CreateDefaultAssociatedGroups           Method      System.Void CreateDefaultAssociatedGroups(string userLogin, string ...
CustomizeCss                            Method      System.Void CustomizeCss(string cssFile)
Delete                                  Method      System.Void Delete()
DeleteUnusedUserResources               Method      System.Void DeleteUnusedUserResources()
Dispose                                 Method      System.Void Dispose()
DoesUserHavePermissions                 Method      bool DoesUserHavePermissions(string login, Microsoft.SharePoint.SPB...
EnsureUser                              Method      Microsoft.SharePoint.SPUser EnsureUser(string logonName)
Equals                                  Method      bool Equals(System.Object obj)
ExportUserResources                     Method      System.Void ExportUserResources(System.Globalization.CultureInfo la...
GetAvailableCrossLanguageWebTemplates   Method      Microsoft.SharePoint.SPWebTemplateCollection GetAvailableCrossLangu...
GetAvailableWebTemplates                Method      Microsoft.SharePoint.SPWebTemplateCollection GetAvailableWebTemplat...
GetCatalog                              Method      Microsoft.SharePoint.SPList GetCatalog(Microsoft.SharePoint.SPListI...
GetChanges                              Method      Microsoft.SharePoint.SPChangeCollection GetChanges(), Microsoft.Sha...
GetDocDiscussions                       Method      Microsoft.SharePoint.SPDocDiscussionCollection GetDocDiscussions(st...
GetFieldLocalizations                   Method      Microsoft.SharePoint.SPLocalizationCollection GetFieldLocalizations...
GetFile                                 Method      Microsoft.SharePoint.SPFile GetFile(string strUrl), Microsoft.Share...
GetFileAsString                         Method      string GetFileAsString(string url)
GetFileOrFolderObject                   Method      System.Object GetFileOrFolderObject(string strUrl)
GetFilePersonalizationInformation       Method      System.Void GetFilePersonalizationInformation(string url, System.Bo...
GetFolder                               Method      Microsoft.SharePoint.SPFolder GetFolder(System.Guid uniqueId), Micr...
GetHashCode                             Method      int GetHashCode()
GetLimitedWebPartManager                Method      Microsoft.SharePoint.WebPartPages.SPLimitedWebPartManager GetLimite...
GetList                                 Method      Microsoft.SharePoint.SPList GetList(string strUrl)
GetListFromUrl                          Method      Microsoft.SharePoint.SPList GetListFromUrl(string pageUrl)
GetListFromWebPartPageUrl               Method      Microsoft.SharePoint.SPList GetListFromWebPartPageUrl(string pageUrl)
GetListItem                             Method      Microsoft.SharePoint.SPListItem GetListItem(string strUrl)
GetListItemFields                       Method      Microsoft.SharePoint.SPListItem GetListItemFields(string strUrl, Pa...
GetListsOfType                          Method      Microsoft.SharePoint.SPListCollection GetListsOfType(Microsoft.Shar...
GetObject                               Method      System.Object GetObject(string strUrl)
GetRecycleBinItems                      Method      Microsoft.SharePoint.SPRecycleBinItemCollection GetRecycleBinItems(...
GetSiteData                             Method      System.Data.DataTable GetSiteData(Microsoft.SharePoint.SPSiteDataQu...
GetSubwebsForCurrentUser                Method      Microsoft.SharePoint.SPWebCollection GetSubwebsForCurrentUser(), Mi...
GetType                                 Method      type GetType()
GetUsageData                            Method      System.Data.DataTable GetUsageData(Microsoft.SharePoint.Administrat...
```

Figure 5-3.   Methods and properties of an SPWeb object

In the example, we select the `IsRootWeb` property, which tells us if the current site is the root site of a site collection, and the `WebTemplate` and `WebTemplateId` properties, which indicate the site definition and configuration (template) used to create the site (in this case, STS1, which corresponds to the Blank Site template).

Our new variable `$spWeb` is an instance of the `Microsoft.SharePoint.SPWeb` type, which lets us access the broad variety of methods and properties offered by this type. In the next example, we use this object's `EnsureUser` method to check if a specific login name belongs to a valid user of a SharePoint site.

```
PS > $spWeb.EnsureUser("powershell\sezel")


UserLogin              DisplayName
---------              -----------
POWERSHELL\sezel       Sergey Zelenov
```

Since the user `sezel` is not currently a known user of the site, the user is added to the site's User Info list.

You can also modify the site through the methods and properties available. In Chapter 4, we used the `Set-SPWeb` cmdlet to change the description of a site. This can also be done directly through the `Description` property available on the object.

```
PS > $spWeb.Description
Home
PS > $spWeb.Description = "Changed through PowerShell"
```

```
PS > $spWeb.Update()
PS > $spWeb.Description
Changed through PowerShell
```

In the example, we begin by retrieving the current description. Then we assign a new string value to the `Description` property, and finally, we use the `Update()` method to commit the changes we made. When we retrieve the object again, the description is changed.

When you are finished working with an object, use the `Dispose()` method to ensure that the object is disposed of correctly.

```
PS > $spWeb.Dispose()
```

This is good practice because `SPWeb`, `SPSite`, and `SPSiteAdministration` objects may take up large amounts of memory. We will discuss disposing objects in more detail in Chapter 7.

Automatic Variables

The Windows PowerShell automatic variables are fixed variables that store state information. Table 5-2 describes these variables.

Variable	Contents
`$$`	The last token in the last line received by the session
`$?`	True or false, depending on the last performed operation
`$^`	The first token from the last line received by the session
`$_`	The current object in the pipeline object
`$args`	An array of values passed to a function or a script
`$ConsoleFileName`	The path of the console file that was most recently used in the session
`$Error`	An array of error objects representing the most recent error that occurred
`$Event`	A `PSEventArgs` object that represents the event that is being processed
`$EventSubscriber`	A `PSEventSubscriber` object that represents the event subscriber of the event that is being processed
`$ExecutionContext`	An `EngineIntrinsics` object that represents the execution context of the Windows PowerShell host
`$false`	Boolean false
`$foreach`	The enumerator of a `foreach` loop
`$Home`	User's home directory

Table 5-2.   Windows PowerShell Automatic Variables (*continued*)

Variable	Contents
`$Host`	Information regarding the current host
`$input`	An enumerator that contains the input passed to a function
`$LastExitCode`	The last exit code of the last program that was run
`$Matches`	Result of the last successful regular expression match
`$MyInvocation`	Information regarding the context under which the script, function, or script block was run
`$NestedPromptLevel`	The current prompt level
`$NULL`	An empty value
`$PID`	The process identifier of the process that is hosting the current Windows PowerShell session
`$Profile`	The full path to the Windows PowerShell profile for the current user
`$PSBoundParameters`	A dictionary of the active parameters and their current values
`$PsCmdlet`	The cmdlet that is being run
`$PsCulture`	The name of the culture currently in use
`$PsDebugContext`	Information about the debugging environment while debugging
`$PsHome`	The full path of the installation directory of Windows PowerShell
`$PsScriptRoot`	The directory from which the script module is being executed
`$PsUICulture`	The name of the user interface culture that is currently in use in the operating system
`$PsVersionTable`	A read-only hashtable containing details about the version of Windows PowerShell
`$Pwd`	The current directory
`$ShellID`	Identifier of the current shell
`$SourceArgs`	Objects that represent the event arguments of the current event
`$SourceEventArgs`	The first object that represents the first event argument that derives from `EventArgs` of the event that is being processed
`$This`	Reference to the current object in script methods and properties
`$true`	Boolean true

Table 5-2. Windows PowerShell Automatic Variables

You can list the variables in Windows PowerShell by using the `Get-ChildItem` or `Get-Variable` cmdlet.

```
PS > Get-ChildItem Variable:
PS> Get-Variable
```

These commands return both automatic variables and user-created variables.

To display the value of a specific automatic variable, simply type the automatic variable's name.

```
PS > $PSHOME
C:\Windows\System32\WindowsPowerShell\v1.0
```

It is also possible to use the value of a variable as input to cmdlets in Windows PowerShell. In the next example, we use the value of the `$PsHome` variable with the `Get-ChildItem` cmdlet to retrieve all items from the Windows PowerShell home directory.

```
PS > Get-ChildItem $PSHOME
```

When working with pipelines and loops in Windows PowerShell, you use the automatic variable `$_` to handle the current object in the pipeline. In Chapter 3, we used the `Select-Object` cmdlet and created a calculated property using a hashtable and the `$_` variable. Other cmdlets support the `$_` variable. Chapter 7 shows examples of its use with the `Where-Object` and `ForEach-Object` cmdlets.

You can get more information about automatic variables by using the `Get-Help` cmdlet.

```
PS > Get-Help about_Automatic_variables
```

Preference Variables

Windows PowerShell includes a set of preference variables that let you customize its behavior. The preference variables affect the environment and how commands behave. Table 5-3 describes the preference variables available in Windows PowerShell.

You can modify the preference variables by changing their value. For example, the following example changes the warning preference to silently continue.

```
PS > $WarningPreference = "SilentlyContinue"
PS > $WarningPreference
SilentlyContinue
```

When you modify a preference variable in Windows PowerShell, the change affects only the current session. In order to make a persistent change to a preference variable, add the modification to a profile script, as this example shows:

```
'$WarningPreference = "SilentlyContinue"' | Out-File $PSHOME\profile.ps1 -Append
```

Variable	Description
$ConfirmPreference	Sets the level of impact that operations have before requesting confirmation: none, low, medium, or high
$DebugPreference	Controls how Windows PowerShell handles debugging messages written by a script or a cmdlet
$ErrorActionPreference	Sets the default error-handling action
$ErrorView	Controls how Windows PowerShell should output errors to the shell
$FormatEnumerationLimit	Determines how many enumerated items are included in a display
$LogCommandHealthEvent	Logs errors and exceptions in command initialization and processing
$LogCommandLifeCycleEvent	Logs the start and stop of a command in a pipeline
$LogEngineHealthEvent	Logs session error and failures
$LogEngineLifeCycleEvent	Logs the opening and closing of a session
$LogProviderLifeCycleEvent	Logs adding and removing of providers in Windows PowerShell
$LogProviderHealthEvent	Logs provider errors
$MaximumAliasCount	Determines how many aliases are permitted in the current session
$MaximumErrorCount	Determines how many errors are saved in the error history
$MaximumFunctionCount	Determines how many functions are permitted in the current session
$MaximumHistoryCount	Determines how many commands are saved in the command history for the current session
$MaximumVariableCount	Determines how many variables are permitted in the current session
$OFS	Output field separator—specifies the character that an element in an array is separated with when the array is converted to a string

Table 5-3.   Windows PowerShell Preference Variables (*continued*)

Variable	Description
$OutputEncoding	Determines the default character encoding used by Windows PowerShell
$ProgressPreference	Determines how Windows PowerShell responds to progress updates generated by a script
$PSEmailServer	Specifies the default e-mail server used by Windows PowerShell cmdlets
$PSSessionApplicationName	Specifies the default application name for a remote command that uses WS-Management technology
$PSSessionConfigurationName	Specifies the default session configuration that is used for PSSessions created in the current session
$PSSessionOption	Establishes the default values for advanced user options in a remote session
$VerbosePreference	Controls how Windows PowerShell handles verbose messages written by a script or a cmdlet
$WarningPreference	Controls how Windows PowerShell handles warning messages written by a script or a cmdlet
$WhatIfPreference	Determines if WhatIf is automatically enabled for every command that supports it

Table 5-3.   Windows PowerShell Preference Variables

A profile script executes each time Windows PowerShell starts. Profile scripts in Windows PowerShell are described in Chapter 8.

Environment Variables

Environment variables store information regarding the operating system environment. You can display the environment variables available using the Get-ChildItem cmdlet.

```
PS > Get-ChildItem env:
```

Here's how to retrieve a specific environment variable:

```
PS > Get-ChildItem env:COMPUTERNAME
```

```
Name                              Value
```

```
- - - -                              - - - - -
COMPUTERNAME                         SPSERVER01
```

To display the value of the environment variable, add its name.

```
PS > $env:COMPUTERNAME
SPSERVER01
```

As with other variables, you can modify an environment variable by changing its value, as in this example:

```
PS > $env:COMPUTERNAME = "NewName"
PS > $env:COMPUTERNAME
NewName
```

As with preference variables, all changes made to the environment variables using Windows PowerShell affect only the current session. To permanently change environment variables, add the modifications to a profile script.

 NOTE   You can also permanently change environment variables through the `SetEnvironmentVariable()` static method available from the `System.Environment` class.

Arrays in Windows PowerShell

An *array* is a container that is used for storing a collection of data elements. An array in Windows PowerShell can contain objects of all types supported by .NET. All arrays are origin zero, meaning that the first element in an array is always at index 0, the second element is at index 1, and so on. Many cmdlets in Windows PowerShell return output in the form of an array.

Here is an example of creating a simple array containing numeric values:

```
PS > $array = 1,2,3
PS > $array
1
2
3
```

You can also create an array using the array subexpression operator @, as shown here:

```
PS > $array = @(1,2,3)
```

You can access specific elements in arrays. To retrieve the first element, type the following:

```
PS > $array[0]
1
```

Notice how we use the value 0 to retrieve the first element, since the indexing of array elements in Windows PowerShell starts with zero. If we used 1, the second element would be returned.

You can change an element in an array by assigning it a new value, as in this example:

```
PS > $array[1] = "Two"
PS > $array
1
Two
3
```

Use the += operator to add an element to an array.

```
PS > $array += "Four"
PS > $array
1
Two
3
Four
```

You can also count the number of elements in an array by using the Count property.

```
PS > $array.Count
4
```

NOTE   The Count property used in this example is actually an alias for the System.Array Length property. It is available through the types.ps1.xml file, which is a built-in XML file that adds several elements to the .NET Framework types in Windows PowerShell.

When cmdlets return more than one result, Windows PowerShell automatically wraps the result into an array. In the following example, we store the output of the Get-SPWebTemplate cmdlet in a variable and use the Count property to check how many elements the array contains.

```
PS > $SPWebTemplate = Get-SPWebTemplate
PS > $SPWebTemplate.Count
50
```

Again, if we want to retrieve the first element, we can simply type the following:

```
PS > $SPWebTemplate[0]
```

Name	Title	LocaleId	Custom
GLOBAL#0	Global template	1033	False

You can also use ranges when retrieving elements in an array.

```
PS > $SPWebTemplate[0..2]
```

Name	Title	LocaleId	Custom
----	-----	--------	------
GLOBAL#0	Global template	1033	False
STS#0	Team Site	1033	False
STS#1	Blank Site	1033	False

It is even possible to use negative numbers when working with arrays. To retrieve the last element in the array, use -1.

```
PS > $SPWebTemplate[-1]
```

Name	Title	LocaleId	Custom
----	-----	--------	------
visprus#0	Visio Process Repository	1033	False

You will see a lot more examples on working with arrays in the upcoming chapters.

Hashtables in Windows PowerShell

Windows PowerShell also includes hashtables, or associative arrays. Hashtables use key/value pairs instead of a numeric index to access the elements.

You can create a hashtable by placing one or more key/value pairs inside @{ }.

```
PS > $hashTable = @{"FirstName"="Jean-Luc";"LastName"="Picard"}
PS > $hashTable
```

Name	Value
----	-----
FirstName	Jean-Luc
LastName	Picard

You can access specific elements in a hashtable in two ways: using dot notation or by typing the key within square brackets. Here's how to use dot notation:

```
PS > $hashTable.FirstName
Jean-Luc
PS > $hashTable.LastName
Picard
```

And here's the square bracket form:

```
PS > $hashTable["FirstName"]
Jean-Luc
PS > $hashTable["LastName"]
Picard
```

You can also send a hashtable down a pipeline and use the `Select-Object` cmdlet to retrieve specific elements.

```
PS > $hashTable | Select @{Name="Name";Expression={$_["FirstName"]}}

Name
----
Jean-Luc
```

To change a key/value pair in a hashtable, you can use either form to access it and assign the new value, as in these examples:

```
PS > $hashTable.FirstName = "William"
PS > $hashTable["LastName"] = "Riker"
PS > $hashTable

Name                     Value
----                     -----
LastName                 Riker
FirstName                William
```

You can also store multiple hashtables in an array. In this example, we store two hashtables in an array.

```
PS > $hashTable = @{"FirstName"="Jean-Luc";"LastName"="Picard"},
@{"FirstName"="William";"LastName"="Riker"}
PS > $hashTable

Name                     Value
----                     -----
LastName                 Picard
FirstName                Jean-Luc
LastName                 Riker
FirstName                William
```

When multiple hashtables are in an array, to access elements in the hashtable, you need to index into a specific element; otherwise, Windows PowerShell will not know which element you want to retrieve.

```
PS > $hashTable[0]

Name                          Value
----                          -----
LastName                      Picard
FirstName                     Jean-Luc


PS > $hashTable[0].FirstName
```

In this example, we retrieve the first hashtable in the array and return the key/value pair.

Summary

In this chapter, we covered the core functionality of Windows PowerShell. The first part of the chapter demonstrated how to use variables to store objects in Windows PowerShell, and we also took a quick dive through methods and properties. Then we looked at arrays and ways of working with them. The last part of the chapter covered hashtables and showed examples of how to use them in Windows PowerShell.

CHAPTER 6 | Operators

Windows PowerShell supports several types of operators, including some interesting and powerful ones that are not typically found in scripting or programming languages. This chapter covers the operators that you will most commonly use when working with Windows PowerShell and SharePoint 2010.

Arithmetic Operators

The basic arithmetic operators include those to add, multiply, subtract, divide, and calculate the remainder of a division. Table 6-1 lists these operators.

Let's take a closer look at the + operator. To add the values 1 and 5 together, you could type this:

```
PS > 1 + 5
6
```

To add a string with a numeric value, use this form:

```
PS > "String" + 5String5
```

It is also possible to add multiple string values to build up a single string. This example uses the + operator to build up a URL from three strings:

```
PS > "http://" + "SPServer01" + "/MySite"
http://SPServer01/MySite
```

You can also add string objects stored in variables together.

```
PS > $url = "http://SPServer01"
PS > $web = "MySite"
PS > $url + "/" + $web
http://SPServer01/MySite
```

Operator	Description
+	Adds two values
–	Subtracts one value from another
*	Multiplies two values
/	Divides one value by another
%	Returns the remainder from a division

Table 6-1.   Windows PowerShell Arithmetic Operators

However, it is not possible to add a string to a numeric value.

```
PS > 1 + ";#" + "Item"
Cannot convert value "String" to type "System.Int32".
Error: "Input string was not in a correct format."
At line:1 char:4
+ 1 + <<<< "String"
    + CategoryInfo          : NotSpecified: (:) [], RuntimeException
    + FullyQualifiedErrorId : RuntimeException
```

Windows PowerShell interprets the first argument as an instance of the type System.Int32. When we try to add a System.String value to a System.Int32 value, an error occurs. Windows PowerShell expects an argument of the type System.Int32, and it is not possible to convert a System.String value containing characters other than numeric ones. The following is the correct way to add the values:

```
PS > "1" + ";#" + "Item"
1;#Item
```

You can also cast the numeric value using the [string] type literal, which is a PowerShell alias for the System.String type.

```
PS > [string]1 + ";#" + "Item"
1;#Item
```

The value on the left side defines the type of the whole operation. You can add a number to a string, since a number can be converted to a string value, as shown in this example:

```
PS > "#Item" + 1
#Item1
```

Here are examples of using the other arithmetic operators:

■ Use the – operator to subtract numeric values:

```
PS > 5 - 4
1
```

■ The - operator also works with negative numbers:

```
PS > -1 - 1
-2
```

■ Use the * operator to multiply values:

```
PS > 5 * 5
25
```

■ You can also multiply string values with a numeric value:

```
PS > "Hello" * 5
HelloHelloHelloHelloHello
```

■ Divide numeric values with the / operator:

```
PS > 9 / 3
3
```

■ Use the modulus (%) operator to calculate remainders:

```
PS > 10 % 3
1
PS > 6 % 2
0
```

Assignment Operators

Assignment operators are used to assign one or more values to a variable, modify values in a variable, or add values to a variable. Table 6-2 shows the assignment operators available in Windows PowerShell.

Operator	Description
=	Sets the value of a variable to the specified value
+=	Increases the value of a variable by the specified value or appends to the existing value
−=	Decreases the value of a variable by the specified value
*=	Multiplies the value of a variable by the specified value or appends the specified value to the existing value
/=	Divides the value of a variable by the specified value
%=	Divides the value of a variable by the specified value and assigns the remainder to the variable
++	Increases the value by one
−−	Decreases the value by one

Table 6-2. Windows PowerShell Assignment Operators

The most common assignment operator is the equal operator (=). You can use the equal operator to assign a value to a variable.

```
PS > $variable = 1
PS > $variable
1
```

You can also assign the same value to multiple variables.

```
PS > $variable1 = $variable2 = 3
PS > $variable1
3
PS > $variable2
3
```

Here are examples of using some of the other assignment operators:

- To increase the value of a variable by a specific value, use the += operator:

```
PS > $variable = "Windows"
PS > $variable += " "
PS > $variable += "PowerShell"
PS > $variable
Windows PowerShell
```

- To decrease a variable with a specific value, use the -= operator:

```
PS > $variable = 5
PS > $variable -= 3
PS > $variable
2
```

- To multiply a variable with a specific value, use the *= operator:

```
PS > $variable = "-"
PS > $variable *= 8
PS > $variable
--------
```

- To increase a numeric value by one, use the ++ operator:

```
PS > $variable = 1
PS > $variable ++
PS > $variable
2
```

- To decrease a numeric value by one, use the -- operator:

```
PS > $variable = 0
PS > $variable --
PS > $variable
-1
```

Comparison Operators

The comparison operators are used to compare values, as well as to find values that match specific patterns. Table 6-3 lists the comparison operators available in Windows PowerShell.

The -eq operator returns True or an array of matching values if it can match the value on the right with one or more values on the left. The operator returns True if an exact match is made.

```
PS > "http://SPServer01" -eq "http://SPServer01"
True
PS > "http://SPServer01" -eq "http://SPServer01/Site"
False
```

In the first example, we use the –eq operator to compare two identical strings. In the second example, we add a few lines to the value on the right. Since the strings are not identical, False is returned.

We can also use the –eq operator to match an argument on the right side with an array of values on the left.

```
PS > "http://SPServer01", "http://SPServer02" -eq "http://SPServer02"
http://SPServer02
```

Operator	Description
-eq	Equal to
-ne	Not equal to
-gt	Greater than
-lt	Less than
-le	Less than or equal to
-ge	Greater than or equal to
-like	Match using the wildcard character (*)
-notlike	Does not match using the wildcard character (*)
-match	Evaluates a regular expression against the operand on the left; returns True if the match is successful
-notmatch	Evaluates a regular expression against the operand on the left; returns True if the match is not successful
-replace	Replaces all or part of a value with the specified value using regular expressions

Table 6-3. Windows PowerShell Comparison Operators

The -ne operator returns True if the left value and the right value are not identical. If the left side of the operation contains multiple values, the operator returns ones that do not match the value on the right.

```
PS > "http://SPServer01" -ne "http://SPServer01"
False
PS > "http://SPServer01","http://SPServer02" -ne "http://SPServer01"
http://SPServer02
```

The -gt operator returns True if the left value is greater than the right value. The -ge operator returns True if the left value is greater than or equal to the right value.

```
PS > (Get-SPSiteAdministration -Identity http://SPServer01).UsersCount
9
PS > (Get-SPSiteAdministration -Identity http://SPServer01).UsersCount -ge 9
True
PS > (Get-SPSiteAdministration -Identity http://SPServer01).UsersCount -gt 9
False
```

In this example, we use the Get-SPSiteAdministration cmdlet to retrieve the number of users of a site. In this case, there are nine users. We then use the –ge operator to check if the number of users is greater than or equal to nine, which returns True. Next, we check if the number of users is greater than nine, which returns False.

To see if the left value is less than the right value, use the -lt operator. The –le operator is for less-than or equal-to comparisons.

```
PS > (Get-SPSiteAdministration -Identity http://SPServer01).UsersCount -lt 9
False
PS > (Get-SPSiteAdministration -Identity http://SPServer01).UsersCount -le 9
True
```

The –like and –notlike operators are similar to the –eq and –ne operators, but instead of matching exact values, they allow wildcards to be used.

```
PS > "http://SPServer01" -like "http://SPServer01"
True
PS > "http://SPServer01/Site" -like "http://SPServer01*"
True
```

In the first example, we use the –like operator to compare two identical strings. Since the strings match, True is returned. In the second example, we use a wildcard character when we compare the values. The wildcard character matches any given character. If the left side of the operation contains multiple values, the operator returns matching values, rather than True or False, as shown in the next example.

```
PS > "http://SPServer01/internal/site1",
>> "http://SPServer01/external/site1" -like "*external*"
>>
http://SPServer01/external/site1
```

For case-sensitive evaluation, use the –clike operator, as demonstrated here:

```
PS > "http://SPServer01" -clike "http://SPServer01"
True
PS > "http://SPServer01" -clike "http://SPSERVER01"
False
```

The following examples demonstrate how to use the –notlike operator.

```
PS > "http://SPServer01" -notlike "http://SPServer01"
False
PS > "http://SPServer01/Site" -notlike "http://SPServer01"
True
PS > "http://SPServer01/Site" -notlike "http://SPServer01*"
False
```

If the left side of the operation contains multiple values, the operation returns values that do not match, as shown here:

```
PS > "http://SPServer01/internal/site1",
>> "http://SPServer01/external/site1" -notlike "*external*"
>>
http://SPServer01/internal/site1
```

The –match and –notmatch operators try to match one or more of the set of string values on the left side of the operation using regular expressions. Regular expressions are a very powerful means of pattern matching (not specific to PowerShell or any other technology), which allow you to create very complex and effective comparisons. Here are some examples:

- Match http://SPServer01/Site with http://SPServer01:

  ```
  PS > "http://SPServer01/Site" -match "http://SPServer01"
  True
  ```

- Match http://SPServer01/Site with a regular expression that checks if the string starts with http://:

  ```
  PS > "http://SPServer01/Site" -match "^http://"
  True
  ```

- Check if http://SPServer01/Site starts with http://, followed by any number of alphanumeric characters, followed by /, followed by any number of alphanumeric characters and ends with an e:

  ```
  PS > "http://SPServer01/Site" -match "^http://\w*/\w*e$"
  True
  ```

As you can see, it is possible to build up complex match patterns using regular expressions. Similar to the –clike operator, -cmatch performs case-sensitive matching.

You can also use multiple values on the left side and match against a value on the right side, as shown in this example:

```
PS > "http://SPServer01/Site",
>> "http://SPServer01",
>> "http://SPServer02" -match "http://SPServer01"
>>
http://SPServer01/Site
http://SPServer01
```

This example returns the left values that match the right value.

The `-replace` operator in Windows PowerShell is used to find and replace substrings in a string value. It assumes its input is a regular expression. You can use the `-replace` operator to search for and replace a specific pattern.

```
PS > "http://SPServer01/Site" -replace "^http","https"
https://SPServer01/Site
```

Here, we replace `http` with `https`. We use the `^` character to match the beginning of the original string.

Here is an example that uses a more complex replacement pattern:

```
PS > "http://SPServer01/Site" -Replace "/{2}\w*/","//SPServer02/"
http://SPServer02/Site
```

This example compares the string `"http://SPServer01/Site"` to the specified pattern and replaces the part of the string that starts with two / characters, contains any number of alphanumeric characters, and ends with another /.

NOTE   Unlike the `-replace` operator, the `Replace()` method available through `System.String` does not accept regular expressions.

Logical Operators

The logical operators are used to combine expressions, allowing you to check multiple conditions in one statement. Expressions on the left and the right side of any of these operators are evaluated (if necessary), converted to Boolean values of `True` or `False`, and then the combination of those values is returned, following the rules of formal logic. Table 6-4 lists the logical operators supported by Windows PowerShell.

With the `-and` operator, you can evaluate multiple expressions. If all the expressions evaluate to true, the Boolean value of `True` is returned.

```
PS > (1 -eq 1) -and (2 -eq 2)
True
PS > (1 -eq 1) -and (2 -eq 3)
False
```

Operator	Description
-and	Returns True when both left and right hand side expressions evaluate to true
-or	Returns True when an expression on at least one side evaluates to true
-xor	Returns True when left and right side expressions have opposite values (one is True and the other is False)
-not	Changes the Boolean value of the expression that follows it for the opposite
!	Same as -not

Table 6-4. Windows PowerShell Logical Operators

The first example returns True, since both expressions evaluate to True. The second example returns False, since the last expression does not evaluate to true.

The –or operator returns True if one or more expressions evaluate to true.

```
PS > (1 -eq 1) -or (2 -eq 2)
True
PS > (1 -eq 1) -or (2 -eq 3)
True
```

The -xor operator returns True only if one of the expressions evaluates to true.

```
PS > (1 -eq 1) -xor (2 -eq 2)
False
PS > (1 -eq 1) -xor (2 -eq 3)
True
```

The -not operator returns True if the right value evaluates to false.

```
PS > -not (1 -eq 1)
False
PS > -not (1 -eq 2)
True
PS > !(1 -eq 2)
True
```

Redirection Operators

By default, Windows PowerShell sends output to the console. However, you can redirect the output to a file by using the redirection operators, which are listed in Table 6-5.

To send the output of a cmdlet to a file, use the > operator. The following example redirects the output of the Get-Command cmdlet to a file named CommandList.txt, and overwrites the file if it exists.

```
PS > Get-Command > CommandList.txt
```

To append content to a file instead of replacing it, use the >> operator:

```
PS > Get-Command >> CommandList.txt
```

The 2> operator redirects all errors that occurred. The following command redirects all errors that occur to a file instead of displaying the error in the PowerShell console, overwriting the file if it already exists.

```
PS > Get-ChildItem C:\nofile.txt 2> Errors.txt
```

To append the errors to the file instead, use the 2>> operator:

```
PS > Get-ChildItem C:\nofile.txt 2>> Errors.txt
```

 NOTE You can also redirect output to a file using cmdlets that handle redirection, such as Out-File.

Operator	Description
>	Sends the output to a file
>>	Appends the output to a file
2>	Sends errors to a file
2>>	Appends errors to a file
2>&1	Sends errors to the success output stream

Table 6-5. Windows PowerShell Redirection Operators

Type Operators

The type operators are used to find or change the type of an object in Windows PowerShell. Table 6-6 lists the type operators available.

You can test if an object is a specific type by using the -is operator.

```
PS > "Hello" -is [System.String]
True
PS > "Hello" -is [System.Int32]
False
```

In the first example, we check if "Hello" is of the type System.String, which returns True. In the second example, we check if "Hello" is of the type System .Int32, which returns False.

To make sure that an object is not a specific type, use the -isnot operator.

```
PS > "Hello" -isnot [System.String]
False
PS > "Hello" -isnot [System.Int32]
True
```

You can convert objects to a specified type using the -as operator.

```
PS > 1.123 -as [System.Int32]
1
```

In this example, we convert the numeric value 1.123 to an object of the type System.Int32.

Operator	Description
-is	Checks if an object is a specified type
-isnot	Checks if an object is not a specified type
-as	Converts an object to a specified type

Table 6-6.   Windows PowerShell Type Operators

Special Operators

Windows PowerShell includes special operators that you can use to perform tasks that cannot be performed by the other operators. Special operators in Windows PowerShell allow you to perform tasks such as dot-sourcing, creating arrays, and more. Table 6-7 lists the special operators that are available.

The range operator (. .) is used to retrieve a specified range from an array.

```
PS > $array = 1,2,3,4,5
PS > $array[0..2]
1
2
3
```

This example retrieves the elements with index 0 to 2.

Operator	Name	Description
. .	Range operator	Indicates a range of values; the first value in the range goes before the operator and the last value goes after it
&	Call operator	Runs a command, script, or script block
.	Dot-sourcing operator	Runs a script and includes the items, functions, and variables in the script to the current scope
: :	Static member operator	Calls the static properties operator and methods of a .NET Framework class
-f	Format operator	Formats strings by using the format method of string objects
$ ( )	Subexpression operator	Returns the result of an expression placed in a parenthetical list
@ ( )	Array subexpression operator	Returns one or more statements as an array
,	Comma operator	As a binary operator, creates an array; as a unary operator, creates an array with one member

Table 6-7.   Windows PowerShell Special Operators

The range operator also accepts negative ranges.

```
PS > $array[-1..-2]
5
4
```

The call operator (&) in Windows PowerShell is used to run commands, scripts, or script blocks. One thing to keep in mind is that the call operator does not interpret parameters. This example demonstrates how to run a command stored in a variable and represented by a string:

```
PS > $myCommand = "Get-SPWeb"
PS > & $myCommand -Identity http://SPServer01

Url
---
http://spserver01
```

Here, we use "Get-SPWeb" as the input string to the variable and specify the arguments when we call the variable.

You can also use the call operator to run script blocks. A script block can contain any amount of code and is defined by braces.

```
PS > & { 1 + 1 }
2
```

The dot-sourcing operator (.) is used to include variables and functions from a script to the current scope. This means that you can store functions and variables in a script and use the dot-source notation to quickly access the functions and variables contained in the script. Here is an example:

```
PS > $variableInScript
PS > . .\myScript.ps1
PS > $variableInScript
This variable is placed in the myScript.ps1 script
```

Here, we first try to call the variable $variableInScript. Since we have not created a variable called $variableInScript in our current session, the command does not return a value. Next, we dot-source our script, which contains the variable $variableInScript. When we call the variable a second time, a value is returned.

The static member operator (::) is used to call static methods and properties of a .NET Framework class. To find out static methods and properties of a class, use the Get-Member cmdlet with the Static switch parameter.

```
PS > [System.Math] | Get-Member -Static
```

Here are some examples of using the static member operator with the static methods and properties of the System.Math class:

- Use the static method Pow() to return the specified number raised to the specified power:

```
PS > [System.Math]::Pow(5,5)
3125
```

- Use Sqrt() to calculate the square root of 9:

```
PS > [System.Math]::Sqrt(9)
3
```

- Call the static property PI, which represents the ratio of a circle to its diameter:

```
PS > [System.Math]::PI
3,14159265358979
```

The format operator (-f) is a binary operator that uses the same formatting rules as the Format() method in the .NET Framework. It takes a string on the left side and an array of values on the right side. Here is an example:

```
PS > "{0}" -f "PowerShell"
PowerShell
```

In this example, the value enclosed in braces represents the index of the element on the right side. Since the format operator allows an array on the right side, you can use more values.

```
PS > "{0}" -f "PowerShell","Windows"
PowerShell
```

With two elements on the right side but one on the left, the operator returns only the first element. If you add a second value on the left side, you can retrieve both values:

```
PS > "{0} {1}" -f "PowerShell","Windows"
PowerShell Windows
```

You can also switch the places of the numeric values to change the output.

```
PS > "{1} {0}" -f "PowerShell","Windows"
Windows PowerShell
```

The subexpression operator ($()) returns the result of one or more statements. If the result contains multiple values, an array is returned. The next example demonstrates how to use the subexpression operator.

```
PS > "There are: $((Get-Command -Noun SP*).Count) SharePoint cmdlets available
 in Windows PowerShell"
There are: 531 SharePoint cmdlets available in Windows PowerShell
```

The array subexpression operator (@()) returns the result of one or more statements as an array. You can use the operator to create a simple array, as shown in this example:

```
PS > @("Windows","PowerShell")
Windows
PowerShell
```

You can access elements in the array by their index.

```
PS > @("Windows","PowerShell")[0]
Windows
PS > @("Windows","PowerShell")[1]
PowerShell
```

The comma operator (,) is a binary operator used to create simple arrays in Windows PowerShell.

```
PS > 1,2,3
1
2
3
```

You can also use the comma operator to place a single line in an array.

```
PS > $array = ,"PowerShell"
PS > $array[0]
PowerShell
```

When you place a comma operator in front of a value, Windows PowerShell treats the value as an element in an array. When you place the statement in a variable and call the first element in the array, the string value is returned.

Summary

The chapter described a variety of operators that we can use to compare and manipulate values in Windows PowerShell.

- **Arithmetic Operators**   These operators allow you to calculate values.
- **Assignment Operators**   These operators allow you to assign one or more values to variables.
- **Comparison Operators**   These operators allow you to compare values and test if values match a specific pattern.
- **Logical Operators**   These operators allow you to combine expressions and check for multiple conditions in one statement.

- **Redirection Operators**   These operators allow you to send the output to a file.
- **Type Operators**   These operators allow you to find or change the type of an object.
- **Special Operators**   These operators allow you to perform specific tasks that other operators are unable to perform.

If you want to find out more information about operators in Windows PowerShell, you can use the Get-Help cmdlet followed by about_Operators.

CHAPTER 7 | Flow Control and Object Disposal

Like other powerful programming and scripting languages, Windows PowerShell supports looping and branching logic. The looping statements in Windows PowerShell let you perform sequences of commands on all members of a collection (such as sites in a site collection) or on only those that meet a particular condition. Windows PowerShell also includes two cmdlets that can be used for flow control. This chapter covers how to use these flow-control facilities, as well as how to dispose of objects.

Conditional Statements

Windows PowerShell supports the conditional statement if/elseif/else, which branches execution based on a condition, and the switch statement, which can handle multiple complex conditions.

The if/elseif/else Statement

The if/elseif/else statement allows you to execute a block of code if a specified condition is met. However, the statement can also execute a block of code if a condition is not met. This statement uses comparison operators to test the condition.

The following is a simple if/elseif/else statement.

```
PS > $url = "http://SPServer01"
PS > if((Get-SPSiteAdministration $url).DiskUsed -gt 20MB) {
>>    "Disk space used is more than 20 MB"
>> } else {
>>    "Disk space used is less than 20 MB"
>> }
>>
Disk space used is less than 20 MB
```

In this example, we use the Get-SPSiteAdministration cmdlet to retrieve the size (the amount of disk space used) of a site collection. We then use an if/else statement to check if this size exceeds 20MB. If so, we return "Disk space used is more than 20MB." If the condition is not met, we return "Disk space used is less than 20MB."

The next example demonstrates the use of the elseif keyword within the if/elseif/else statement.

```
PS > $url = "http://SPServer01"
PS > if((Get-SPSiteAdministration $url).DiskUsed -gt 20MB) {
>>    "Disk space used is more than 20 MB"
>> } elseif((Get-SPSiteAdministration $url).DiskUsed -gt 10MB) {
>>    "Disk space used is more than 10 MB"
>> } else {
```

```
>>    "Disk space used is less than 10 MB"
>> }
>>
Disk space used is more than 10 MB
```

The elseif keyword lets you introduce another condition and a corresponding additional execution branch. You can add any number of elseif keywords to an if/elseif/else statement.

The switch Statement

The switch statement is a series of if statements and is used to evaluate a condition against a number of potential matches. The switch statement matches the expression with each of the conditions, and if a match is found, an action associated with the condition is performed. If more than one condition applies, the switch statement will execute each of the applicable conditions.

The following is a simple switch statement.

```
PS > $a = 1
PS > switch($a) {
>> 1 { "contains one" }
>> 2 { "contains two" }
>> }
>>
contains one
```

In this example, we choose an action based on the value in parentheses after the switch keyword. The value is matched with each of the conditions. If a match is found, the action associated with that condition is performed.

The default comparison operator used by the switch statement is the -eq operator. It is possible to use other operators when using the switch statement, as the next example demonstrates.

```
PS > $url = "http://SPServer01"
PS > switch((Get-SPSiteAdministration $url).DiskUsed) {
>>    {$_ -gt 20MB} { "Disk space used is more than 20 MB"; Break }
>>    {$_ -gt 10MB} { "Disk space used is more than 10 MB"; Break }
>>    {$_ -gt 5MB} { "Disk space used is more than 5 MB"; Break }
>>    Default { "Disk space used is less than 5 MB" }
>> }
>>
Disk space used is more than 10 MB
```

In this example, the values in parentheses are the amount of disk space used. The value is then matched against the patterns in each clause, and if a match is found, the corresponding clause is executed. Since a Break is used at the end of each condition, the switch stops as soon as a match is made. The Default clause is used to perform an action if none of the switch values match the pattern. Notice how we use the $_ variable to reference the input object.

The switch statement supports a couple of options that you can use to control the pattern matching. By default, the switch statement is case-insensitive. You can perform a case-sensitive pattern match with the -Casesensitive option.

```
PS > $url = "http://SPServer01"
PS > switch -CaseSensitive ($url) {
>>    "http://SPServer01" {"matches http://SPServer01"; Break }
>>    "http://SPSERVER01" {"matches http://SPSERVER01"; Break }
>>    default {"no match found"}
>> }
>>
matches http://SPServer01
```

We can also use wildcard pattern matching with the switch statement. Here is an example:

```
PS > $url = "http://SPServer01"
PS > switch -WildCard -CaseSensitive ($url) {
>> "http*[S]*" {"Starts with 'http' and contains a upper-case S"; Break }
>> "http*[s]*" {"Starts with 'http' and contains a lower-case s"; Break }
>> }
>>
Starts with 'http' and contains a upper-case S
```

In this example, first we check if the value of the variable $url starts with a 'http' and contains an uppercase S. Then we check if the value of the variable $url starts with 'http' and contains a lowercase s. Since the first pattern matches the variable, the corresponding clause is executed.

The switch statement also supports regular expressions, which let you create complex pattern matches. Here is an example:

```
PS > $url = "http://SPServer01"

PS > switch -regex ($url) {

>> "^(http|https)://{2}" {"match found"}

>> }

>>

match found
```

In this example, we test if the value of the variable $url starts with 'http' or 'https' followed by the : character and two / characters.

Looping Statements

The looping statements in Windows PowerShell include `for`, `while`, `do/while`, and `foreach`.

The for Loop

The `for` loop is a construct used to run commands in a statement block for as long as the specified condition evaluates to true. The `for` loop is often used to iterate through an array or other type of collection and run a set of commands against each of its elements.

Here is an example of a simple `for` loop:

```
PS > for($i = 1; $i -le 5; $i ++) { $i }
1
2
3
4
5
```

The example returns the value of `$i` as long as `$i` is less than or equal 5. Each time the `for` loop evaluates, the condition increments the value by 1.

The `for` loop is often used to loop through an array and run a command on each element in the array. Here is an example:

```
PS > $array = 1,2,3,4,5
PS > for($i = 0; $i -lt ($array.count); $i ++) { $array[$i] * 10 }
10
20
30
40
50
```

In this example, we first create an array holding the values 1 to 5. We then use the array in the `for` loop to specify how many times the loop should run. Notice how we place the array within parentheses in order to calculate the number of times the `for` loop should run.

You can also use the `for` loop to iterate through a collection of sites, as shown in this example:

```
PS > $url = "http://SPServer01"
PS > $spWebs = Get-SPSite -Identity $url | Get-SPWeb
PS > for($i = 0; $i -lt $spWebs.Count; $i ++) {
>> $spWebs[$i] | Select-Object -Property Url, Created
>> }
```

```
Url                           Created
---                           -------
http://spserver01             3/28/2010 11:44:11 PM
http://spserver01/Web1        4/10/2010 10:15:03 PM
http://spserver01/Web10       4/10/2010 10:15:37 PM
http://spserver01/Web2        4/10/2010 10:15:21 PM
http://spserver01/Web3        4/10/2010 10:15:23 PM
http://spserver01/Web4        4/10/2010 10:15:26 PM
http://spserver01/Web5        4/10/2010 10:15:28 PM
http://spserver01/Web6        4/10/2010 10:15:29 PM
http://spserver01/Web7        4/10/2010 10:15:31 PM
http://spserver01/Web8        4/10/2010 10:15:33 PM
http://spserver01/Web9        4/10/2010 10:15:35 PM'
```

Here, we use the `Get-SPSite` and `Get-SPWeb` cmdlets to retrieve all the sites in a specific site collection and store them in the `$spWebs` variable. First, we use the `$spWebs` variable in the test pipeline of the `for` loop to determine how many times the loop needs to run. Notice how we use the `count` property to retrieve the number of sites. In the command block, we use the same variable to return an array containing all sites, and then retrieve each individual site in a new iteration of the loop, using the index notation and the `$i` variable. Finally, we pipe the site object to the `Select-Object` cmdlet and retrieve the `Url` and `Created` properties.

The do/while Loop

The `while` and `do/while` loops are language constructs used to run a command block as long as a condition evaluates to true.

Here is an example on a simple `while` loop:

```
PS > $i = 0
PS > while ($i -le 4) { "`$i = $i"; $i++ }
$i = 1
$i = 2
$i = 3
$i = 4
```

This example repeats the command block as long as the value of the `$i` variable is not equal to 4. The variable is incremented in the code block. We also use a backtick character (`` ` ``) to comment away `$i` in the output. The backtick character is typically used to return variable names in the output.

The `do/while` loop is a variation of the `while` loop. In the `while` loop, the condition is checked in the beginning of the loop. In the `do/while` loop, the condition is checked in the end of the loop. Here is an example of a `do/while` loop:

```
PS > do { $i++; "`$i = $i";} while ($i -le 4)
$i = 1
$i = 2
```

```
$i = 3
$i = 4
$i = 5
```

In this example, the loop increases by one as long as the variable is less than or equal to 4. Notice how the value 5 is returned in the output. This happens because the while condition is still true when the variable $i is equal to 5.

The foreach Loop

The foreach loop is a construct used to iterate through a series of values in a collection of items. A block of code contained within braces is used to execute a statement for each item in the collection.

Here is an example of a basic foreach loop:

```
PS > $items = 1,2,3,4,5
PS > foreach($item in $items) { $item }
1
2
3
4
5
```

The example iterates through each element in the array and performs the operation specified in the block of code on each element.

You can also use the foreach loop when working with SharePoint 2010. The example below demonstrates how to iterate through items in a site collections recycle bin and display the items Web, Title, and also display who deleted the item.

```
PS > foreach($i in (Get-SPSite http://SPServer01).RecycleBin) {
>>    @{"Web"=$i.Web}
>>    @{"Item"=$i.Title}
>>    @{"DeletedBy" = $i.DeletedBy}
>> }
>>
Name             Value
----             -----
Web              Team Site
Item             Tasks
DeletedBy        POWERSHELL\sezel
```

Flow-Control Cmdlets

Windows PowerShell also includes two cmdlets that rely on scriptblocks : ForEach-Object and Where-Object. A ScriptBlock is a chunk of PowerShell code enclosed in braces. Note that scriptblocks are also used in functions, filters, and variables. In fact, anything that you can type in a Windows PowerShell prompt can be placed in a scriptblock.

The ForEach-Object Cmdlet

ForEach-Object is a flow-control cmdlet that is used to perform an operation on each object in a pipeline. It uses the automatic variable $_ to represent the current object and processes one object at a time. The operation to perform is described within a script block.

The ForEach-Object cmdlet has the alias foreach, so you can use that instead of typing the full cmdlet name. When you use foreach in a pipeline, Windows PowerShell interprets the command as the ForEach-Object cmdlet. However, when you use foreach at the beginning of a command, the foreach *construct* is used instead of the ForEach-Object cmdlet. The foreach construct is used to iterate through a series of values in a collection of items, and basically works in the same way as the ForEach-Object cmdlet. The difference lies in how the objects are processed, the foreach statement stores the whole collection in memory before processing while the ForEach-Object cmdlet reads one object at the time. Another difference is that the foreach statement does not use the $_ variable. Instead the loop variable is specified in the construct.

Here is a simple example of how to use the ForEach-Object cmdlet:

```
PS > $num = 1,2,3,4,5
PS > $num | ForEach-Object { $_ }
1
2
3
4
5
```

Notice how we use $_ to work with the current object being processed by the ForEach-Object cmdlet.

Here is an example of using the foreach alias:

```
PS > $num | foreach { $_ }
1
2
3
4
5
```

Since we are sending an array through a pipeline, Windows PowerShell interprets the foreach command as the ForEach-Object cmdlet.

You can access specific properties and methods on each object passed to the ForEach-Object cmdlet. Here is an example where we take an array of two string values as input and use the ToUpper() method on each object.

```
PS > $strings = "windows","powershell"
PS > $strings | ForEach-Object { $_.ToUpper() }
WINDOWS
POWERSHELL
```

You can also use the ForEach-Object cmdlet to perform operations on multiple sites in a site collection, as demonstrated in this example:

```
PS > $url = "http://SPServer01"
PS > Get-SPSite -Identity $url | Get-SPWeb | ForEach-Object {
>> "$($_.url) has $($_.Lists.Count) lists"
>> }
http://spserver01 has 24 lists
http://spserver01/Web1 has 9 lists
http://spserver01/Web2 has 1 lists
http://spserver01/Web3 has 7 lists
http://spserver01/Web4 has 2 lists
http://spserver01/Web5 has 1 lists
http://spserver01/Web6 has 7 lists
http://spserver01/Web7 has 2 lists
http://spserver01/Web8 has 6 lists
```

In this example, we pipe the sites retrieved with Get-SPWeb to the ForEach-Object cmdlet. We then return the URL and the number of lists in each site. Notice how we place the $_ variable in a subexpression to access the properties of the current object being processed by the cmdlet.

In the previous examples, we used a single scriptblock to describe the operation performed on each object passed to the ForEach-Object cmdlet. It is possible to add two additional scriptblocks: one that runs before the first object is processed and one that runs when all objects have been processed. You can add the additional scriptblocks using the Begin, Process, and End parameters supported by the ForEach-Object cmdlet as demonstrated in this example:

```
PS > Get-SPSite -Identity http://SPServer01 | Get-SPWeb |
>> ForEach-Object  -Begin {Get-Date} `
>> -Process {"$($_.url) has $($_.Lists.Count) lists"} `
>> -End {Get-Date}
>>

Sunday, June 27, 2010 1:59:03 PM
http://spserver01 has 24 lists
http://spserver01/Site1 has 9 lists
http://spserver01/Site2 has 1 lists
```

```
http://spserver01/Site3 has 7 lists
http://spserver01/Site4 has 2 lists
http://spserver01/Site5 has 1 lists
http://spserver01/Site6 has 7 lists
http://spserver01/Site7 has 2 lists
http://spserver01/Site8 has 6 lists
Sunday, June 27, 2010 1:59:03 PM
```

Here, we pipe the sites retrieved with Get-SPWeb to the ForEach-Object cmdlet. We then use the Begin parameter to display the current date and time. The Process parameter uses the current object being processed and displays the URL, followed by the number of lists in the current site. Finally, the End parameter is used to display the date and time after all of the objects have been processed.

The Where-Object Cmdlet

The Where-Object cmdlet is used to select objects from a collection based on the conditions specified in its scriptblock. Each element coming in through the pipeline is evaluated, and if the result evaluates to true, the element is passed through. If the result evaluates to false, the element is ignored. Like the ForEach-Object cmdlet, Where-Object uses the $_ automatic variable to host the current pipeline element.

Here is an example of using the Where-Object cmdlet:

```
PS > $num = 1,2,3,4,5
PS > $num | Where-Object  {-not ( $_ % 2 )}
2
4
```

In this example, we send an array of numeric characters through a pipeline and use the Where-Object cmdlet to check if any of the elements in the array are even.

You can also use logical operators to test different values.

```
PS > $num | Where-Object  {-not ( $_ % 2 ) -or $_ -eq 5 }
2
4
5
```

In this example, we check if any of the elements in the array are even or equal to 5.

You can pass cmdlets through a pipeline and perform evaluations on the objects returned by a cmdlet.

```
PS > Get-SPSite -Identity http://SPServer01 | Get-SPWeb |
>> Where-Object { $_.LastItemModifiedDate -lt $(Get-Date 5/5/2010) }

Url
---
http://spserver01
http://spserver01/Site1
http://spserver01/Site2
```

Here, we pipe the sites retrieved with Get-SPWeb to the Where-Object cmdlet. We then check if the LastItemModifiedDate is less than May 5, 2010. Three sites meet the criteria in the example.

You can go one step further and send the objects to the ForEach-Object cmdlet and perform additional operations on the objects that meet the criteria.

```
PS > Get-SPSite -Identity http://SPServer01 | Get-SPWeb |
>> Where-Object { $_.LastItemModifiedDate -lt $(Get-Date 5/5/2010) } |
>> ForEach-Object { $_.Author }

UserLogin            DisplayName
---------            -----------
POWERSHELL\sezel      Sergey Zelenov
POWERSHELL\maka      Mattias Karlsson
POWERSHELL\nigo      Niklas Goude
```

In this example, we use the ForEach-Object cmdlet to return the author of the sites that meet the criteria.

Object Disposal

SPWeb, SPSite, and SPSiteAdministration objects can sometimes take up large amounts of memory, so using any of these objects in PowerShell requires proper memory management. Normally, instances of these objects obtained through cmdlets such as Get-SPWeb are disposed of automatically at the end of the pipeline, but this does not happen to instances stored in variables.

The Start-SPAssignment and Stop-SPAssignment cmdlets were introduced to spare script authors the need to dispose of each such object individually. Instead, you can associate multiple objects with an assignment store, and then dispose of them all correctly and efficiently with one command.

Dispose Method

If you want to do a straightforward task, such as change the description of a site, use the cmdlets available, which dispose of the objects at the end of the pipeline. Here is an example:

```
PS > $url = "http://SPServer01"
PS > Get-SPWeb -Identity $url | Set-SPWeb -Description "Hello"
```

If you want to change properties that are not available through the Set-SPWeb cmdlet, such as enabling or disabling the tree view on a single site, the simplest way is to store an instance of an SPWeb object in a variable, change the TreeViewEnabled property, use the `Update()` method, and finally use the `Dispose()` method when the change is committed to dispose of the object. Here is an example of this approach:

```
PS > $spWeb = Get-SPWeb -Identity $url
PS > $spWeb.TreeViewEnabled = $True
PS > $spWeb.Update()
PS > $spWeb.Dispose()
```

The Start-SPAssignment and Stop-SPAssignment Cmdlets

In the previous example, we disposed of the object using the `Dispose()` method. As mentioned earlier, it is also possible to dispose of objects using the `Start-SPAssignment` and `Stop-SPAssignment` cmdlets.

There are basically three levels of assignments:

- **No assignment** Applies when an object of the type `SPWeb`, `SPSite`, or `SPSiteAdministration` is not assigned to a variable and is disposed of automatically.
- **Simple assignment** All objects are assigned to the global assignment store.
- **Advanced assignment** Objects are assigned to named stores and disposed of when the specific store is disposed.

In the following example, we store an object of the type `SPWeb` in a variable and dispose of it using a simple assignment.

```
PS > Start-SPAssignment -Global
PS > $spWeb = Get-SPWeb -Identity $url
PS > $spWeb.TreeViewEnabled = $True
PS > $spWeb.Update()
PS > Stop-SPAssignment -Global
```

When iterating through multiple sites in a site collection, the simple assignment lets you associate multiple objects with an assignment store, and then dispose of them all correctly and efficiently with a single command, as shown in this example:

```
PS > Start-SPAssignment -Global
PS > $spSite = Get-SPSite -Identity $url
PS > $spSite | Get-SPWeb -limit All | ForEach-Object {
>> $spWeb = $_
>> $spWeb.TreeViewEnabled = $True
>> spWeb.Update()
>> }
PS > Stop-SPAssignment -Global
```

Here, we first use the `Start-SPAssignment` cmdlet with the `Global` switch parameter. Then we iterate through multiple sites in a site collection and change the `TreeViewEnabled` property on each site. When the last site is processed, we dispose of the objects using the `Stop-SPAssignment` cmdlet.

The previous example might seem like a good way to update multiple sites and handle the disposal with a few simple cmdlets. But suppose that the site collection contains a thousand sites. An instance object for each site would then be stored in the global assignment store, and would not be disposed of until the final site was updated. This is obviously not a good approach for large site collections.

A better way when iterating through large site collections is to use the advanced assignment when storing objects returned from cmdlets in variables and using the `Dispose()` method to dispose of objects stored in variables created in a loop, as demonstrated in this example:

```
PS > $spAssignment = Start-SPAssignment
PS > $spSite = Get-SPSite -Identity $url -AssignmentCollection $spAssignment
PS > $spSite | Get-SPWeb -limit All | ForEach-Object {
>> $spWeb = $_
>> $spWeb.TreeViewEnabled = $True
>> spWeb.Update()
>> $spWeb.Dispose()
>> }
PS > Stop-SPAssignment $spAssignment
```

Here, we assign the instance object returned from the `Get-SPSite` cmdlet to an advanced assignment store. Then we iterate through each site in the site collection using the `ForEach-Object` cmdlet. In the script block, we store the current object in a variable and change a property. When we are finished with the object, we call the `Dispose()` method to immediately dispose of the object before handling the next object passed to the `ForEach-Object` cmdlet. Finally, when the `ForEach-Object` cmdlet has processed all objects in the pipeline, we use `Stop-SPAssignment` to dispose of the object assigned to the `$spAssignment` variable.

Summary

In this chapter, we covered flow control and looping. You also saw examples on how and when to dispose of objects using Windows PowerShell.

- **Conditional statements**   The `if`/`elseif`/`else` branches execution based on a condition. The `switch` statement lets you use multiple conditions and supports pattern matching.

- **Looping statements**   The `for` loop iterates through a collection of objects. The `while` and `do`/`While` loops execute as long as condition evaluates True.

- **foreach- and ForEach-Object**   The `foreach` loop stores the entire collection in memory before processing while the `ForEach-Object` cmdlet processes one object at the time.

- **Object disposal** objects of the type `SPWeb`, `SPSite` or `SPSiteAdministration` require proper memory management so consider disposing of them correctly.

CHAPTER 8 | Functions, Scripts, and Remoting

Thish chapter completes the introduction to Windows PowerShell in SharePoint 2010 by covering three important components: functions, execution policies, and scripts. We will also look at running Windows PowerShell remotely.

Windows PowerShell Functions

Functions are used in most programming and scripting languages. A *function* is a named block of code that can be referred to from within Windows PowerShell. When a function's name is called, the list of statements contained in the function is executed.

A function may accept input in the form of arguments, the values of which can then be used by the code inside the function. The output from a function can be stored in a variable, passed to another function, passed to a cmdlet, or written to one of the output streams.

A function is declared with the keyword `function`, and the associated code is placed within a script block. Here is an example of a basic function:

```
PS > function Hello {
>>    "Hello $env:username"
>> }
>>
PS > Hello
Hello nigo
```

When we call the function `Hello`, the block of code contained in the function is executed, and the output is returned to the session.

A function also accepts arguments, as this example shows:

```
PS > function foo { $args }
PS > foo 1 2 3
1
2
3
```

This function uses the automatic variable `$args` to return the arguments passed to the function. When we call the function and pass the arguments 1, 2, and 3, they are returned to the session.

Like cmdlets, functions can have parameters. One way to define a parameter is to place a variable within parentheses after the function's name. Here is an example of a function with two named parameters:

```
PS > function username ($firstname, $lastname) {
>> "FirstName: $firstname"
>> "LastName: $lastname"
>> }
>>
```

The two named parameters to the function are $firstname and $lastname. When we call the function, each argument passed to the function will be bound to the corresponding parameter. If we simply type two arguments after we call the function, the arguments will bind to the corresponding parameter based on the argument's position.

```
PS > username Niklas Goude
FirstName: Niklas
LastName: Goude
```

You can also bind the arguments to a named parameter by typing the parameter's name before the argument:

```
PS > username -firstname Niklas -lastname Goude
FirstName: Niklas
LastName: Goude
```

This way, you do not need to enter the arguments in positional order. For example, you can input the last parameter first:

```
PS > username -lastname Goude -firstname Niklas
FirstName: Niklas
LastName: Goude
```

By adding a type to a named parameter, you can control the type of argument that the function accepts. Here is an example:

```
PS > function addition ([int]$val1, [int]$val2) { $val1 + $val2 }
PS > addition 2 3
5
```

If we try to input a string value to this function, it returns an error.

```
PS > addition 2 "three"
addition : Cannot process argument transformation on parameter 'val2'.
Cannot convert value "three" to type "System.Int
32". Error: "Input string was not in a correct format."
At line:1 char:9
+ addition <<<<  2 "three"
    + CategoryInfo          : InvalidData: (:) [addition], ParameterBindin...
mationException
    + FullyQualifiedErrorId : ParameterArgumentTransformationError,addition
```

You can also create switch parameters that can either evaluate to True or False. Switch parameters do not require any input; you can simply type the function's name followed by the name of the switch parameter. Here is an example:

```
PS > function TV([switch]$on) {
>> if($on) { "The television is on" }
```

```
>> else { "The television is off" }
>> }
PS > TV
The television is off
PS > TV -on
The television is on
```

When we call the function TV without entering the switch parameter's name, the variable $on is set to False, and The television is off is returned. If we do type the switch parameter's name, the variable $on is set to True, and The television is on is returned.

You can add other types of named parameters to a function as well. In the next example, we create a named parameter of the type System.uri to check if a URL is valid.

```
PS > function Check-Url([uri]$url) {
>>    if($url.AbsoluteUri -ne $Null -and $url.Scheme -match 'http|https') {
>>      $true
>>    } else {
>>      $false
>>    }
>> }
```

The Check-Url function has one parameter: $url. When we call the function, the argument passed to the function needs to be bound to the corresponding parameter, which can happen either by the parameter's name or position. If we simply type the argument value after the function's name, the argument will be bound to the parameter based on the argument's position. Since we have only one parameter in this example, the argument will be bound to the $url parameter.

It is also possible to specify the type of parameter the function will accept (if there are multiple parameters, type information will also be used in the binding process, after the name and position). Notice how we use the type System.Uri—an object representation of a uniform resource identifier (URI), which, according to Microsoft Developer Network (MSDN), is "a compact representation of a resource available to your application on the intranet or Internet." We then check if the value of its AbsoluteURI property is not null and that the Scheme property value (which represents the protocol) contains either http or https. If the condition evaluates to true, True is returned; if not, False is returned. This is a quick way of testing if a URL supplied is in the correct format. We can call the function by typing its name followed by the URL that we want to check.

```
PS > Check-Url -url http://SPServer01
True
```

Windows PowerShell Scripts

Scripts in Windows PowerShell are basically sequences of commands stored in a text file. A script in Windows PowerShell must have the file name extension .ps1 and can contain functions such as the ones described in the previous section. Like functions, scripts in Windows PowerShell can use parameters to accept input.

Windows PowerShell was designed with security in mind. One security feature is that files with the extension .ps1 are associated with Notepad, rather than Windows PowerShell. This prevents users from accidentally clicking a script and executing it unintentionally.

Another security feature is the *execution policy*, which controls how scripts can be executed. Before we get started with writing scripts, let's take a quick tour of the execution policies in Windows PowerShell.

Setting the Execution Policy

Windows PowerShell supports execution policies that let you define criteria for allowing scripts to execute. The execution policies for the local computer and current users are stored in the registry. The following are the Windows PowerShell execution policies:

- **Restricted**   This is the default policy. It permits commands and functions to be run in the Windows PowerShell console, but will not run scripts.

- **AllSigned**   This policy allows execution of scripts, but requires them to be digitally signed by a trusted publisher, including scripts written on your local computer.

- **RemoteSigned**   This policy allows scripts written on the local computer to be executed, but does not allow execution of scripts downloaded or received by e-mail, unless they are digitally signed.

- **Unrestricted**   With this policy, Windows PowerShell runs all scripts, but displays a warning for scripts originating from the Internet.

 NOTE   Windows PowerShell (or any component of the operating system) can tell whether or not a script or file originating from the Internet is trusted by the zone information contained in a specified alternative data stream of the file. All it takes to turn an Internet file into a local file is opening the file's properties and clicking the Unblock button (this applies to Windows XP SP2 and Internet Explorer 7 and later).

You can use the `Get-ExecutionPolicy` cmdlet to retrieve the current execution policy on the local computer.

```
PS > Get-ExecutionPolicy
Restricted
```

In this example, the policy is set to Restricted, which is the default.

To set a Windows PowerShell execution policy, you need elevated privileges. To run Windows PowerShell with elevated privileges, right-click the Windows PowerShell icon and click Run as Administrator.

 NOTE   Since there is no User Access Control (UAC) in Windows XP or Windows Server 2003, the Run as Administrator option does not apply to those operating systems.

You can now use the `Set-ExecutionPolicy` cmdlet to change the execution policy. Here's an example of changing the policy to RemoteSigned:

```
PS > Set-ExecutionPolicy RemoteSigned

Execution Policy Change
The execution policy helps protect you from scripts that you do not trust.
Changing the execution policy might expose
you to the security risks described in the about_Execution_Policies help topic.
Do you want to change the execution policy?
[Y] Yes  [N] No  [S] Suspend  [?] Help (default is "Y"): Y
```

Executing Scripts

Let's start by creating a simple script and executing it. The following code is placed in a file named myScript.ps1.

```
# One-line comments in scripts are written after a number sign.
$args
<#
Block Comments can be written over
multiple lines.
#>
```

The script starts with a comment, which is preceded by a # sign to indicate it is a comment. Next, it uses the automatic variable `$args` to display the arguments passed to the script. It ends with a block comment, which is written over multiple lines and enclosed with <# and #> characters.

Run the script as follows:

```
PS > .\myScript.ps1 "hey" "hey" "my" "my"
hey
hey
my
my
```

Windows PowerShell does not execute scripts in the current directory by default. You need to explicitly tell Windows PowerShell that the script is placed in the current directory by typing . \ before the script name. Alternatively, you can type its full path:

```
PS > C:\Scripts\myScript.ps1 "hey" "hey"
hey
hey
```

If the directory name contains whitespace, you can use the call operator (&) to execute the script. Here's an example:

```
PS > & 'C:\My Scripts\myScript.ps1' "hey"
hey
```

Using Parameters in Scripts

The `param` statement is used to add parameters to scripts. The `param` statement must be the first executed line of code in a script (except for comments or comment-based help). Script parameters work in the same way as function parameters, as discussed earlier in this chapter.

The following shows a basic script using parameters.

```
param([string]$firstname, [string]$lastname)
"FirstName: $firstname"
"LastName: $lastName"
```

We can execute the script by typing . \, the script name (myScript.psi in this example), followed by the parameters.

```
PS > .\myScript.ps1 -firstname Niklas -lastname Goude
FirstName: Niklas
LastName: Goude
```

Writing Comment-Based Help Topics in Scripts

Cmdlets in Windows PowerShell include a help topic that describes how to use the cmdlets in Windows PowerShell. When writing scripts, you can add a custom comment-based help topic using a comment block (enclosed with <# and #>) containing at least one keyword. Some of the valid keywords are `synopsis`, `description`, `parameter` (followed by the parameter name), `example`, `inputs`, `outputs`, `notes`, `links`, `component`, `role`, and `functionality`. Here is an example that demonstrates how to add a comment-based help topic to a script in Windows PowerShell:

```
<#
.SYNOPSIS
Displays firstname and lastname
```

```
.DESCRIPTION
The myScript.ps1 script displays the firstname and lastname.

.PARAMETER firstname
Specifies the users firstname

.PARAMETER lastname
specifies the users lastname

.OUTPUTS
System.String. myScript.ps1 returns a string with the users firstname and lastname

.EXAMPLE
PS >  .\myScript.ps1 Niklas Goude
FirstName: Niklas
LastName: Goude

#>

param([string]$firstname, [string]$lastname)
"FirstName: $firstname"
"LastName: $lastName"
```

When a comment-based help topic is added to a script, you can use the `Get-Help` cmdlet to display the help topic in the session. Here is how we could display the help topics added to the previous script:

```
PS > Get-Help .\myScript.ps1 -Examples

NAME
    C:\Scripts\myScript.ps1

SYNOPSIS
    Displays firstname and lastname

    ------------------------- EXAMPLE 1 -------------------------

    PS >.\myScript.ps1 Niklas Goude


    FirstName: Niklas
    LastName: Goude
```

Using Functions in Scripts

You can add functions in a script by placing them at the top of the script. (This might seem strange if you are used to VBScript.) Since Windows PowerShell reads the script from top to bottom, an error will occur if a function is called before it has been read into memory.

Here is an example of a Windows PowerShell script that includes a function:

```
param([string]$Identity)

function Check-Url([uri]$url) {
  if($url.AbsoluteUri -ne $Null -and $url.Scheme -match 'http|https') {
    $true
  } else {
    $false
  }
}

if(Check-Url -url $Identity) {
  Get-SPWeb -Identity $Identity
} else {
  Write-Host "Invalid URL"
}
```

This script starts with a `param` statement, where we define the script parameters. Here, we use the type `System.String` for the input parameter. Next, we add our function to the script. At the bottom of the script, we add our code that executes when the script is run. We start off by validating the URL passed to the script. If the URL is valid, the script attempts to run the `Get-SPWeb` cmdlet. If not, the script returns `Invalid URL`.

Customizing Windows PowerShell with Profile Scripts

Profile scripts run automatically when Windows PowerShell starts. Using profile scripts, you can customize the Windows PowerShell environment and add commands, aliases, functions, variables, snap-ins, and drives to every Windows PowerShell session that you start. Windows PowerShell supports the four basic profile scripts shown Table 8-1.

Path	Filename	Shells	User
$PSHOME\	profile.ps1	All shells	All users
$PSHOME\	Microsoft.PowerShell_ profile.ps1	Microsoft. PowerShell shell	All users
$HOME\My Documents\ WindowsPowerShell\	profile.ps1	All shells	Current user
$HOME\ My Documents\ WindowsPowerShell\	Microsoft.PowerShell_ profile.ps1	Microsoft. PowerShell shell	Current user

Table 8-1. Windows PowerShell Profile Scripts

Table 8-1 shows how different profile scripts affect different users and shells. For instance, a profile script named profile.ps1 placed in the Windows PowerShell root folder affects all users. A profile script with the same name placed in the user's home folder affects only that user.

For example, if we wanted all Windows PowerShell sessions to start by displaying "Hello" followed by the current user's name, we would create a new profile script in the Windows PowerShell root folder and place the following code in that profile script:

```
PS > '"Hello $env:USERNAME"' | Out-File $PSHOME\profile.ps1
```

 NOTE Running the command may require administrative privileges.

Windows PowerShell Remoting

Windows PowerShell offers great remote features through Windows Remote Management. Windows Remote Management is the Microsoft implementation of the WS-Management console protocol, which is a SOAP-based protocol designed as a common way for exchanging management information between heterogeneous systems.

To run Windows PowerShell remotely, you need to enable Windows Remote Management, which is included in Windows 7 and Windows Server 2008 Release 2. Enabling Windows Remote Management requires administrative privileges.

Figure 8-1 demonstrates running the Enable-PSRemoting cmdlet to configure the computer to receive Windows PowerShell remote commands that are sent using the WS-Management protocol. With this set up, you can run Windows PowerShell commands remotely from a different computer on the network.

```
PS > Enable-PSRemoting

WinRM Quick Configuration
Running command "Set-WSManQuickConfig" to enable this machine for remote management through WinRM service.
 This includes:
    1. Starting or restarting (if already started) the WinRM service
    2. Setting the WinRM service type to auto start
    3. Creating a listener to accept requests on any IP address
    4. Enabling firewall exception for WS-Management traffic (for http only).

Do you want to continue?
[Y] Yes  [A] Yes to All  [N] No  [L] No to All  [S] Suspend  [?] Help (default is "Y"): Y
WinRM already is set up to receive requests on this machine.
WinRM has been updated for remote management.
Created a WinRM listener on HTTP://* to accept WS-Man requests to any IP on this machine.
WinRM firewall exception enabled.


Confirm
Are you sure you want to perform this action?
Performing operation "Registering session configuration" on Target "Session configuration "Microsoft.PowerShell32" is
not found. Running command "Register-PSSessionConfiguration Microsoft.PowerShell32 -processorarchitecture x86 -force"
to create "Microsoft.PowerShell32" session configuration. This will restart WinRM service.".
[Y] Yes  [A] Yes to All  [N] No  [L] No to All  [S] Suspend  [?] Help (default is "Y"): Y
PS >
```

Figure 8-1. Enabling Windows Remote Management

Running SharePoint 2010 cmdlets in a remote session also has two additional implications that you must consider:

- **Authentication**   The Windows Remote Management (or WinRM, which is the "backbone" for PowerShell remoting) supports a variety of authentication mechanisms, from clear password-based to Kerberos. However, since many of the SharePoint 2010 cmdlets communicate directly with the SQL server, they require a means of securely delegating a user's credentials from the remote client through the SharePoint 2010 server and onto the backend server (scenario commonly known as "double hop"). The authentication protocol that does this best for WinRM is Microsoft's Credential Security Support Provider (CredSSP), which means it must be enabled for you to be able to use SharePoint 2010 cmdlets and object model remotely. You can enable CredSSP on the server using the following command:

```
PS > Enable-WSManCredSSP -Role Server
```

It is also required to enable CredSSP on each client as demonstrated here:

```
PS > Enable-WSManCredSSP -role client -delegatecomputer
SPServer01.powershell.nu
```

- **Memory Limit**   WinRM implements a set of quotas for remote users, designed to make the service more robust and reliable. One of such quotas is the maximum amount of memory that can be allocated to a remote shell, which by default is set to 150MB. Now, some SharePoint 2010 cmdlets can potentially use large amounts of memory (even with all the memory management logic in place), which means they can fail if run in this default configuration. If you run SharePoint 2010 cmdlets remotely you should consider increasing the quota setting to at least 1000MB as demonstrated here:

```
PS > Set-Item WSMan:\localhost\Shell\MaxMemoryPerShellMB 1000
```

Entering a Remote Session

You can start a remote session against the target computer with the Enter-PSSession cmdlet:

```
PS > Enter-PSSession -ComputerName SPServer01.powershell.nu `
>> -Authentication CredSSP -Credential powershell\administrator
```

This starts an interactive session with a remote computer using CredSSP authentication. During the session, all commands that you type run on the remote host. You can stop the remote session with the Exit-PSSession cmdlet:

```
PS > Exit-PSSession
```

To run commands against multiple remote computers, combine the `New-PSSession` and `Invoke-Command` cmdlets. The `New-PSSession` cmdlet creates persistent connections to remote computers. The `Invoke-Command` cmdlet runs a script block on the computers specified in the `New-PSSession` cmdlet. Here's an example:

```
PS > $Session = New-PSSession `
>> -ComputerName SPServer01.powershell.nu, Server1.powershell.nu `
>> -Authentication CredSSP -Credential powershell\administrator
PS > Invoke-Command -Session $Session -ScriptBlock {
>>    "Running Remote commands on: $($Env:COMPUTERNAME)"
>>    $regKey = "hklm:software\microsoft\shared tools\web server extensions\14.0"
>>    if(Test-Path -Path $regKey) {
>>      if(get-itemProperty -Path $regKey |
>>        Where-Object { $_.SharePoint -eq "Installed" }) {
>>         "$($Env:COMPUTERNAME) is running SharePoint 2010"
>>      } else {
>>         "$($Env:COMPUTERNAME) is not running SharePoint 2010"
>>      }
>>    } else {
>>      "$($Env:COMPUTERNAME) is not running SharePoint 2010"
>>    }
>> }
>>
Running Remote commands on: SERVER1
SERVER1 is not running SharePoint 2010
Running Remote commands on: SPSERVER01
SPSERVER01 is running SharePoint 2010
```

In the script block in this example, we check if the remote computer has the registry key `HKLM\Software\Microsoft\Shared Tools\Web Server Extensions\14.0` using the `Test-Path` cmdlet. If the key exists, we check if the SharePoint string value is equal to `Installed`. Depending on the outcome of condition evaluation, we then output an informational message stating whether SharePoint is installed on that particular server.

 NOTE   Checking the registry for keys and values is a quick and simple way to verify that SharePoint 2010 is installed on the server.

Running SharePoint 2010 Cmdlets Remotely

Windows PowerShell includes the `Add-PSSnapin` cmdlet, which is used to add registered snap-ins to the current session. After a snap-in is added, you can use cmdlets and providers that the snap-in supports. When SharePoint 2010 is installed, it also installs a Windows PowerShell snap-in for SharePoint. You can use the snap-in to run cmdlets included in SharePoint 2010 remotely.

```
PS > Enter-PSSession -ComputerName SPServer01.powershell.nu `
>> -Authentication CredSSP -Credential powershell\administrator

[SPServer01.powershell.nu]: PS > Get-PSSnapin -Registered


Name        : Microsoft.SharePoint.PowerShell
PSVersion   : 1.0
Description : Register all administration Cmdlets for Microsoft SharePoint Server

[SPServer01.powershell.nu]: PS > Add-PSSnapin Microsoft.SharePoint.PowerShell
```

In this example, we use the `Enter-PSSession` cmdlet to start an interactive session on the server `SPServer01`. We then use the `Get-PSSnapin` cmdlet to retrieve all registered snap-ins. Since the server has SharePoint 2010 installed, `Microsoft.SharePoint.PowerShell` is returned. We can add the snap-in with the `Add-PSSnapin` cmdlet and invoke all the cmdlets available in SharePoint 2010 remotely. In a standard remote Session each pipeline, function, or script is run on its own thread. To start a remote session that runs pipelines, functions, and scripts on the same thread, you have to create a custom session configuration on every server in the farm that you want to manage remotely. This example demonstrates how to create a custom session configuration.

```
PS > Register-PSSessionConfiguration -Name SharePoint -ThreadOptions ReuseThread
```

When starting a remote session against a server in the farm that contains a custom session configuration, you can simply use the ConfigurationName parameter as demonstrated in this example:

```
PS > Enter-PSSession -ComputerName SPServer01.powershell.nu `>> -Authentication
CredSSP -Credential powershell\administrator `>> -ConfigurationName SharePoint
```

Summary

In this chapter, we covered the use of functions, execution policies, and scripts in Windows PowerShell. Finally, we looked at a few examples of running Windows PowerShell remotely.

This concludes Part II of the book. In next part, you will learn how you to use Windows PowerShell with SharePoint 2010 in "real life."

PART III | SharePoint 2010 and PowerShell: Real-World Solutions

CHAPTER 9 | Scripted Installation

S harePoint 2010 can be installed in either of two ways: using a wizard that takes you through the different steps or by using a script. Using the scripted installation option not only gives you more options to control the setup, but it also provides the opportunity to reuse the script over and over again to achieve the exact same result. Therefore, a scripted installation should be a part of your disaster and recovery plan to make sure you can quickly rebuild your environment in case of a disaster.

Imagine that you are about to set up a proof-of-concept (POC) or test environment of SharePoint 2010 to evaluate and test the new features for your organization. This will most likely be the case whether you are about to implement SharePoint for the first time or you are upgrading from a previous SharePoint version. It is also likely that you will need to reinstall this environment several times during your evaluation. Also, you might want to set up additional staging environments when you are finished with your testing and evaluation. In these cases, scripted installations will save you a lot of work.

SharePoint 2010 offers a set of PowerShell cmdlets to perform the necessary installation steps. In this chapter, we will go through a basic setup to demonstrate the cmdlets. Then we will put together a reusable PowerShell script that you can use as is or modify to suit your particular needs.

Scripted Installation of SharePoint 2010 Using Windows PowerShell

When the binaries are installed on the server (we will not go through the actual installation of the SharePoint binaries in this chapter) and we have a Microsoft SQL Server instance available, the first thing we need to do is create a configuration database. The configuration database is the heart of a SharePoint farm and contains more or less all global settings. Without the configuration database, a SharePoint farm would not function.

To create this new database we use the `New-SPConfigurationDatabase` cmdlet. This cmdlet requires that we specify the database name and the name of the database server instance, as well as the name of the content database associated with the Central Administration web application, the credentials of the farm account to use, and the passphrase used when adding extra servers to the farm.

So, to begin, we specify the name of the database. Storing information in variables allows us to reuse the variables.

```
PS > $dbName = "NimaIntranet_ConfigDB"
```

Setting the database name is an option available when performing a setup using Windows PowerShell (or STSADM). If you use the graphical configuration wizard described later in this chapter, this is not possible. This is one of the main reasons for using a scripted installation: You are able to control the database name and align it with corporate naming standards.

We also specify the name of the SQL Server instance that we will use and the name for the Central Administration content database.

```
PS > $dbServer = "SQLServer01"
PS > $centralAdmindbName = "NimaIntranet_Admin_ContentDB"
```

The New-SPConfigurationDatabase cmdlet also requires the Passphrase parameter. A *passphrase* is a new addition in SharePoint 2010. It is a "farm password" used for generating the farm encryption key (master key), which is used for securing managed accounts and credentials stored in the Secure Store Service. In addition, the passphrase is used when adding new servers to the farm.

The Passphrase parameter requires an object of the type System.Security .SecureString as input. By using the ConvertTo-SecureString cmdlet, we can create a secure string in Window PowerShell, as in this example:

```
PS > $securePassPhrase =
>> (ConvertTo-SecureString -String "pass@word1" -AsPlaintext -Force)
```

The SecureString cmdlets in Windows PowerShell use the Windows Data Protection API when working with secure strings. This API is the standard way a Windows program protects sensitive data. The encryption key is based on logon credentials.

We also add the credentials used for the farm administrator account using the FarmCredentials parameter. The parameter requires a System.Management .Automation.PSCredential object as input. Windows PowerShell includes the Get-Credential cmdlet, which prompts the user for password (or a username and password) and returns a PSCredential object to the session. However, since we are going for an automated installation, we will create a PSCredential object using the New-Object cmdlet. Before we can create a PSCredential object, we need to create a secure string containing the user password, since the PSCredential object constructor accepts only secure strings as input for the password argument.

```
PS > $userName = "powershell\administrator"
PS > $password = "P@ssword1"
PS > $securePassword =
>> ConvertTo-SecureString -string $password -AsPlainText -Force

PS > $psCredentials =
>> New-Object -TypeName System.Management.Automation.PSCredential `
>> -ArgumentList $userName, $securePassword
```

Now that we have collected all the necessary input information and stored it conveniently in variables, we can go ahead and run the New-SPConfigurationDatabase cmdlet:

```
PS > New-SPConfigurationDatabase -DatabaseName $databaseName `
>> -DatabaseServer $databaseServer `
>> -AdministrationContentDatabaseName $centralAdminDatabase `
>> -Passphrase $securePassPhrase -FarmCredentials $psCredentials
```

The next step in the process of installing a SharePoint 2010 farm is to install the Help files. If a custom Help file or only a specific file should be used, you can use the LiteralPath parameter. In most cases, you will use the All parameter to install all available Help collections, like this:

```
PS > Install-SPHelpCollection -All
```

We also want to enforce security for all resources, including files, folders, and registry keys. This is done by using the Initialize-SPResourceSecurity cmdlet:

```
PS > Initialize-SPResourceSecurity
```

Now we need to install the necessary services and features in our farm. The services are installed using the Install-SPService cmdlet. The cmdlet installs all services, service instances, and service proxies specified in the registry on the server. Install-SPService also supports the Provision parameter used for stand-alone servers only.

The features are installed using the Install-SPFeature cmdlet. The cmdlet supports the AllExistingFeatures switch parameter, which installs all the existing features on the server.

The following example demonstrates how to use these two cmdlets.

```
PS > Install-SPService
PS > Install-SPFeature -AllExistingFeatures
```

We can manage the SharePoint 2010 environment through the Central Administration site, but before we can access it, we must provision a new site using the New-SPCentralAdministration cmdlet. The cmdlet creates a new web application with the Central Administration site collection at the root, using the port and authentication provider specified with the parameters Port and WindowsAuthProvider, as shown in the following example.

```
PS > New-SPCentralAdministration -Port 8000 -WindowsAuthProvider "NTLM"
```

The last step in the installation is to copy the shared application data to the web application folders. We can achieve this using the Install-SPApplicationContent cmdlet.

```
PS > Install-SPApplicationContent
```

TIP   Since none of the cmdlets used in this scenario produce any output, you can use the `Verbose` switch parameter on the cmdlets to get a detailed output of what each actually does. An example is `Install-SPApplicationContent -Verbose`.

Automate a SharePoint 2010 Installation

The preceding examples show the basic steps used to provision a new SharePoint 2010 farm. We can automate the procedure of creating new SharePoint 2010 farm by placing the following code in a script named New-SPInstallation.ps1.

```
<#
.SYNOPSIS
Automates a SharePoint 2010 installation.

.DESCRIPTION
The script automates a SharePoint 2010 installation.
Requires that the binaries are installed on the server.

.PARAMETER databaseName
Name of the configuration database.

.PARAMETER databaseServer
Name of the database server.

.PARAMETER centralAdminDatabase
Name of the Central Administration content database.

.PARAMETER port
Port to use.

.PARAMETER windowsAuthProvider
NTLM or Kerberos, default set to NTLM.

.PARAMETER userName
Farm Administrator account in the format 'domain\username'.

.PARAMETER password
Password for the Farm Administrator account.

.PARAMETER passPhrase
Farm password, used to add new machines to the farm.

#>
```

```
param(
    [string]$databaseName,
    [string]$databaseServer,
    [string]$centralAdminDatabase,
    [string]$port,
    [string]$windowsAuthProvider = "NTLM",
    [string]$userName,
    [string]$password,
    [string]$passPhrase
)

# Converting password strings to secure strings
$securePassword = ConvertTo-SecureString -String $password -AsPlainText -Force
$securePassPhrase = ConvertTo-SecureString -String $passPhrase -AsPlainText -Force

# Creating a PSCredential object
$psCredentials =

New-Object -TypeName System.Management.Automation.PSCredential `
-ArgumentList $userName, $securePassword

# New Configuration Database
New-SPConfigurationDatabase -DatabaseName $databaseName `
-DatabaseServer $databaseServer `
-AdministrationContentDatabaseName $centralAdminDatabase `
-Passphrase $securePassPhrase -FarmCredentials $psCredentials

# Install help files
Install-SPHelpCollection -All

# Install services
Install-SPService

# Install Features
Install-SPFeature -AllExistingFeatures

# Create a new Central Administration
New-SPCentralAdministration -Port $port -WindowsAuthProvider $windowsAuthProvider

# Copy shared application data
Install-SPApplicationContent
```

We can run the script by typing the following:

```
PS > .\New-SPInstallation.ps1 -databaseName "NimaIntranet_ConfigDB" `
>> -databaseServer "SQLServer01" `
```

```
>> -centralAdminDatabase "NimaIntranet_Admin_ContentDB" -port 5057 `
>> -userName "powershell\administrator" `
>> -password "SecretP@ssw0rd" -passPhrase "J0inD0main"
```

The New-SPInstallation.ps1 script creates a new configuration database and installs the help collections, the services required, and all existing features. It also sets up Central Administration and adds shared application content.

 TIP A number of solutions for scripted installations using Windows PowerShell are available on the Internet. One is the Microsoft-provided SPModule, which can be found on TechNet (http://technet.microsoft.com/en-us/library/cc262839.aspx#section1). You can also find solutions on Codeplex; for example, AutoSPInstaller is available from that site (http://autospinstaller.codeplex.com/).

Connecting and Disconnecting Servers with Windows PowerShell

What if you want to scale out and add more servers to your farm? This can be accomplished using the Connect-SPConfigurationDatabase cmdlet. When using the cmdlet, you need to specify the configuration database name, database server, and the passphrase you used when you created the farm (as in the previous example).

```
PS > $securePassPhrase =
>> (ConvertTo-SecureString -String "pass@word1" -AsPlaintext -Force)
PS > Connect-SPConfigurationDatabase -DatabaseName "NimaIntranet_ConfigDB" `
>> -DatabaseServer "SQLServer01" -PassPhrase $securePassPhrase
```

If you are unsure of the name of your configuration database, you can use the Get-SPFarm cmdlet to retrieve it (on a server that is already part of the farm):

```
PS > Get-SPFarm
```

The counterpart to the Connect-SPConfigurationDatabse cmdlet is the Disconnect-SPConfigurationDatabase cmdlet. The Disconnect-SPConfigurationDatabase cmdlet differs from the Connect-SPConfigurationDatabase cmdlet in that you do not need to specify the configuration database name, farm administration account name, or passphrase. You simply need to make sure that the account you execute the command as has sufficient permissions. The cmdlet detects to which configuration database the server is connected.

```
PS > Disconnect-SPConfigurationDatabase -confirm:$false
```

The confirm parameter is a switch parameter. If it's omitted, you will need to confirm that you want to take the action before it will be performed by the cmdlet.

Additional Functionality in SharePoint 2010

After the binaries are installed for SharePoint 2010, you will notice that the Start menu on your server includes an application group named Microsoft SharePoint 2010 Products. Here, you will find the SharePoint 2010 Products Configuration Wizard, which guides you through essentially the same steps we have gone through using Windows PowerShell, but using a graphical interface rather than cmdlets. If you have worked with SharePoint products before, you find this interface familiar. (One difference is the new Passphrase dialog box, which appears if you have not selected the Standalone option during the installation of the binaries.)

The SharePoint 2010 Products Configuration Wizard could be run as an alternative to a scripted installation or when patching the environment with a cumulative update or service pack. With the wizard, you are also able to connect and disconnect servers from your farm, as shown in Figure 9-1.

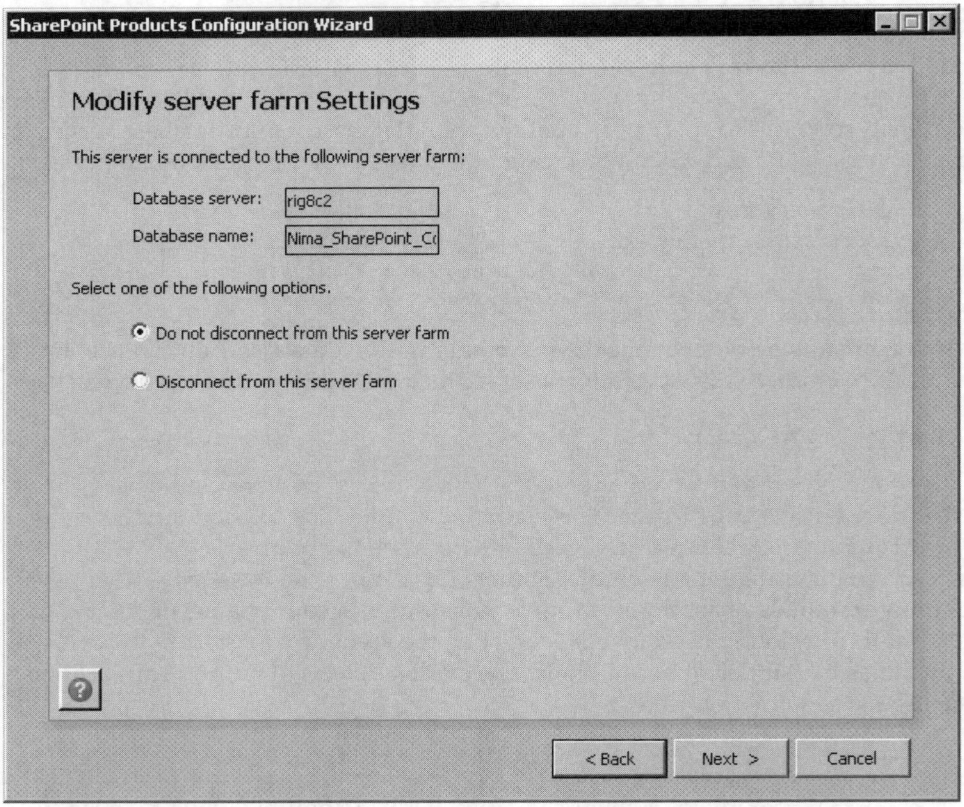

Figure 9-1. Disconnecting a server with the SharePoint 2010 Products Configuration Wizard

Psconfig.exe is the command-line version of the SharePoint 2010 Products Configuration Wizard tool, which can be found in the %COMMONPROGRAMFILES%\ Microsoft Shared\Web Server Extensions\14\BIN folder. With psconfig.exe, you are able to run command lines in a script and provision a SharePoint 2010 farm, similar to what we have done with Windows PowerShell in this chapter. However, PowerShell has clear advantages when you have several different farm configurations and need to reprovision those different versions regularly. This is quite common for organizations that have a SharePoint framework consisting of different staging environments like a development farm, a test farm, a user acceptance testing (UAT) farm, and one or many production farms. Using psconfig.exe and Windows command batch files, you would need to create separate scripts with hard-coded values. With Windows PowerShell, you can create one script and multiple configuration files—most likely in XML, as it is extremely easy to work with in Windows PowerShell.

If you have psconfig.exe scripts for provisioning a SharePoint 2007 farm, it's quite possible they will work with SharePoint 2010, with no or minimal changes. However, we recommend that you look into changing your old scripts so that they use Windows PowerShell, since almost all scripts you will create from now on will be Windows PowerShell scripts. This will help you create a unified script library based on the same language.

Summary

In this chapter, we demonstrated how to use Windows PowerShell to script a SharePoint 2010 installation. Key reasons for doing scripted installations are that you have the opportunity to specify the name of your configuration database and all installations will always look the same. Windows PowerShell also offers cmdlets to add new servers or to remove servers from the farm.

As an alternative to scripted installation, SharePoint 2010 offers a configuration wizard that can take you through the steps to provision a new farm using a graphical user interface.

Scripted installations can also be done using psconfig.exe, which is the command-line version of the SharePoint 2010 Products Configuration Wizard.

CHAPTER 10 | Working with Web Applications

Afterr setting up a SharePoint 2010 farm, it is time to look into how to create and manage Web applications using Windows PowerShell. In this chapter, we will demonstrate how to create and extend a Web application and show examples of how to manage solution packages.

In the first scenario, we will create a Web application that will host a collaboration area for teams, projects, and meeting workspaces. Since collaboration areas are often used together with partners and vendors that do not have access to the corporate network, we will set up a new Web application and extend it to the Extranet zone. Extending a Web application to the Extranet zone allows external users to authenticate against a separate directory service using Forms-based authentication instead of the company's Active Directory.

The second scenario demonstrates how you can work with solution packages in SharePoint 2010. In some environments, solution packages need to be updated on a regular basis. You can automate these steps using Windows PowerShell.

Extending a Web Application

In Chapter 4, we looked at how to manage Web applications using the SharePoint 2010 cmdlets. Now it is time to put the cmdlets to action. Let's start with creating a Web application that will be used as the base for our Extranet solution. Before creating a Web application, we should create a managed account (a new feature in SharePoint 2010 described in Chapter 2) to use for the application pool in which the new Web application will run.

Creating Managed Accounts

To create a new managed account, you use the `New-SPManagedAccount` cmdlet. If a managed account already exists, you can retrieve the account using the `Get-SPManagedAccount` cmdlet.

This example demonstrates how to create a new managed account using the `New-SPManagedAccount` cmdlet with a `PSCredential` object containing the username and password as input. Note that the account used must be an existing account in Active Directory.

```
PS > $userName = "powershell\managedaccount"
PS > $password = "C0mplexP@ssw0rd!"
PS > $securePassword =
>> ConvertTo-SecureString -String $password -AsPlainText -Force

PS > $psCredentials =
>> New-Object System.Management.Automation.PSCredential `
>> -ArgumentList $userName, $securePassword
```

```
PS > New-SPManagedAccount -Credential $psCredentials
```

UserName	PasswordExpiration	Automatic Change	ChangeSchedule
--------	-----------------	--------	--------------
POWERSHELL\manage...	6/6/2010 5:02:45 AM	False	

After we have added a new managed account, we can use the `Set-SPManagedAccount` cmdlet with the `AutogeneratePassword` switch parameter.

```
PS > Set-SPManagedAccount -Identity "powershell\managedaccount" `
>> -AutoGeneratePassword -Confirm:$False
```

This creates a secure password that fulfills the password complexity policy. It also sets the property `Automatic Change` to `True` so that SharePoint handles the password change automatically.

NOTE In Windows Server 2008 R2 (and earlier versions), the local security policy is set to require a minimum password age of one day. If you create or change the password of an account in Active Directory and set it up as a managed account in SharePoint 2010, within 24 hours, the `-AutoGeneratePassword` switch parameter will generate the following error: "The password does not meet the password policy requirements."

Create a New Web Application

Next, we set up the specifications for a new Web application, including its name, internal host header, internal URL, port, application pool, and managed account. We also specify the name of the content database to maintain a naming standard. (If a name for the content database is not specified, the content database will get an autogenerated name.) In this example, we store the values used in a set of variables.

```
PS > $waName = "Collaboration Area"
PS > $databaseName = "SharePoint_Workspace_ContentDB_01"
PS > $internalHostHeader = "workspace.nima.net"
PS > $internalUrl = "http://workspace.nima.net"
PS > $port = "80"
PS > $appPool = "SharePoint_Workspaces_applicationPool"
PS > $appPoolUser = Get-SPManagedAccount -Identity "powershell\managedaccount"
```

We want to separate the Web application from the Intranet as much as we can. Part of the solution for this is creating a separate service application proxy group. When creating Web applications, we have the option to specify the proxy group using the `ServiceApplicationProxyGroup` parameter, but before we can specify a new proxy group, we must create one. We can use the `New-SPServiceApplicationProxyGroup` cmdlet to create a new proxy group as shown in the next example. (Service applications and service application proxy groups will be described in detail in Chapter 18.)

```
PS > $saProxy = New-SPServiceApplicationProxyGroup -Name Workspaces
```

We are setting up an Extranet solution where users sitting on the corporate network will access the site using Windows authentication, and partners and vendors will access the site through an Extranet zone using Forms-based authentication. Therefore, we need to create a Web application using Claims-based authentication to be able to extend it, and turn on Forms-based authentication on the extended Web application instance.

To enable Claims-based authentication on a Web application, we need to create a new authentication provider using the `New-SPAuthenticationProvider` cmdlet and disable Kerberos authentication.

```
PS > $spAuth = New-SPAuthenticationProvider -DisableKerberos:$true
```

Next, we create a Web application using the `New-SPWebApplication` cmdlet and use the variables as input to the cmdlet's parameter.

```
PS > New-SPWebApplication -Name $waName -ApplicationPool $appPool `
>> -ApplicationPoolAccount $appPoolUser -URL $internalUrl `
>> -HostHeader $internalHostHeader -Port $port `
>> -DatabaseName $databaseName `
>> -ServiceApplicationProxyGroup $saProxy -AuthenticationProvider $spAuth
```

Extending the New Web Application

After we have created a new Web application, we can extend it using the `New-SPWebApplicationExtension` cmdlet. When extending a Web application, we need to specify which Zone we want to use: Default, Intranet, Extranet, Internet, or Custom. A new Web application instance will always use the Default zone. Extending a Web application lets us add an additional zone. In this example, we will use the Extranet zone.

We also need to create another authentication provider and specify the membership provider and role manager used for the Forms-based authentication. In this example, we store the values we will use with the `New-SPWebApplicationExtension` cmdlet in a set of variables.

```
PS > $name = "Extranet"
PS > $hostHeader = "Extranet.nima.net"
PS > $url = "http://Extranet.nima.net"
PS > $zone = "Extranet"
PS > $membershipProvider = "CustomMemberShipProvider"
PS > $roleprovider = "CustomRolesProvider"
PS > $spAuth = New-SPAuthenticationProvider -ASPNETMembershipProvider `
>> $membershipProvider -ASPNETRoleProviderName $roleprovider
```

We then retrieve the existing Web application using the `Get-SPWebApplication` cmdlet, pipe the Web application to the `Set-SPWebApplication` cmdlet, and extend the Web application.

```
PS > Get-SPWebApplication $internalUrl |
>> New-SPWebApplicationExtension -Name $name -Zone $zone `
>> -URL $url -HostHeader $hostHeader -Port 80 `
>> -AuthenticationProvider $spAuth
```

Scripting the Extranet Solution

Implementing Forms-based authentication also requires an update of the `web.config` file for the corresponding Web application zone instance, Central Administration, and the Security Token Service. The configuration required depends on the type of provider. The following script, `Set-FBAConfig.ps1`, is an example of how this could be automated using Windows PowerShell. The script configures an Extranet application for Forms-based authentication against Active Directory and grants Full Control rights to the current user.

```
<#.SYNOPSIS
 A generic function that makes modifications to the
 web.config file found at the specified path.
.PARAMETER webapplication
 Web Application url
#>
param([string]$webApplication)
function Edit-WebConfig ($servers, $configPath) {
 # Process each server
 $servers | Foreach-Object {
  # Transform the local path to a UNC path for the
  # server being currently processed
  $configPath = "\\{0}\{1}" -f
   $_, ($configPath -replace ":", "`$");
  # Create an instance of XmlDocument class containing
  # the web.config file using PowerShell's
  # [xml] type accelerator, and store it in a variable
  $config = [xml](Get-Content $configPath);
  # Check if the web.config file contains required
  # configuration sections and add them if needed
  if($config.configuration["system.web"] -eq $null) {
   $config.configuration.AppendChild(
    $config.CreateElement("system.web")) | Out-Null;
  }
  if($config.configuration.SelectSingleNode(
   "system.web"
  )["membership"] -eq $null) {
   $config.configuration.SelectSingleNode("system.web").AppendChild(
```

```
    $config.ImportNode(
      ([xml]"<membership><providers></providers></membership>")["membership"],
      $true
    )
  ) | Out-Null;
}
if($config.configuration.SelectSingleNode(
  "system.web"
)["roleManager"] -eq $null) {
  $config.configuration.SelectSingleNode("system.web").AppendChild(
    $config.ImportNode(
      (
        [xml]"<roleManager enabled='true'><providers></providers></roleManager>"
      )["roleManager"],
      $true
    )
  ) | Out-Null;
} else {
  # Add the 'enabled='true'' attribute to the roleManager node
  $attrEnabled = $config.CreateAttribute("enabled");
  $attrEnabled.psbase.Value = "true";
  $config.Configuration."system.web".roleManager.SetAttributeNode(
    $attrEnabled
  ) | Out-Null;
}
# If the web.config file being processed is the one for the
# Central Administration application, add the defaultProvider attribute
# to the roleManager node
if ($configPath -eq "\\{0}\{1}" -f $_,($caConfigPath -replace ":","`$")) {
  $attrDefaultProvider = $config.CreateAttribute("defaultProvider");
  $attrDefaultProvider.psbase.Value = "AspNetWindowsTokenRoleProvider";
  $config.Configuration."system.web".roleManager.SetAttributeNode(
    $attrDefaultProvider
  ) | Out-Null;
}
# Add the required sections to the web.config file
$memProv = $config.configuration."system.web".membership.SelectSingleNode(
  "providers"
);
if (
  $memProv.SelectSingleNode("add[@name='CustomMemberShipProvider']") -eq $null
) {
  $memProv.AppendChild(
    $config.ImportNode(([xml]$CustomMemberShipProvider)["add"], $true)
  ) | Out-Null;
}
$roleProviders =
  $config.Configuration."system.web".roleManager.SelectSingleNode("providers")
```

```
  if ($roleProviders.SelectSingleNode(
    "add[@name='CustomRolesProvider']"
  ) -eq $null) {
    $roleProviders.AppendChild(
      $config.ImportNode(([xml]$CustomRolesProvider)["add"], $true)
    ) | Out-Null;
  }
  # Save the modified XML to the original web.config location
  $config.Save($configPath);
 }
}


# Bind to the target Web application
$wa = Get-SPWebApplication $webApplication;
# Bind to the Central Administration Web application
$ca = Get-SPWebApplication -IncludeCentralAdministration |
 Where-Object {$_.IsAdministrationWebApplication};
# Obtain the names of all the servers hosting the target
# Web application and store them in an array
$waServers = @($wa.WebService.Instances |
 Where-Object { $_.Status -eq "Online" } |
  Foreach-Object {$_.Server.Address});
# Obtain the names of all the servers hosting the Central Administration
# Web application and store them in an array
$caServers = @($ca.WebService.Instances |
 Where-Object { $_.Status -eq "Online" } |
  Foreach-Object {$_.Server.Address});
# Obtain the physical local path of the web.config file for the
# IIS virtual server that the target Web application's
# Extranet zone is extended onto
$waExtranetConfigPath =
Join-Path -Path $wa.IisSettings[
 [Microsoft.SharePoint.Administration.SPUrlZone]"Extranet"
].Path -ChildPath web.config;
# Obtain the physical local path of the
# web.config file for the IIS virtual server
# that the Central Administration Web application is extended onto
$caConfigPath = Join-Path -Path $ca.IisSettings[
 [Microsoft.SharePoint.Administration.SPUrlZone]"Default"
].Path -ChildPath web.config;
# Bind to the IIS virtual server on one of the web- front-end servers
# that hosts SharePoint Service Application proxies
$wsHost = ([adsi]("IIS://{0}/W3SVC" -f $caServers[0])).psbase.Children |
 Where-Object {$_.ServerComment -eq (Get-SPServiceHostConfig).IisSiteName};
# Obtain the physical local path of the web.config file
# for the virtual directory that hosts the Security Token Service
$stsWSConfigPath =
Join-Path -Path (($wsHost.psbase.children |
```

```
   Where-Object {$_.Name -eq "ROOT"}).psbase.children |
     Where-Object {((Get-SPSecurityTokenServiceConfig).Parent.Applications |
       Foreach-Object { $_.Name }) -contains $_.Name}).Path -ChildPath web.config;
# Bind to the Active Directory domain that the current server is member of
$dom = [System.DirectoryServices.ActiveDirectory.Domain]::GetCurrentDomain();
# Bind to one of the domain controllers at random
$dc = $dom.DomainControllers[0];
# Initialize a string variable containing the
# Roles Provider configuration section
$CustomRolesProvider =
  '<add name="CustomRolesProvider" ' +
  'type="Microsoft.Office.Server.Security.LdapRoleProvider, ' +
  'Microsoft.Office.Server, Version=14.0.0.0, ' +
  'Culture=neutral, PublicKeyToken=71e9bce111e9429c" ' +
  'server="' + $dc.Name + '" port="389" useSSL="false" ' +
  'groupContainer="CN=Users,DC=' + ($dom.Name -replace "\.", ",DC=") +
  '" groupNameAttribute="cn" groupNameAlternateSearchAttribute=' +
  '"samAccountName" groupMemberAttribute="member" ' +
  'userNameAttribute="sAMAccountName" dnAttribute="distinguishedName" ' +
  'groupFilter="(ObjectClass=group)" userFilter="(ObjectClass=person)" ' +
  'scope="Subtree" />'
# Initialize a string variable containing the
# Membership Provider configuration section
$CustomMemberShipProvider =
  '<add name="CustomMemberShipProvider" ' +
  'type="Microsoft.Office.Server.Security.LdapMembershipProvider, ' +
  'Microsoft.Office.Server, Version=14.0.0.0, Culture=neutral, ' +
  'PublicKeyToken=71e9bce111e9429c" ' +
  'server="' + $dc.Name + '" port="389" useSSL="false" ' +
  'userDNAttribute="distinguishedName" userNameAttribute="sAMAccountName" ' +
  'userContainer="CN=Users,DC=' + ($dom.Name -replace "\.", ",DC=") +
  '" userObjectClass="person" userFilter="(ObjectClass=person)" ' +
  'scope="Subtree" otherRequiredUserAttributes="sn,givenname,cn" />'
# Call the Edit-WebConfig function to modify the
# web.config file(s) for the Central Administration Web application
Edit-WebConfig $caServers $caConfigPath;
# Call the Edit-WebConfig function to modify the
# web.config file(s) for the Security Token Service Web application
Edit-WebConfig $waServers $stsWSConfigPath;
# Call the Edit-WebConfig function to modify the
# web.config file(s) for the target Web application (Extranet zone)
Edit-WebConfig $waServers $waExtranetConfigPath;
# Create a new user policy for the current user and the 'Full Control' role
$admpolicy =
 $wa.ZonePolicies("Extranet").Add(
  (New-SPClaimsPrincipal -Identity "CustomMemberShipProvider:$env:username" `
   -IdentityType FormsUser
  ).ToEncodedString(),$env:username
 );
```

```
$admpolicy.PolicyRoleBindings.Add($wa.PolicyRoles["Full Control"]);
# Commit policy change to the target Web application
$wa.Update();
```

You can run the script by typing the following:

```
PS > .\Set-FBAConfig.ps1 -webApplication http://Extranet.nima.net
```

Deploying Solution Packages

In this scenario, we will address the need for frequent updates of solution packages. We will create a Windows PowerShell script that can be used to install or update the solutions in SharePoint 2010. We'll start by reviewing the cmdlets used to manage solution packages in SharePoint 2010.

Using Cmdlets to Manage Solution Packages

The `Get-SPSolution` returns the SharePoint solutions in a farm.

```
PS > Get-SPSolution
```

If you want to retrieve a specific solution, use the `-Identity` parameter and specify the solution's name as input.

You can also check if a solution exists using the `-not` operator and the `Where-Object` cmdlet. If it doesn't exist, the command will return `True`.

```
PS > -not(Get-SPSolution | Where-Object { $_.name -eq "Project_Template.wsp" })
True
```

After making sure that a solution package does not exist, you can add a new solution using the `Add-SPSolution` cmdlet. When adding a solution using the `Add-SPSolution` cmdlet, you need to specify the solution file's path using the `-LiteralPath` parameter. The parameter does not accept wildcards, so you must type the complete path.

```
PS > Add-SPSolution -LiteralPath e:\SolutionDeployment\Project_Template.wsp
```

Once the solution is added to the solution store, you can deploy it globally or to a specific Web application using the `Install-SPSolution` cmdlet. Before installing the solution, you should check if the solution contains any Web application-specific resources that need to be deployed to the root of each target Web application. You can get this information by using the `Get-SPSolution` cmdlet and selecting the `ContainsWebApplicationResource` property.

```
PS > Get-SPSolution project_template.wsp |
>> Select-Object -property ContainsWebApplicationResource
```

```
ContainsWebApplicationResource
------------------------------
                           True
```

If the solution has any Web application-specific resources, you should deploy it either to all Web applications using the –AllWebApplications switch parameter or to a specific Web application using the –WebApplication parameter.

A solution can also contain a Code Access Security (CAS) policy, which is a solution for preventing untrusted code from performing privileged actions. You can check if a solution contains a CAS policy by using the Get-SPSolution cmdlet and selecting the ContainsCasPolicy property.

```
PS > Get-SPSolution project_template.wsp |
>> Select-Object -property ContainsCasPolicy


ContainsCasPolicy
-----------------
             True
```

To deploy a solution with CAS policies, use the –CASPolicies switch parameter. The existing CAS policies will be merged with the CAS policies in the solution package.

NOTE In some cases, you may not want to merge the CAS policies, even if the ContainsCasPolicy parameter is set to True.

A solution package can also contain assemblies that need to be added to the Global Assembly Cache (GAC). If it does, you can use the –GACDeployment switch parameter. This example demonstrates how to add a solution to all Web applications, merge the existing CAS policies, and add the assemblies to the GAC:

```
PS > Get-SPSolution project_template.wsp |
>> Install-SPSolution -AllWebApplications -CASPolicies -GACDeployment
```

When updating solutions in SharePoint 3.0, you could use the STSADM upgradesolution operation, but it had some limitations that sometimes made it necessary to first retract the solution and remove it from the solution store, and then add and deploy the updated solution. In SharePoint 2010, you can use the Update-SPSolution cmdlet instead. The cmdlet is used to update an existing solution, without first retracting and deleting it. The cmdlet requires that you specify the solution identity followed by the path to the updated solution.

```
PS > Update-SPSolution -identity project_template.wsp `
>> -LiteralPath e:\SolutionDeployment\project_template.wsp
```

The Update-SPSolution cmdlet should be used if the solution package has been updated using the UpgradeActions feature introduced in SharePoint 2010. Otherwise, it is recommended that you retract and delete the solution before reinstalling it. When retracting a solution, you can force the retraction timer job to execute using the `Start-SPAdminJob` cmdlet. The cmdlet requires that the SharePoint Administration Service be stopped. In the next example, we create a function named `Restart-SPAdminV4`, which restarts the SharePoint Administration Service and forces the timer jobs to execute.

```
function Restart-SPAdminV4([switch]$adminJob) {
  Stop-Service SPAdminV4
  if($adminJob) { Start-SPAdminJob }
  Start-Service SPAdminV4
}
PS > $spSolution = Get-SPSolution -identity project_template.wsp
PS > if($spSolution.Deployed) {
>> if($spSolution.ContainsWebApplicationResource) {
>> $spSolution | Uninstall-SPSolution -AllWebApplications -Confirm:$false
>> } else {
>> $spSolution | Uninstall-SPSolution -Confirm:$false
>> }
>> Restart-SPAdminV4 -adminJob
>> do{ Start-Sleep -Seconds 1 } while ($spSolution.Deployed)
>> $spSolution | Remove-SPSolution -Confirm:$false
>> }
```

   In this example, we check if a solution is deployed; if it is, we retract it using the `Uninstall-SPSolution` cmdlet. We also check if the solution contains any Web application resources using the `ContainsWebApplicationResource` property; if it does, we retract the solution from all Web applications. Next, we use the `Restart-SPAdminV4` function to force the retraction timer job to execute. Then we wait for the `Deployed` property to equal `False` using a `do/while` loop. Finally, we delete the solution using `Remove-SPSolution`.

Scripting Solution Package Updates

The following script automates the solution package deployment steps demonstrated in the previous examples.

```
<#
.SYNOPSIS
Deploys a solution package.

.PARAMETER solution
path to solution package.

.PARAMETER webApplication
Web applications to install solutions on,
if solution has Web application resources
```

```
.PARAMETER gacDeployment
Deploy to GAC

.PARAMETER casPolicy
Deploy CAS policies

.PARAMETER update
Update a solution instead of
retracting and removing.
#>

param(
  [string]$solution,
  [array]$webApplication,
  [switch]$gacDeployment,
  [switch]$casPolicy,
  [switch]$update
)


# stops the SPAdminV4 service and runs Start-SPAdminJob
function Restart-SPAdminV4([switch]$adminJob) {
  Stop-Service SPAdminV4
  if($adminJob) { Start-SPAdminJob }
  Start-Service SPAdminV4
}
# Check if Snap-in is loaded
if(-not(
 Get-PSSnapin | Where { $_.Name -eq "Microsoft.SharePoint.PowerShell"})
) {
  Add-PSSnapin Microsoft.SharePoint.PowerShell;
}
# Check if solution exists.
$spSolution = Get-SPSolution -Identity (Split-Path $solution -Leaf) `
-ErrorAction SilentlyContinue


# Check if solution exists and should be removed
if($spSolution -AND -not($update)) {
  # Check if solution is deployed
  if($spSolution.Deployed) {
    # Check if solution has Web application resources
    Write-Host "Retracting Solution."
    if($spSolution.ContainsWebApplicationResource) {
      $spSolution | Uninstall-SPSolution -AllWebApplications -Confirm:$false
    } else {
      $spSolution | Uninstall-SPSolution -Confirm:$false
```

```
      }
    }
    Restart-SPAdminV4 -adminJob
    # Wait for solution
    do { Start-Sleep -Seconds 1 } while ($spSolution.Deployed)
    # Remove solution
    Write-Host "Removing Solution."
    $spSolution | Remove-SPSolution -Confirm:$false
    # nullify $spSolution
    $spSolution = $null
}
# Check if solution does not exist
if(-not($spSolution)) {
    # Add solution
    Write-Host "Adding Solution."
    $spSolution = Add-SPSolution -LiteralPath $solution
}
# check if solution contains Web application resources
if($spSolution.ContainsWebApplicationResource -AND -not($webApplication)) {
    Write-Host "The solution $solution contains Web application resources"
    Write-Host "please specify Web applications."
    return;
}
if(-not($spSolution.Deployed)) {
    # Check if there are application-level resources
    if ($spSolution.ContainsWebApplicationResource) {
        # Install solution on each specified Web application
        foreach($wa in $webapplication) {
            Write-Host "Deploying solution to $wa."
            Install-SPSolution -identity $spSolution.Name -Webapplication $wa `
                -GACDeployment:$gacDeployment -CASPolicies:$casPolicy -force
        }
    } else {
        # Install solution on Farm
        Write-Host "Deploying solution to Farm."
        Install-SPSolution -identity $spSolution.Name `
            -GACDeployment:$gacDeployment -CASPolicies:$casPolicy -force
    }
} else {
    # Check if there are application-level resources
    if ($spSolution.ContainsWebApplicationResource) {
        # Update solution on each specified Web application
        foreach($wa in $webapplication) {
            Write-Host "Updating solution on $wa,"
```

```
        Update-SPSolution -identity $spSolution.Name -Webapplication $wa `
          -LiteralPath $solution -GACDeployment:$gacDeployment `
          -CASPolicies:$casPolicy -force
      }
    } else {
      # Update solution on Farm level
      Write-Host "Updating solution on Farm."
      Update-SPSolution -identity $spSolution.Name -LiteralPath $solution `
        -GACDeployment:$gacDeployment -CASPolicies:$casPolicy -force
    }
  }


Restart-SPAdminV4 -adminJob
# Wait for solution
do { Start-Sleep -Seconds 1 } while (-not($spSolution.Deployed))
```

You can run the script by calling it from a Windows PowerShell console window, as follows:

```
PS > .\Deploy-SPSolution.ps1 -solution C:\solutions\solution.wsp `
>> -gacDeployment -casPolicy
```

Additional Functionality in SharePoint 2010

Central Administration offers a lot of opportunities when it comes to managing Web applications in a SharePoint 2010 farm. With the new Ribbon user interface, the task has become much easier than in previous versions.

In the first scenario in this chapter, we created and extended a Web application—a task that is rather simple to complete from Central Administration. However, in some cases, you may need to create a lot of Web applications, and this type of repetitive task is much easier to perform using a script. The first example also demonstrated how to enable Forms-based authentication using the new Claims-based security architecture, which also can be done from Central Administration. In Figure 10-1, you can see that when creating a new Web application and selecting the Claims-based authentication option and Forms-based authentication, you have the option to specify the membership provider and role provider.

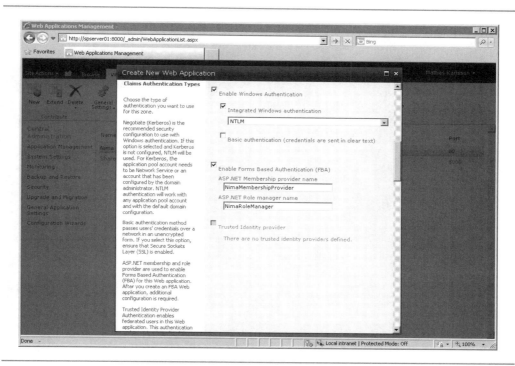

Figure 10-1. Creating a new Web application that will use Forms-based authentication

In Central Administration, under the System Settings | Farm Management | Manage farm solutions, you can see the solutions installed in your farm, as shown in Figure 10-2. The main limitation here is that you are not able to add new solutions to the solution store or upgrade existing solutions. Those two tasks must be performed using Windows PowerShell. When a solution is added or updated using Windows PowerShell, you can deploy, retract, and delete the solution from Central Administration. When deploying solutions, you have the opportunity to specify the target Web application and the time to perform the actual deployment, just as with Windows PowerShell.

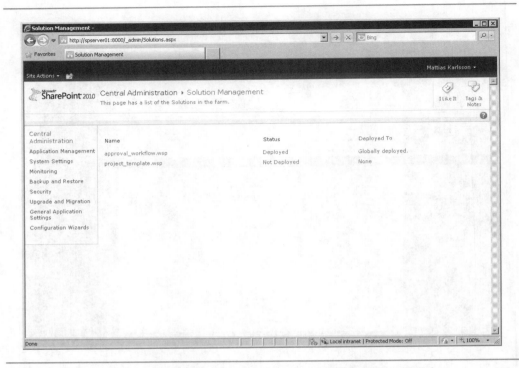

Figure 10-2.   List of solutions added and deployed to the SharePoint 2010 farm

Summary

In this chapter, we demonstrated how to manage Web applications using Windows PowerShell by extending and setting the authentication providers. We also presented examples of how to specify additional settings, such as the content database name and application proxy group. When setting up a new Web application, we used a managed account that we created using Windows PowerShell. Using different managed accounts for different Web applications lets us improve security and significantly decrease the risk of downtime in a SharePoint 2010 farm.

The other scenario in this chapter showed how to manage solutions in SharePoint 2010 by using the `Get-SPSolution`, `Install-SPSolution`, and `Add-SPSolution` cmdlets.

CHAPTER 11 | Working with Site Collections

A common requirement when setting up new SharePoint environments is to create a lot of new site collections. For instance, you may have a new project collaboration area where each of the running projects within a company should get its own site to be able to collaborate more efficiently. In this chapter, we will look at how to automate the creation of site collections in SharePoint 2010.

In our first scenario, we will start with a Microsoft Excel spreadsheet containing a number of projects (or site names) that need to be created. You will see how simple it is to use this spreadsheet with Windows PowerShell to automatically create sites and set properties like, owner, title, and description.

In our second scenario, we will create a simple solution for ordering new site collections and have the sites automatically created when the necessary information is provided. We will use a SharePoint list that we modify with a couple of new columns. Then, using a Windows PowerShell script, we will be able to find new items in the list and create the site collection based on the information about those items.

Creating Site Collections Based on an Excel Spreadsheet

In this scenario, our IT department has created a Microsoft Excel 2010 spreadsheet containing a list of all the currently running projects. Each project requires a new site collection. The Excel spreadsheet has the following column headings:

- Project Name
- Project Description
- Project Manager
- Project Manager Logon Name
- Department
- Cost Center
- Project Type

Before looking into how to create all the site collections, let's see how we can work with Excel 2010 using Windows PowerShell.

Working with Excel Spreadsheets

In this example, we will use the Connection object in ADO. ADODB.Connection is used to read, edit, and update databases such as Microsoft Access, and it can also be used to read data in Excel spreadsheets. We can create an instance of the ADODB .Connection object using the New-Object cmdlet.

```
PS > $excelConnection= New-Object -ComObject "ADODB.Connection"
```

Next, we open a connection to the Excel spreadsheet using the `Open` method supported by the `Connection` object. When creating a connection string to an Excel spreadsheet, we use the OLE DB provider and specify the path to the Excel file.

```
PS > $file = "C:\Documents\projects.xlsx"
PS > $excelConnection.Open(
>> "Provider=Microsoft.ACE.OLEDB.12.0;Data Source=" +
>> "$file;Extended Properties=Excel 12.0;"
>> )
```

After we have established a connection to the Excel spreadsheet, we can execute a query that retrieves the values from the spreadsheet. This example demonstrates how we pass the query to the `Execute` method:

```
PS > $strQuery = "Select * from [Sheet1$]"
PS > $objRecordSet = $excelConnection.Execute($strQuery)
```

Notice how we use `Sheet1$` in the query, which is the name of the sheet from which we want to retrieve the data. By default, Excel spreadsheets are named `Sheet1`, `Sheet2`, `Sheet3`, and so on. If you have a worksheet with a custom name, use that name in the query.

Before looping through the fields and retrieving the values, we should get the field names since we will use them later. We can retrieve the field names from the `Fields` property. Here, we use the `Select-Object` cmdlet to retrieve the fields:

```
PS > $fields = $objRecordSet.Fields | Select-Object -Property Name
```

Next, we move to the first record in the recordset using the `MoveFirst` method. The first record represents the first row in the Excel spreadsheet.

```
PS > $objRecordSet.MoveFirst()
```

Finally, we loop through the records and retrieve the values from the Excel spreadsheet.

```
PS > do {
>> $obj = New-Object -TypeName PSObject
>> $fields | ForEach-Object {
>> $obj |
>>   Add-Member -MemberType NoteProperty -Name $_.Name `
>>   -Value $objRecordSet.Fields.Item($_.Name).Value
>> }
>> $obj
>> $objRecordSet.MoveNext()
>>} until ($objRecordSet.EOF)
```

We use a `do until` loop to go through each record in the recordset. We start the loop by creating a custom object, which we will use to store the output. We then loop through each field using the `ForEach-Object` cmdlet and use the current field's name as input to the `Item` parameterized property to retrieve the field value. Using the field name and field value with the `Add-Member` cmdlet, we are able to store the information in a custom object. After the record's fields and values are stored in the custom object, the object is returned. Finally, we use the `MoveNext` method to move on to the next row and repeat the procedure. The loop continues until the `EOF` (end of file) property evaluates to true.

After the loop completes, we tidy up our objects using the `Close` method.

```
PS > $objRecordSet.Close()
PS > $excelConnection.Close()
```

The following shows the complete `Get-Excel` function that we can use to read information from an Excel spreadsheet.

```
function Get-Excel([string]$File) {

  $excelConnection = New-Object -ComObject "ADODB.Connection"

  $excelConnection.Open(
    "Provider=Microsoft.ACE.OLEDB.12.0;Data Source=" +
    "$File;Extended Properties=Excel 12.0;"
  )
  $strQuery ="Select * from [Sheet1$]"
  $objRecordSet = $excelConnection.Execute($strQuery)
  $fields = $objRecordSet.Fields | Select-Object -Property Name

  $objRecordSet.MoveFirst()

  do {
    $obj = New-Object -TypeName PSObject
    $fields | ForEach-Object {
      $obj |
      Add-Member -MemberType NoteProperty -Name $_.Name `
      -Value $objRecordSet.Fields.Item($_.Name).Value
    }
    $obj
    $objRecordSet.MoveNext()

  } until ($objRecordSet.EOF)

  $objRecordSet.Close()
  $excelConnection.Close()
}
```

When we run the function, the rows in the Excel spreadsheet are returned as custom objects, as shown in Figure 11-1.

```
PS > Get-Excel C:\Documents\Projects.xlsx

Project Name              : tintrax
Project Description       : Coordinating the work
Project Manager           : Joya Anthony
Project Manager Logon Name : joan
Department                : Coordination
Cost Center               : 1298
Project Type              : Internal

Project Name              : Tin-tech
Project Description       : Technical reviews and advice
Project Manager           : Sergey Zelenov
Project Manager Logon Name : seze
Department                : Technical Solutions
Cost Center               : 1376
Project Type              : Internal

Project Name              : Sildax
Project Description       : Managing the workers
Project Manager           : Roger Stewart
Project Manager Logon Name : rost
Department                : Management
Cost Center               : 1946
Project Type              : Internal

Project Name              : Aplamlam
Project Description       : Customer interaction
Project Manager           : Mikael Svensen
Project Manager Logon Name : misv
Department                : Sales
Cost Center               : 1864
Project Type              : Internal

Project Name              : Lattex
Project Description       : System maintenance
Project Manager           : Carl Anderson
Project Manager Logon Name : caan
Department                : Engineering
Cost Center               : 1982
Project Type              : Internal

Project Name              : Tincan
Project Description       : Cleaning and maintenance
Project Manager           : Andreas Irving
Project Manager Logon Name : anir
Department                : Maintenance
Cost Center               : 1655
Project Type              : Internal
```

Figure 11-1.   Results of the Get-Excel function

Creating the Site Collections

We can store the output from the Get-Excel function in a variable that we can use to loop through each project and create a site collection using the New-SPSite cmdlet.

```
PS > $projects = Get-Excel -file C:\Documents\project.xlsx
```

TIP   Windows PowerShell supports the Import-Csv and Export-Csv cmdlets, which let you work with comma-separated files. This means that you can achieve the same result as demonstrated in the previous example by saving the Excel file as CSV and running $projects = Import-Csv -Path C:\Documents\project.csv.

Now it is a simple procedure to create the site collections in SharePoint 2010 using the ForEach-Object cmdlet.

```
PS > $projects | ForEach-Object {
>> New-SPSite -url http://nimaintra.net/sites/$($_.'Project Name') `
>> -Name $($_.'Project Name') -Description $($_.'Project Description') `
>> -OwnerAlias $($_.'Project Manager Logon Name') `
```

```
>> -Template "STS#0"
>> }
>>

Url
---
http://nimaintra.net/sites/tintrax
http://nimaintra.net/sites/Tin-tech
http://nimaintra.net/sites/Sildax
http://nimaintra.net/sites/Aplamlam
http://nimaintra.net/sites/Lattex
http://nimaintra.net/sites/Tincan
http://nimaintra.net/sites/Kaviar
http://nimaintra.net/sites/Lotphase
http://nimaintra.net/sites/Tinzennix
http://nimaintra.net/sites/Spanex
```

We go through each object stored in the $projects variable using the ForEach-Object cmdlet. Then we use the New-SPSite cmdlet to create new site collections, with the object property values as input. Since the property names include spaces, we place the names within quotation marks. As each New-SPSite command completes, the URL of the newly created site collection is displayed in the Windows PowerShell console.

Creating Site Collections Based on Items in a SharePoint 2010 List

Another way to automate creation of site collections is to use information stored in a SharePoint 2010 list. Before we dig into the script, let's take a look at the SharePoint 2010 list.

Working with SharePoint 2010 Lists

We will use a custom list named Request Site that contains the items for new site collections. Table 11-1 shows the columns in this custom list.

When creating a script that automates the creation of site collections in SharePoint 2010, we need a solution for detecting new items in the list. If a new item exists in the list, we will create a site collection based on the item. Let's go through this step by step.

First, we need to bind to the target SharePoint 2010 list. We can do this using the GetList method of the SPWeb class, which accepts a list's URL as input.

```
PS > $spWeb = Get-SPWeb -Identity "http://nimaintra.net"
PS > $spList = $spWeb.GetList("Lists/Request Site")
```

Column Name	Column Type
Site name	Changed name of the default Title column
Site description	Multiple lines of text
Site owner	Person or group
Department	Single line of text
Cost center	Single line of text
Project type	Choice (drop-down menu) Internal Vendor Partner
Status	Choice (drop-down menu) Requested Created
Comment	Multiple lines of text

Table 11-1. Custom Columns Created in the Request Site List

The Status field in the list will act as identifier of new items in this example. If the status is set to Requested, the item will be processed by the script. If the status is set to Created, the item will be skipped.

The Status field's default value is set to Requested, but how do we prevent users from changing the value to Created manually? A simple but effective trick is to hide the field from the user. Here's how to do this:

```
PS > $spField = $spList.Fields["Status"]
PS > $spField.ShowInNewForm = $False
PS > $spField.ShowInEditForm = $False
PS > $spField.Update()
PS > $spField = $null
```

We create an instance of the SPField object and set the properties ShowInNewForm and ShowInEditForm to False. We then make sure the changes persist in SharePoint by calling the Update method.

We can use the same approach for the Comment field, which will be used to add comments to each item.

Next, we store the list items in an array. We use the `Items` property of the `SPList` object and pipe all list items to the `Where-Object` cmdlet to retrieve specific list items where the value of the Status field equals Requested.

```
PS > $items = $spList.Items | Where-Object {
>> $_["Status"] -eq "Requested" }
```

 NOTE When you use the `Items` property on an `SPList` object, all the list items in the list are read into memory, meaning that large lists may consume a lot of memory. If you are working with large lists, it is a good idea to instead use the `SPList` object methods, such as `GetItemById` and `GetItems`, which support Collaborative Application Markup Language (CAML) queries. You will see examples of how to work with list items using CAML queries and the `GetItemById` method in Chapter 15.

This array contains all list items where the status equals Requested. We can use the `ForEach-Object` cmdlet to loop through each list item in the array and create a site collection based on the list item's property values.

```
PS > $items | ForEach-Object {
>> $siteName = $_["Site name"] -Replace "\W","";
>> $siteURL = $url + "sites/" + $siteName;
>> $userID = $_["Site owner"] -Replace "\d*;#","";
>> $user = Get-SPUser -Web $url -Identity $userID;
>> New-SPSite -url $siteURL -Name $($_["Site name"]) `
>> -Description $($_["Site description"]) -OwnerAlias $user -Template "STS#0";
>> $_["Status"] = "Created";
>> $_["Comment"] = "Site $siteURL created";
>> $_.Update();
>> }
```

We start by replacing nonalphanumeric characters in the Site name field value using the `-replace` operator, which accepts regular expressions as a pattern to search for, as described in Chapter 6. The `\W` character represents all nonalphanumeric characters. When we use Windows PowerShell to retrieve a value from a person or group field, such as the Site owner field here, the string returned contains the user's ID, followed by the `;#` characters, followed by the user's display name. Since we want the user login name or an `SPUser` object as input to the `New-SPSite` cmdlet, we need to replace the unwanted characters and use the `Get-SPUser` cmdlet.

The last step performed in the `ForEach-Object` cmdlet is updating the current item's status to `Created`. Updating the items helps us to keep track of which items we have already processed, allowing us to rerun the script without processing the same item twice. We also add a comment in the Comment field and call the `Update` method to commit the changes we made to the list item to the SharePoint 2010 content database.

Scripting the Site Collection Creation

The following script contains all the code used in this solution. The script also checks if the site collection already exists before adding a new site collection and adds a comment in the Comment field depending on the outcome.

```
<#
.SYNOPSIS
Automates creation of site collections
based on information stored in a SharePoint 2010 list.

.DESCRIPTION
The script automates creation of site collections
based on a SharePoint List containing various settings
required.

.PARAMETER listURL
URL of the source list.

.PARAMETER field
Name of the field to be used for filtering items, default is set to 'Status'.

.PARAMETER pattern
Value to be used for filtering items, default is set to 'Requested'.
#>

param(
  $listURL,
  $field = "Status",
  $pattern = "Requested"
)

# Check if Snap-in is loaded
If (-not(
 Get-PSSnapin | Where-Object { $_.Name -eq "Microsoft.SharePoint.PowerShell"})
) {
  Add-PSSnapin Microsoft.SharePoint.PowerShell;
}

# Convert special characters to quoted UTF-8 format
$webUrl = [Microsoft.SharePoint.Utilities.SPEncode]::UrlDecodeAsUrl($listUrl);

# Iterate through each segment
-1..-((([uri]$listURL).Segments).Count | ForEach-Object {
  if ($spWeb -eq $null) {
    $webUrl = $webUrl -replace `
```

```
        [Microsoft.SharePoint.Utilities.SPEncode]::UrlDecodeAsUrl(
          ([uri]$listURL).Segments[$_]
        );
      $spWeb = Get-SPWeb -Identity $webUrl -ErrorAction SilentlyContinue
  }
}

# Get the list
$spList = $spWeb.GetList($listURL);
# Store list items in an array
$items = $spList.Items | Where-Object { $_[$field] -eq $pattern }

# Check if the array contains information
if ($items -ne $null) {
  # Loop through list item collection
  $items | ForEach-Object {

    # Build site URL and replace non-alphanumeric characters
    $siteName = $_["Site name"] -Replace "\W","";
    $siteURL = $webURL + "sites/" + $siteName;

    # Check if site collection already exists
    if(Get-SPSite -Identity $siteURL -ErrorAction SilentlyContinue) {

      # Site already exists
      Write-Host "Site $siteURL already exists";

      # Updating comments
      $_["Comment"] = "Site already exists, choose a new name";
      $_.Update();

    } else {
      # Get the user ID
      $userID = $_["Site owner"] -Replace "\d*;#","";
      # Check if User exists

      if(
       Get-SPUser -Web $webUrl -Identity $userID -ErrorAction SilentlyContinue
      ) {
        $user = Get-SPUser -Web $webUrl -Identity $userID
      } else {
        $user = New-SPUSer -Web $webUrl -UserAlias $userID
      }
```

```
    # Create site collection
    New-SPSite -url $siteURL -Name $_["Site name"] `
    -Description $_["Site description"] -OwnerAlias $user -Template "STS#0";

    # Update the list item
    $_["Status"] = "Created";
    $_["Comment"] = "Site $siteURL created";
    $_.Update();
    }
  }
}


# Dispose SPWeb
$spWeb.Dispose()
```

This example demonstrated some of the ways you can work with SharePoint 2010 lists. In Chapter 14, we will describe how to access, modify, and manage lists in more detail.

You can run the script against the Request Site list manually by typing the following:

```
PS > .\Create-RequestedSites.ps1 `
>> -listURL "http://nimaintra.net/Lists/Request Site"
```

When you do not specify the field or pattern, the default values are used. The script checks the list for list items where the Status field equals Requested and creates new site collections based on the list items retrieved. Finally, the script updates the list items' Status field to Created and adds a comment indicating the site was created in the Comment field.

You can also set up a scheduled task that runs the script once per day, automating the creation of new site collections.

Additional Functionality in SharePoint 2010

New site collections can be created from Application Management and Site Collections in Central Administration. However, it is not possible to import a list of sites or automate the creation of site collections through Central Administration.

SharePoint 2010 also has a Self-Service Site Collection Management feature, which allows users with the Use Self-Service Site Creation permission to create new site collections, as shown in Figure 11-2. The disadvantage of this feature is that the administrator loses control over the naming standards.

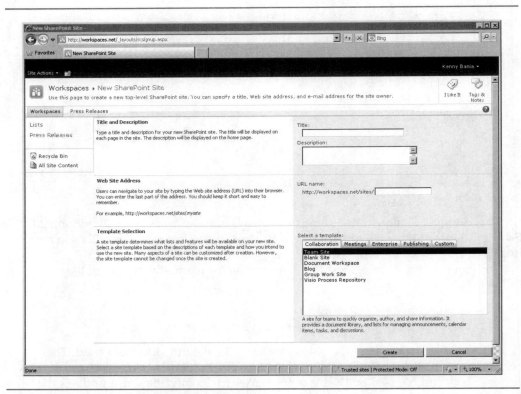

Figure 11-2. The Self-Service Site Collection creation form

Another feature available in SharePoint 2010 is Site Use Confirmation and Deletion, which allows administrators to set up rules for when sites should be deleted. The settings page, shown in Figure 11-3, lets you specify how often a site owner will receive an e-mail to confirm that the site is still in use. It is then possible to automatically delete the site if a confirmation is not received after a specific number of notifications.

Figure 11-3.   The Site Use Confirmation and Deletion settings in Central Administration

Summary

In this chapter, we looked at how to create new site collections using Windows PowerShell. You've seen the convenience Windows PowerShell offers when performing repetitive tasks.

The first example showed how to work with Excel spreadsheets, and how easy it is to gather information from one source and use it to automate tasks in the Windows environment. Using Windows PowerShell to enumerate through Excel spreadsheet, CSV files, or even a SQL Server database allows you to automate the creation of hundreds of site collections in a way that is not possible through Central Administration.

In the second example, we looked at how to connect to a SharePoint list and use the information stored in the list items to create new site collections. SharePoint lists and list items will be covered in detail in Chapters 14 and 15.

CHAPTER 12 | Managing Sites

A s discussed in the previous chapter, SharePoint 2010 offers some functionality to automatically delete site collections that are not confirmed to be in use. However, this is available only at the site collection level with the out-of-the box tools. But what if we want to have the same kind of functionality for sites?

Imagine that we have thousands of sites within a site collection (which is often the case when working with meeting workspaces, for example). We want to know which sites have not been used for the last 180 days, and send an e-mail message to the people responsible for those sites. For our solution, we will need to identify sites that have not been used within the time period, get the contact information for the people to receive e-mail, and send the e-mail.

Validating Site Usage

The Get-SPWeb cmdlet allows us to work with sites and subsites in SharePoint 2010. When we use the Get-SPWeb cmdlet, an instance of the SPWeb class is returned. The SPWeb class in SharePoint 2010 has the LastItemModifiedDate property, which we can use to check if anything has been changed in the site within a specific time span.

To begin, we need to create a DateTime object, which we will use to perform the comparison of dates against. In this example, we create a DateTime object containing the date of 180 days ago.

```
PS > $lastModified = (Get-Date).AddDays(-180)
```

First, we use the Get-Date cmdlet to get the current date, placing it within parentheses to make sure it is evaluated first. Then we call the AddDays method on the resulting System.DateTime object, passing it a negative value so that the corresponding number of days are subtracted, rather than added, from the current date.

We can then use the DateTime object stored in the lastModified variable and compare it to the LastItemModifiedDate to retrieve all subsites that have not been modified within the last 180 days.

```
PS > $url = "http://nimaintra.net"
PS > $objSelected = Get-SPSite $url | Get-SPWeb -limit All |
>> Where-Object { $_.LastItemModifiedDate -le $lastModified } |
>> Select-Object -Property Url, Title, Description,
>> @{Name="Modified";Expression={$_.LastItemModifiedDate}},
>> @{Name="email";Expression={$_.RequestAccessEmail}},
>> @{Name="authorEmail";Expression={$_.Author.Email}},
>> @{Name="inactive";Expression={
>> (Getdate).Subtract($($_.LastItemModifiedDate)).Days}}
```

We use the `Where-Object` cmdlet to filter out the subsites that do not satisfy our criteria. We then use the `Select-Object` cmdlet to limit the set of properties returned to the URL, title, and description.

We also create calculated hash table properties based on other site properties. Hash table-based properties allow us to set custom names for the properties, as well as to perform advanced calculations to obtain a value. In the first three hashtable-based properties, we set custom names and get the values from the `SPWeb` object directly. In the last hash table property, the expression consists of a calculation that results in the number of days that the subsite has not been used.

 NOTE   This example identifies sites where nothing has been updated for a specific number of days. Realize that this might not mean that the site is not in use. For instance, the site could be an archive or a FAQ that contains information that is not frequently updated. When using this type of approach, you should evaluate if the criteria used is applicable for your environment, so that sites that are used are not deleted.

Getting Site Contact Information

Since sites do not use the same primary and secondary administrator concept as site collections, we need to find a way to get the e-mail address for the person responsible for each site. For this information, we can look at the site settings to see if the Allow requests for access setting is enabled, as shown in Figure 12-1. This is a standard setting, accessible from the Site Permissions page of each site, which contains the e-mail address of the person who will receive site permission request e-mail messages. However, access requests are not enabled by default. Our work-around will retrieve the username of the person who created the site and try to send an e-mail to that user.

Since we are planning on sending an e-mail to the address set in the `RequestAccessEmail` property, it is a good idea to check if the property contains any information (as noted, this value is not set by default). If the `RequestAccessEmail` property is not set, we will use the `Author` property, which contains an `SPUser` object representing the user who created the site. The user object contains a property that stores the user's e-mail address, which we can use instead of the value of the `RequestAccessEmail` property.

We can use the `ForEach-Object` cmdlet to loop through all subsites, check the `RequestAccessEmail` property value, and set it to the e-mail address of the user who created the site if the value is null or empty.

```
PS > $objSelected | ForEach-Object {
>> if ([string]::IsNullOrEmpty($_.email)) { $_.email = $_.authorEmail }
>> }
```

It is possible to use comparison operators to check if a string value is null or empty, but here, we use a quicker way: the static method `IsNullOrEmpty` of the `System.String` class.

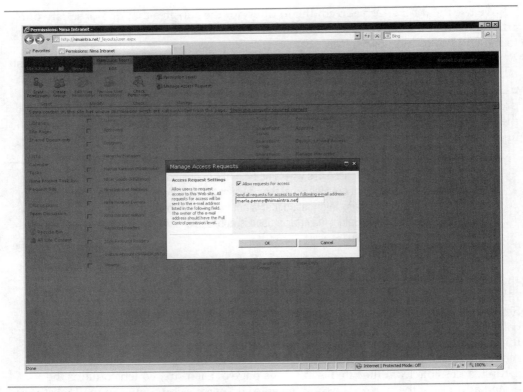

Figure 12-1.   The Manage Access Requests dialog box

> **NOTE**   Static methods and properties relate only to information about the concept that the class
> represents. If you want to find out more about static methods and properties available on a class,
> you can pipe the type to the Get-Member cmdlet and use the Static parameter supported by
> the cmdlet: [string] | Get-Member -Static.

Now that we have collected all the necessary information and stored it in an array
of objects, we can send an e-mail to all the e-mail addresses where the sites have been
inactive for at least 180 days. In order to send an e-mail with Windows PowerShell, we
need to know the SMTP server and the e-mail address from which we will send the
e-mail. We can retrieve the information from the Web application.

```
PS > $smtp =
>> ((Get-SPWebApplication $url).OutboundMailServiceInstance).Server.Address
PS > $from = (Get-SPWebApplication $url).OutboundMailSenderAddress
```

We retrieve the SMTP server address using the `OutboundMailServiceInstance` property of the `SPWebApplication` class. This returns an object containing information about the service. The object contains a `Server` property, which is an object of type `Microsoft.SharePoint.Administration.SPServer`, from which we retrieve the server's address. The `OutboundMailSenderAddress` property is of the type `System.String`, so we do not need to retrieve additional properties to get the sender address. In both previous examples, we place the cmdlets within parentheses to avoid needing to store the resulting object in an intermediary variable.

The last step is to loop through the array stored in the `objSelected` variable and send e-mail messages to the addresses set in the `RequestAccessEmail` property. We can do this with the Windows PowerShell `Send-MailMessage` cmdlet. This cmdlet has parameters that we can use to customize the e-mail.

For our solution, we will send the body of the e-mail as HTML, but before we can send the e-mail, we need to convert the message to HTML. This can be done using the `ConvertTo-Html` cmdlet. Note that because this cmdlet returns an array where each high-level element is represented by a separate object, we also must join those elements into a single string using the static `Join` method of the familiar `System.String` class.

```
PS > $objSelected | ForEach-Object {
>> $subject = "The site $($_.Title) has been inactive in $($_.inactive) days"
>> $body = [string]::Join("`n",($_ |
>> ConvertTo-Html -Property Url, Title, Description, Modified, email, inactive))
>> Send-MailMessage -To $_.email -From $from -Subject $subject `
>>  -Body $body -SmtpServer $smtp -BodyAsHtml
>> }
```

Here, we loop through each object in the array stored in the `objSelected` variable. We then use the object's `Title` and inactive properties to build up the subject. The body of the e-mail is based on the properties of the object and converted to HTML using the `ConvertTo-Html` cmdlet. Finally, we use the `Send-MailMessage` cmdlet to send the e-mail.

Check Site Usage Script

The following is the complete `Mail-SiteOwner` script.

```
<#
.SYNOPSIS
Checks if sites have been modified within a given timespan.

.DESCRIPTION
The script checks if sites within a site collection
have been modified within a specified timespan. If the switch
-sendMail is used, the script sends an email to the
address specified in the RequestAccessEmail property.
```

```
.PARAMETER url
Site Collection URL.

.PARAMETER days
Days to check, default set to 180.

.PARAMETER sendMail
Sends an email to the address specified in the RequestAccessEmail property.

#>

param(
  [string]$url,
  [int32]$days = 180,
  [switch]$sendMail
)
# Check if Snap-in is loaded
if (-not(
  Get-PSSnapin | Where-Object { $_.Name -eq "Microsoft.SharePoint.PowerShell"})
) {
  Add-PSSnapin Microsoft.SharePoint.PowerShell;
}

# create DateTime object 30 days back.
$lastModified = (Get-Date).Subtract((New-TimeSpan -Days $days))

Get-SPSite $url | Get-SPWeb | ForEach-Object {
  # Check when the last item was modified
  if($_.LastItemModifiedDate -le $lastModified) {

    # Store web information in object

    $objSelected = $_ | Select-Object Url, Title, Description,
      @{Name="Modified";Expression={$_.LastItemModifiedDate}},
      @{Name="email";Expression={$_.RequestAccessEmail}},
      @{Name="inactive";Expression={
      (Get-date).Subtract($($_.LastItemModifiedDate)).Days
      }}

    # if string is null or empty, use author email instead
    if ([string]::IsNullOrEmpty($objSelected.email)) {
      $objSelected.email = $_.Author.Email
    }

    # Check if mail should be sent
    if ($sendMail -and $objSelected.email) {

      # Get SMTP Settings.
      $smtp =
```

```
    ((Get-SPWebApplication $url).OutboundMailServiceInstance).Server.Address
    $from = (Get-SPWebApplication $url).OutboundMailSenderAddress

    # Store subject in a variable
    $subject = "The site $($_.Title) has been inactive in $days days"

    # Body as html
    $body = [string]::Join("`n", ($objSelected |
     ConvertTo-Html -Property Url, Title,
     Description, Modified, email, inactive))

    Send-MailMessage -to $objSelected.email -from $from -Subject $subject `
    -Body $body -SmtpServer $smtp -BodyAsHtml
    }

    # Return information to PowerShell
    return $objSelected
  }
}
```

You can run the script by typing the following:

```
PS > .\Mail-SiteOwner.ps1 -url http://nimaintra.net `
>> -days 180 -sendMail
```

The script checks all the sites within a site collection. If a site has not been modified within the last 180 days, an e-mail is sent to the RequestAccessEmail address. If no address is set, the e-mail is sent to the e-mail address of the site's creator (if available).

Additional Functionality in SharePoint 2010

SharePoint 2010 does not offer any tools to handle sites that have not been used for a specific amount of time, and such sites could potentially use up a lot of unnecessary storage in the content database. However, it is possible to build workflows using Microsoft Visual Studio that would do something very similar to what we have done using Windows PowerShell in this chapter.

In a document management system, it is usually important to use expiration policies on each document or item. SharePoint 2010 supports this and offers the opportunity to create retention approval workflows and information management policies. Information management policies can be applied to a specific list to affect the items within the list or on a content type. You can use a policy to specify rules for what will happen to documents or lists that have not been modified for a specific amount of time. Figure 12-2 shows an example of creating such a policy.

When creating an information management policy, you specify the action to take when items are not modified within the configured time span. You have the option to specify a disposition approval workflow, which can include sending an e-mail to the

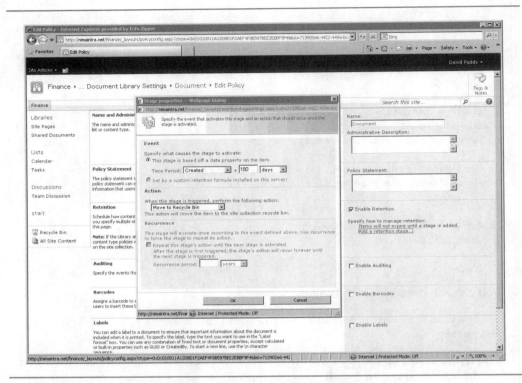

Figure 12-2. Creating a new information management policy

user who created the item or document. The disposition approval workflow is one of the workflows shipped with SharePoint 2010, and it can be used on a list or content type.

Summary

In this chapter, we looked at how we can get information about a site using Windows PowerShell. In the sample scenario, we retrieved information about when each site was last modified and, with the help of a `DateTime` object, we retrieved all the sites that had not been modified during the last 180 days. We also looked at a couple of other properties of the `SPWeb` object that can be very useful in these kinds of scenarios. We checked to see if the site used the Allow requests for access setting, and where it did not, we retrieved the e-mail address of the user who created the site, using the `Author` property. Finally, we retrieved the SMTP settings from the Web application and used these settings to send an e-mail to the users responsible for the unused sites.

Finally, we briefly discussed the opportunities SharePoint 2010 offers when it comes to setting up retention periods using information management policies and disposition workflows. These settings are limited to only documents and list items.

CHAPTER 13 | Managing the Look and Feel of Sites

A s with earlier versions of SharePoint, you can change the appearance of sites by applying different themes. However, in SharePoint 2010, themes are based on .thmx files, as used by the Microsoft Office suite. This means that you can create a theme in Microsoft PowerPoint, for example, and apply it to a SharePoint site. In our first scenario, we will look into how to work with themes and change the theme on a site.

Next, we will explore how to change the site icon, title, and description using Windows PowerShell.

Our final examples demonstrate how to manage and modify the navigation of sites. This can be useful when you want to have a unified look and feel for the navigation, as well as when you add or remove menu items. For instance, you might want all the sites to have a navigation item pointing to a specific page or site.

Managing Themes

This scenario demonstrates how you can work with themes in SharePoint 2010 using Windows PowerShell. We will show examples of how to get a site's current theme, retrieve a list of all available themes in a site collection, and apply a new theme to a site.

Getting the Current Theme

Let's start with retrieving a site's current theme. First, use the Get-SPWeb cmdlet to bind to the site.

```
PS > $spWeb = Get-SPWeb -Identity http://nimaintra.net
```

The SPWeb object is then used with the static GetThemeUrlForWeb method provided by the Microsoft.SharePoint.Utilities.ThmxTheme class and stored in the variable theme.

```
PS > $theme =
>> [Microsoft.SharePoint.Utilities.ThmxTheme]::GetThemeUrlForWeb($spWeb)
```

If the site uses the default theme, an empty string is returned by this method. Otherwise, the method returns a string containing the relative path to the theme.

Next, we check if the variable contains a value. If it does, we use the static Open method provided by the Microsoft.SharePoint.Utilities.ThmxTheme class. This method has six overloads where each one of them accepts two parameters: an SPSite object and a theme URL.

```
PS > if (-not([string]::IsNullOrEmpty($theme))) {
>> [Microsoft.SharePoint.Utilities.ThmxTheme]::Open($spWeb.Site, $theme) |
>> Format-List -Property @{Name="Theme";Expression={$_.Name}},
>> @{Name="Type";Expression={$_.ThemeType}},
>> @{Name="RelativeUrl";Expression={$_.ServerRelativeUrl}},
```

```
>> @{Name="Description";Expression={$_.AccessibleDescription}}
>>
>> } else {
>> Write-Host "Default theme is used"
>> }
PS > $spWeb.Dispose()
```

In this example, we use an `if` statement to check if the `theme` variable contains a value. If the condition evaluates to `True`, we use the `Open` method supported by the `ThmxTheme` class to retrieve the theme that is currently used on the site, and use the `Format-List` cmdlet to display specific properties. If the variable `theme` is null or empty, we use the `Write-Host` cmdlet and return a message. Finally, we dispose of the object using the `Dispose()` method.

The following is the complete `Get-SPTheme` function.

```
function Get-SPTheme([string]$url) {
  $spWeb = Get-SPWeb -Identity $url
  $theme = [Microsoft.SharePoint.Utilities.ThmxTheme]::GetThemeUrlForWeb($spWeb)
  if (-not([string]::IsNullOrEmpty($theme))) {
    [Microsoft.SharePoint.Utilities.ThmxTheme]::Open($spWeb.Site, $theme) |
      Format-List -Property @{Name="Theme";Expression={$_.Name}},
      @{Name="Type";Expression={$_.ThemeType}},
      @{Name="RelativeUrl";Expression={$_.ServerRelativeUrl}},
      @{Name="Description";Expression={$_.AccessibleDescription}}
  } else {
    Write-Host "Default theme is used"
  }
  $spWeb.Dispose()
}
```

You can use the function by typing the following:

```
PS > Get-SPTheme -url http://nimaintra.net/subsite
```

Getting the Available Themes

SharePoint 2010 includes a number of site themes, such as Azure, Berry, and Bittersweet. We can retrieve a list of all themes available in a site collection using the `GetManagedThemes` method of the `Microsoft.SharePoint.Utilities.ThmxTheme` class.

```
PS > $spSite = Get-SPSite -Identity http://nimaintra.net
PS > [Microsoft.SharePoint.Utilities.ThmxTheme]::GetManagedThemes($spSite)
PS > $spSite.Dispose()
```

When we use the `GetManagedThemes` method, `ThmxTheme` objects are returned using default formatting for .NET classes that have no specific formatting rules associated with them—a flat list of all public properties. If we want to return only specific properties, we can pipe the results to the `Select-Object` cmdlet.

The `Get-SPThemeName` function demonstrated next uses a URL as parameter to access a site collection and then calls the static `GetManagedThemes` method, piping the results to the `Select-Object` cmdlet to return the `Name` property.

```
function Get-SPThemeName([string]$url) {
  $spSite = Get-SPSite -Identity $url
  [Microsoft.SharePoint.Utilities.ThmxTheme]::GetManagedThemes($spSite) |
  Select-Object -Property Name
  $spSite.Dispose()
}
```

You can use this function by typing the following:

```
PS > Get-SPThemeName -url http://nimaintra.net
```

Setting a New Theme

`ThmxTheme` objects support the `ApplyTo` method, which we can use to set a new theme for a site. When applying a new theme to a site, we first create an instance of the `ThmxTheme` class using the static method `GetManagedThemes`. We can use the `Where-Object` cmdlet to filter on the name of the theme we want to use.

```
PS > $spWeb = Get-SPWeb -Identity http://nimaintra.net
PS > $thm =
>> [Microsoft.SharePoint.Utilities.ThmxTheme]::GetManagedThemes($spWeb.Site) |
>> Where-Object { $_.Name -eq "Berry" }
```

In this example, we use the `Where-Object` cmdlet to retrieve the `ThmxTheme` object where the value of the `Name` property equals `Berry`.

Next, we can use the `ApplyTo` method on the `ThmxTheme` object to change the theme of a site in SharePoint 2010 to the Berry theme in this example. The `ApplyTo` method takes two arguments: an `SPWeb` object and a `shareGenerated` Boolean value.

```
PS > $thm.ApplyTo($spWeb, $true)
PS > $spWeb.Dispose()
```

The `Set-SPTheme` function is used to change the theme of a site in SharePoint 2010. The following is the complete function.

```
function Set-SPTheme([string]$url, [string]$theme) {
  $spWeb = Get-SPWeb $url
  $thm =
  [Microsoft.SharePoint.Utilities.ThmxTheme]::GetManagedThemes($spWeb.Site) |
  Where-Object { $_.Name -eq $theme }
  $thm.ApplyTo($spWeb, $true)
  $spWeb.Dispose()
}
```

Here is an example of running the function to change the theme to Azure:

```
PS > Set-SPTheme -url http://nimaintra.net -theme Azure
```

If we want to apply the same theme to multiple sites, we can use the Get-SPSite and Get-SPWeb cmdlets and pipe the retrieved site objects to the Set-SPTheme function.

```
PS > Get-SPSite -Identity http://nimaintra.net | Get-SPWeb | ForEach-Object {
>> Set-SPTheme -url $_.Url -theme Azure }
```

To revert to the default theme, use the static SetThemeUrlForWeb method of the Microsoft.SharePoint.Utilities.ThmxTheme class. The method has two overload definitions. One of the overloads takes two arguments: an SPWeb object and a theme URL. The second overload also supports a shareGenerated parameter. In the next example, we set the theme URL to null, which resets the site to the default theme.

```
PS > $spWeb = Get-SPWeb -Identity http://nimaintra.net
PS > [Microsoft.SharePoint.Utilities.ThmxTheme]::SetThemeUrlForWeb(
>> $spWeb, $null)
```

The SetThemeUrlForWeb method can also be used to apply a new theme to a site, just as we did with the ApplyTo method of the ThmxTheme class in a previous example.

```
PS > $thm =
>> [Microsoft.SharePoint.Utilities.ThmxTheme]::GetManagedThemes($spWeb.Site) |
>> Where { $_.Name -eq "Berry" }
PS > [Microsoft.SharePoint.Utilities.ThmxTheme]::SetThemeUrlForWeb(
>> $spWeb, $thm.ServerRelativeUrl)
PS > $spWeb.Dispose()
```

Changing the Site Logo, Title, and Description

We can modify the site logo, as well as its title and description, by changing the properties of the corresponding SPWeb object.

Changing the Logo

In this scenario, we will look at how easy it is to change the logo of a site. A site logo is the small image that appears to the left of the site title, in the top-left corner of your site's pages.

First, we bind to the site using the Get-SPWeb cmdlet.

```
PS > $spWeb = Get-SPWeb -Identity http://nimaintra.net
```

The SPWeb object returned by the Get-SPWeb cmdlet supports SiteLogoUrl and SiteLogoDescription properties that we can use to set a new site logo and a description. In this example, we use an image that exists in a picture library within the site.

```
PS > $spWeb.SiteLogoUrl = "http://nimaintra.net/Pictures/Image.bmp"
PS > $spWeb.SiteLogoDescription = "My Image"
```

After we have set the properties, we use the Update method to commit the changes we have made to the site, and finally dispose of the object.

```
PS > $spWeb.Update()
PS > $spWeb.Dispose()
```

By placing the code in a function, we can reuse it on multiple sites without needing to retype the code every time. Here is an example on a function, Set-SPSiteLogo, that sets the site logo and the site logo description:

```
function Set-SPSiteLogo([string]$url, [string]$logoUrl,
[string]$description) {
  $spWeb = Get-SPWeb -Identity $url
  $spWeb.SiteLogoUrl = $logoUrl
  $spWeb.SiteLogoDescription = $description
  $spWeb.Update()
  $spWeb.Dispose()
}
```

You can run the function by typing the following:

```
PS > Set-SPSiteLogo -url http://nimaintra.net -description "My image" `
>> -logoUrl http://nimaintra.net/Pictures/Image.bmp
```

Changing the Title and Description

Both the title and description of a site in SharePoint 2010 are available as properties on a corresponding SPWeb object. These properties allow us to change the title and description with only a few lines of code, as this example shows:

```
PS > $spWeb = Get-SPWeb -Identity http://nimaintra.net
PS > $spWeb.Title = "New Title"
PS > $spWeb.Description = "New Description"
PS > $spWeb.Update()
PS > $spWeb.Dispose()
```

Here, we create an instance of an SPWeb object and set the Title property to New Title and the Description property to New Description. When we call the Update method, the changes are committed.

We can also use the more convenient `Set-SPWeb` cmdlet, which allows us to perform the same actions on a single line of code.

```
PS > Set-SPWeb http://nimaintra.net -Description "New Description"
```

Managing Navigation

Along with the top navigation control, SharePoint 2010 can, out of the box, present navigation items in the left-side navigation pane using the Quick Launch bar or using the Tree View navigation. Both the Quick Launch navigation and the Tree View controls can be displayed at the same time, but usually only one is used.

Enabling the Tree View

The Tree View navigation control can be useful in scenarios where there are deeper structures or when easy access to lists and libraries are important.

To enable the Tree View, set the `TreeViewEnabled` property to `True`.

```
PS > $spWeb = Get-SPWeb -Identity http://nimaintra.net
PS > $spWeb.TreeViewEnabled = $true
PS > $spWeb.Update()
PS > $spWeb.Dispose()
```

Managing the Quick Launch Navigation

The Quick Launch navigation control can be enabled or disabled using the `QuickLaunchEnabled` property.

```
PS > $spWeb = Get-SPWeb -Identity http://nimaintra.net
PS > $spWeb.QuickLaunchEnabled = $true
PS > $spWeb.Update()
PS > $spWeb.Dispose()
```

In some scenarios, it is useful to add new navigation nodes to the Quick Launch bar. We can use Windows PowerShell to add any number of navigation nodes to the Quick Launch bar on any number of sites with a few simple lines of code. The first step is to create an instance of a `SPNavigationNode` object. The constructor contains two overloads. The first overload supports two arguments as input: a title and a URL. The second overload also supports a Boolean value that determines if the URL is external. In this case, *external* means external to the current site collection. By default, the value is set to `False`. To add a link to an external site, we set the value to `True`.

```
PS > $node = New-Object Microsoft.SharePoint.Navigation.SPNavigationNode `
>> -ArgumentList "bing", "http://www.bing.com", $true
```

Once we have an SPNavigationNode object stored in a variable, we can add the node to the Quick Launch bar on a site. There are three different methods that we can use when adding nodes to the Quick Launch bar: Add, AddAsFirst, and AddAsLast.

The Add method requires two arguments: the node to add and the previous node.

```
PS > $spWeb = Get-SPWeb -Identity http://nimaintra.net
PS > $previousNode = $spWeb.Navigation.QuickLaunch |
>> Where { $_.Title -eq "Lists" }
PS > $spWeb.Navigation.QuickLaunch.Add($node, $previousNode)
PS > $spWeb.Dispose()
```

Notice how we create a variable holding the previous node. The new node is added after the specified node.

We can add nodes to the top or to the bottom of the Quick Launch bar with the AddAsFirst or AddAsLast method, respectively. These methods require only the new node as input. The following example shows how to add a node to the bottom of the bar.

```
PS > $spWeb = Get-SPWeb -Identity http://nimaintra.net
PS > $spWeb.Navigation.QuickLaunch.AddAsLast($node)
PS > $spWeb.Dispose()
```

As always with Windows PowerShell, if you repeat it—script it. The following function, New-SPQuickLaunchNode, adds nodes to the Quick Launch bar.

```
function New-SPQuickLaunchNode(
  [string]$url,
  [string]$nodeURL,
  [string]$nodeTitle,
  [switch]$isExternal,
  [switch]$addAsFirst
) {
$spWeb = Get-SPWeb -Identity $url
if ($isExternal) {
  $node =
    New-Object Microsoft.SharePoint.Navigation.SPNavigationNode $nodeTitle,
      $nodeUrl, $true;
} else {
  $node =
    New-Object Microsoft.SharePoint.Navigation.SPNavigationNode $nodeTitle,
      $nodeUrl;
}
if ($addAsFirst) {
  $spWeb.Navigation.QuickLaunch.AddAsFirst($node);
} else {
```

```
   $spWeb.Navigation.QuickLaunch.AddAsLast($node);
  }
  $spWeb.Dispose();
}
```

Here is an example of using the function to add a node named Finance:

```
PS > New-SPQuickLaunchNode -url http://nimaintra.net `
>> -nodeURL /finance -nodeTitle "Finance"
```

In this example, we add an internal site. When adding internal sites, we can type a relative URL instead of the full URL.

The function also supports the `IsExternal` switch, which we can use when adding external links (external to the current site collection) and the `AddAsFirst` switch that adds the new node at the top of the Quick Launch bar.

Managing Top Navigation

The top navigation, or global navigation, control in each site can be configured so that it inherits the same navigation structure as its parent site. We can set the top navigation to inherit the parent's navigation items using the `UseShared` property, which accepts a Boolean value.

```
PS > $spWeb = Get-SPWeb -Identity http://nimaintra.net
PS > $spWeb.Navigation.UseShared = $true
PS > $spWeb.Dispose()
```

It is also possible to add new nodes to the top navigation. This requires that we create an instance of an `SPNavigationNode` object. This example shows how to add a node at the end of the top navigation bar:

```
PS > $spWeb = Get-SPWeb -Identity http://nimaintra.net
PS > $spWeb.Navigation.TopNavigationBar.AddAsLast($node)
PS > $spWeb.Dispose()
```

The following function, `New-SPTopNavigation`, adds nodes to the top navigation bar.

```
function New-SPTopNavigation (
  [string]$url,
  [string]$nodeURL,
  [string]$nodeTitle,
  [switch]$isExternal,
  [switch]$addAsFirst
  ) {
```

```
$spWeb = Get-SPWeb -Identity $url;

if ($isExternal) {
  $node =
   New-Object Microsoft.SharePoint.Navigation.SPNavigationNode $nodeTitle,
    $NodeUrl, $true;
} else {
  $node =
   New-Object Microsoft.SharePoint.Navigation.SPNavigationNode $nodeTitle,
    $NodeUrl;
}

if ($addAsFirst) {
  $spWeb.Navigation.TopNavigationBar.AddAsFirst($node);
} else {
  $spWeb.Navigation.TopNavigationBar.AddAsLast($node);
}

$spWeb.Dispose();
}
```

Here is an example of using the function to add links to sites in the same site collection to the top navigation bar:

```
PS > New-SPTopNavigation -url http://nimaintra.net -nodeURL /Project `
>> -nodeTitle "Project"
```

If we want to add an external link, we can use the IsExternal switch.

```
PS > New-SPTopNavigation -url http://nimaintra.net `
>> -nodeURL http://www.powershell.nu `
>> -nodeTitle "PowerShell.nu" -isExternal
```

Additional Functionality in SharePoint 2010

As mentioned previously, SharePoint themes are now based on .thmx files, as used by the Microsoft Office suite. Out of the box, a number of themes are available, but we have the opportunity to upload custom .thmx files to the themes gallery and apply them to a site.

Themes can be managed from the Site Settings page, as shown in Figure 13-1. You can modify themes directly. For instance, you can change the color of default text or the font that should be used within the site.

Figure 13-1.   Modifying themes through the user interface

Similarly, the global navigation and Quick Launch bar controls can be configured from the Site Settings page of each site, as shown in Figure 13-2. These options allow you to specify if the navigation should be inherited and what sort order should be applied. You can also add and remove items from the navigation.

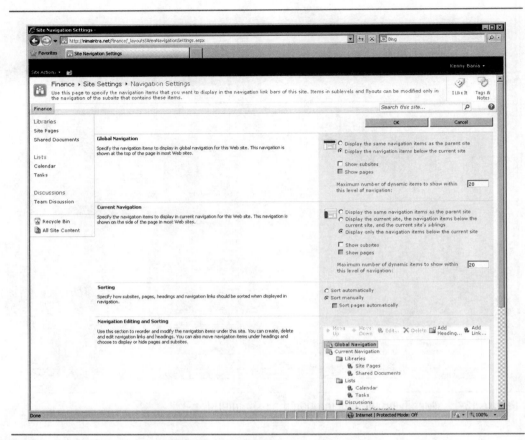

Figure 13-2.   Modifying navigation through the user interface

Summary

In this chapter, we looked at how to modify the look and feel of a site using Windows PowerShell. In the first scenario, we demonstrated how to manage themes by retrieving the current theme from a site, displaying all themes available in a site collection, and applying new themes to a site.

In the second scenario, we created a Windows PowerShell function that changed the site icon to use the URL we passed to the function. This was achieved by changing the properties of the corresponding SPWeb object. We also looked at changing the site title and description.

The chapter continued with examples of how to customize navigation by adding new items to the Quick Launch bar and to the global navigation.

The theme and navigation settings can be changed through the user interface. However, when you want to apply themes, logos, or navigation items to many sites or throughout the whole SharePoint environment, using Windows PowerShell is easier and more efficient.

CHAPTER 14 | Working with SharePoint Lists

One of the most powerful features in SharePoint from an end-user perspective is the ease of creating and customizing lists with columns and views so that they suit their business needs. Managing lists, columns, and views is not usually a day-to-day task for SharePoint administrators, but occasionally, you may need to work with them. For instance, you might need to create or modify a large number of columns in different lists on different sites—creating a Windows PowerShell script that automates this task will save you hours of work.

In this chapter, we will look at several ways that Windows PowerShell can assist with list management. In our first scenario, we will create both out-of-the-box and custom lists, and demonstrate how to wrap Windows PowerShell code in reusable functions. In our second scenario, we will take the lists created in the first scenario and modify them by adding new columns.

SharePoint offers a very powerful way to sort and filter the data in lists with the use of list views. The third scenario in this chapter shows how to modify existing list views and create new custom list views using Windows PowerShell.

The examples in this chapter also describe the concepts of optimizing the performance and minimizing memory utilization when working with lists using Windows PowerShell.

Managing SharePoint Lists

Using Windows PowerShell, you can create any of the types of lists supplied with SharePoint 2010, as well as custom lists.

Creating a New List

Let's start with creating a new Contacts list. The first step is to bind to the site that will contain the new list.

```
PS > $spWeb = Get-SPWeb -Identity "http://nimaintra.net/site"
```

You can use the ListTemplates property of the SPWeb object to see the available list templates. In this example, we choose to return the name and description of each of the available templates.

```
PS > $spWeb.ListTemplates | Select-Object -Property Name, Description |
>> Format-Table -AutoSize
Name                             Description
----                             -----------
Document Library                 A place for storing documents or oth...
Form Library                     A place to manage business forms lik...
Wiki Page Library                An interconnected set of easily edit...
Picture Library                  A place to upload and share pictures.
Links                            A list of web pages or other resources.
```

```
Announcements                          A list of news items, statuses and o...
Contacts                               A list of people your team works wit...
Calendar                               A calendar of upcoming meetings, dea...
Discussion Board                       A place to have newsgroup-style disc...
Tasks                                  A place for team or personal tasks.
Project Tasks                          A place for team or personal tasks. ...
Issue Tracking                         A list of issues or problems associa...
Custom List                            A blank list to which you can add yo...
Custom List in Datasheet View          A blank list which is displayed as a...
External List                          Create an external list to view the ...
Survey                                 A list of questions which you would ...
Asset Library                          A place to share, browse and manage ...
Custom Workflow Process                Custom Workflow Process tracking lis...
Data Connection Library                A place where you can easily share f...
Workflow History                       This list is used by SharePoint to s...
No Code Workflows                      Gallery for storing No Code Workflows
Data Sources                           Gallery for storing data source defi...
No Code Public Workflows               Gallery for storing No Code Public W...
```

When creating a list in SharePoint 2010 programmatically, you use the `Add` method of the `SPListCollection` class. This method has seven overloads (method signatures, or ways in which the method can be called). The one we will be using for our example accepts three parameters: the list title, description, and template type to be used. The title and description parameters are both of the type `System.String`, and the template parameter is of the type `SPListTemplateType`, so we need to provide an instance of this type as value for this parameter.

Here, we create a variable containing the Contacts list template type, which we obtain from the `Microsoft.SharePoint.SPListTemplateType` enumeration:

```
PS > $listTemplate = [Microsoft.SharePoint.SPListTemplateType]::Contacts
PS > $spListCollection = $spWeb.Lists
PS > $spListCollection.Add("My Contacts","Description",$listTemplate)
```

Why do we need this intermediary `spListCollection` variable? Why not call the `Add` method directly with `$spWeb.Lists.Add`? If we used the `Add` method directly and repeated the command ten times, the metadata for all available lists in the site would be loaded ten times. Storing the lists collection in a variable and working with that variable minimizes the amount of memory consumed, since the lists are loaded only once.

Creating a Custom List

You can also create custom lists.

```
PS > $listTemplate = $spWeb.ListTemplates |
>> Where-Object { $_.Name -eq "Custom List" }
PS > $spListCollection.Add("My Custom List","Description",$listTemplate)
```

Instead of passing it an instance of the SPListTemplateType class, we retrieve an SPListTemplate object from the ListTemplates property and store it in a variable that we use when creating the list.

The GetNames static method of the System.Enum class displays the correct enumeration values for the list templates types.

```
PS > [System.Enum]::GetNames("Microsoft.SharePoint.SPListTemplateType")
```

You can also use the ListTemplates collection and select the Name and Type properties.

```
PS > $spWeb.ListTemplates |
>> Format-Table -AutoSize -Property @{Label="Template
Name";Expression={$_.Name}},
>> @{Label="Type";Expression={[int]$_.Type};Alignment="Left"}
```

This approach displays only the templates available in a particular site (based on a particular site template).

We can ease list creation by using a function, such as the following New-SPList function.

```
function New-SPList (
  [string]$url,
  [string]$name,
  [string]$description,
  [string]$template,
  [switch]$showTemplate
) {
$spWeb = Get-SPWeb -Identity $url
if ($showTemplate) {
  $spWeb.ListTemplates |
    Format-Table -AutoSize -Property `
      @{Label="Template Name";Expression={$_.Name}},
      @{Label="Type";Expression={[int]$_.Type};Alignment="Left"};
} else {
  $spListCollection = $spWeb.Lists
  $spListCollection.Add($name, $description, $template)
}
$spWeb.Dispose()
}
```

You can use the function by typing the following:

```
PS > New-SPList -url http://nimaintra.net/site -name "My Calendar" `
>> -description "My Custom Calendar" -template 106
```

In this example, we use a numeric value as input to the `Template` parameter. To find out a template's corresponding numeric `Type` value, you can use the `showTemplate` switch parameter.

```
PS > New-SPList -url http://nimaintra.net/site -showTemplate
```

When creating a list using the SharePoint object model and the simple `Add` method overload that we used in our function, the list may not appear on the Quick Launch navigation bar (based on the value of the `OnQuickLaunch` property of the corresponding list template), so we may need to add this link manually. We can achieve this by setting the `OnQuickLaunch` property to `True`. The property is provided by the `SPList` class, so first we need to retrieve an instance of `SPList` containing the list we just created.

Getting List Instances

The simplest way of getting a instance of our new list is by typing this:

```
PS > $spWeb.Lists["My Calendar"]
```

The problem with this line of code is that it loads the metadata of all available lists, then performs a comparison of the `Title` property, and finally returns the lists where the title matches. This approach might consume a lot of memory if performed against a site with many lists.

A better approach is to use the `GetList` method supported by `SPWeb`. The `GetList` method accepts a list's full or relative URL as input. In this example, we use a site-relative URL:

```
PS > $spList = $spWeb.GetList("/Lists/My Calendar")
```

The following `Get-SPList` function also retrieves a list instance.

```
function Get-SPList([uri]$url) {
  # Nullify variables $site, $web and $list
  $site = $web = $list = $null
  # Get site collection
  $site = New-Object -TypeName Microsoft.SharePoint.SPSite `
  -ArgumentList $(
  [Microsoft.SharePoint.Utilities.SPEncode]::UrlDecodeAsUrl($url.AbsoluteUri)
  );
  # Get site-relative URL
  $webURL = ([Microsoft.SharePoint.Utilities.SPEncode]::UrlDecodeAsUrl(
  $url.AbsoluteUri)
  ) -replace $site.Url;
  # Remove query information if included
  if (-not [string]::IsNullOrEmpty($url.Query)) {
    $webURL = $webURL.Replace($url.Query, [string]::Empty);
  }
```

```
# Process the array of segments backwards,
# removing segments one by one from the end of the URL,
# until the URL of the lowest level subsite is identified
-1..-($url.Segments.Count) | ForEach-Object {
  if ($web -eq $null) {
    # Once the correct URL is obtained, initialize a variable containing an
    # instance of SPWeb class for the lowest level subsite
    if($webUrl -eq "/"){
     $identity = $webUrl
    } else {
     $identity = $webUrl.Trim("/")
    }
    $web = Get-SPWeb -Site $site -Identity $identity `
     -ErrorAction SilentlyContinue;
    $webUrl =
    $webUrl -replace `
     [Microsoft.SharePoint.Utilities.SPEncode]::UrlDecodeAsUrl(
       $url.Segments[$_]
     );
  }
}
if ($web -ne $null) {
  0..($url.Segments.Count - 1) | ForEach-Object {
    $listUrl += $url.Segments[$_];
    if ($list -eq $null) {
      $list = $(trap {continue}; $web.GetList($listUrl.TrimEnd("/")));
    }
  }
}
$web.Dispose();
$site.Dispose();
return $list;
}
```

You can use the function by typing the following:

```
PS > $spList = Get-SPList -url "http://nimaintra.net/site/Lists/My Calendar"
```

 NOTE   From this point on, we'll use the Get-SPList function in all functions and scripts that handle lists and libraries in SharePoint 2010.

Adding Lists to the Quick Launch Bar

When you have retrieved an instance of SPList using any of the methods demonstrated previously, you can set the OnQuickLaunch property to True and update the list. This will add a link to a list in the Quick Launch bar.

```
PS > $spList.OnQuickLaunch = $true
PS > $spList.Update()
```

The Set-SPListOnQuickLaunch function shown next demonstrates how to add and remove lists from the Quick Launch navigation. The function uses the Get-SPList function presented in the previous section to retrieve an instance of SPList.

```
function Set-SPListOnQuickLaunch ([uri]$url, [switch]$add,
[switch]$remove) {
  # Use the Get-SPList function to retrieve a list
  $spList = Get-SPList -url $url
  if($spList) {
    if($add) {
      $spList.OnQuickLaunch = $true;
    }
    if($remove) {
      $spList.OnQuickLaunch = $false;
    }
    $spList.Update();
  }
}
```

The Set-SPListOnQuickLaunch function either adds or removes a link to a list from the Quick Launch bar. To add a list, type this:

```
PS > Set-SPListOnQuickLaunch `
>> -url "http://nimaintra.net/site/Lists/My Calendar" -add
```

To remove a list, use the –remove switch.

```
PS > Set-SPListOnQuickLaunch `
>> -url "http://nimaintra.net/site/Lists/My Calendar" -remove
```

Deleting Lists

You can also delete lists in SharePoint 2010 using Windows PowerShell. Simply retrieve the list using the Get-SPList function, and then use the Delete method provided by the SPList class.

```
PS > $spList = Get-SPList -url "http://nimaintra.net/site/Lists/My Calendar"
PS > $spList.Delete()
```

The following is a function that you can use to delete a list from SharePoint 2010.

```
function Remove-SPList ([string]$url) {
  # Use the Get-SPList function to retrieve a list
  $spList = Get-SPList -url $url
```

```
  if($spList) {
    $spList.Delete();
  }
}
```

Run the `Remove-SPList` function as follows:

```
PS > Remove-SPList -url "http://nimaintra.net/site/Lists/My Calendar"
```

 NOTE   Lists in SharePoint 2010 have other properties that you can manipulate using Windows PowerShell. You can use the `Get-Member` cmdlet to find out more about the available methods and properties of the `SPList` class.

Managing SharePoint Fields

You can also add fields to lists using Windows PowerShell. You can display the available types of fields using the `FieldTypeDefinitionCollection` property of the `SPWeb` class. In the following example, we send the output through a pipeline to the `Select-Object` cmdlet and display the `TypeName` and `TypeDisplayName` properties.

```
PS > $spWeb.FieldTypeDefinitionCollection |
>> Select-Object -Property TypeName, TypeDisplayName
```

TypeName	TypeDisplayName
Counter	Counter
Text	Single line of text
Note	Multiple lines of text
Choice	Choice
MultiChoice	Choice
GridChoice	Rating Scale
Integer	Integer
Number	Number
Decimal	Decimal
Currency	Currency
DateTime	Date and Time
Lookup	Lookup
Boolean	Yes/No
User	Person or Group
URL	Hyperlink or Picture

Here, we've shown only a fraction of the field types available in SharePoint 2010.

Creating a New Field

Before we add a field to a list, we first retrieve the list using the Get-SPList function.

```
PS > $spList = Get-SPList -url "http://nimaintra.net/site/Lists/My Custom List"
```

To create a field in a SharePoint 2010 list, you use the Add method provided by the SPFieldCollection class. Here, we create a simple Text type field in a SharePoint list:

```
PS > $spFieldType = [Microsoft.SharePoint.SPFieldType]::Text
PS > $spList.Fields.Add("TextField",$spFieldType,$false)
```

In this example, we create an SPFieldType object with the value Text and store it in the variable spFieldType. We then use the Add method and pass in the field's display name, followed by the variable spFieldType, followed by Boolean False. The last parameter in this overload of the Add method specifies whether the new field is required to always contain a value. Our example creates a new text field in the list with the display name of TextField that will not require any input. An additional Boolean parameter you can use with the Add method compacts the field name to eight characters if set to True.

The following wraps the field-creation code in a reusable function.

```
function New-SPTextField([string]$url, [string]$field,[switch]$required) {
  # Use the Get-SPList function to retrieve a list
  $spList = Get-SPList -url $url
  if($spList) {
    $spFieldType = [Microsoft.SharePoint.SPFieldType]::Text
    $spList.Fields.Add($field, $spFieldType, $required)
  }
}
```

Here's an example of using this function to create a new mandatory text field named My Field, in the My Custom List list:

```
PS > New-SPTextField -url "http://nimaintra.net/site/Lists/My Custom List" `
>> -field "My Field" -required
```

A field in SharePoint 2010 has a few properties that you can set to change how the field is displayed. Before you can change the properties of a field, you need to retrieve it. You can either use the GetField method provided by the SPFieldCollection class or simply index into the collection.

```
PS > $spField = $spList.Fields.GetField("My Field")
PS > $spField = $spList.Fields["My Field"]
```

The first example demonstrates how to use the GetField method to retrieve an existing field and store the object in a variable. The second example demonstrates how to index into the collection. Note that both forms are case-sensitive.

You can use the `Get-Member` cmdlet to display all the methods and properties available on the object.

```
PS > $spField | Get-Member
```

Many of the properties available are "get/set," meaning that you can get the values from the properties and set new values. Here's how to set a description for the field:

```
PS > $spField.Description = "A Simple Text Field"
```

It is also possible to hide the field from various forms in SharePoint. In the next example, we hide the field from the Edit Item form so that when end users try to edit a list item in SharePoint 2010, they will not be able to edit the text field, since it will simply not appear.

```
PS > $spField.ShowInEditForm = $false
PS > $spField.Update()
```

We call the `Update` method to commit the changes to the SharePoint 2010 content database.

You can add other types of fields as well, such as `Note`, `Number`, `Decimal`, `Currency`, and so on. Here is an example on adding an `Integer` type field using Windows PowerShell:

```
PS > $spFieldType = [Microsoft.SharePoint.SPFieldType]::Integer
PS > $spList.Fields.Add("NumericField", $spFieldType, $false)
```

This new field will accept only numeric values.

Adding a Choice Field

Adding a `Choice` type field is a little different since it requires additional information regarding the possible choices. You can store the choices in an instance of the `System.Collections.Specialized.StringCollection` class, as shown in this example:

```
PS > $choices = New-Object System.Collections.Specialized.StringCollection
PS > $choices.Add("First Choice")
PS > $choices.Add("Second Choice")
PS > $choices.Add("Third Choice")
```

Now that we have our choices stored in a variable, we can use the variable when creating a `Choice` type field.

```
PS > $spFieldType = [Microsoft.SharePoint.SPFieldType]::Choice
PS > $spList.Fields.Add("ChoiceField",$spFieldType,$false,$false,$choices)
```

We use the `choices` variable to associate a list of options with the field.

The following demonstrates how to wrap this code in a function.

```
function New-SPChoiceField(
  [string]$url,
  [string]$field,
  [array]$choices,
  [switch]$required
  ) {
  # Use the Get-SPList function to retrieve a list
  $spList = Get-SPList -url $url
  if($spList) {
    $spFieldType = [Microsoft.SharePoint.SPFieldType]::Choice
    $colChoices = New-Object System.Collections.Specialized.StringCollection
    foreach ($choice in $choices) {
      $colChoices.Add($choice) | Out-Null
    }
    $spList.Fields.Add($field,$spFieldType,$required,$false,$colChoices)
  }
}
```

Run the function by typing the following:

```
PS > New-SPChoiceField -url "http://nimaintra.net/site/Lists/My Custom List" `
>> -field 'Pick One' -choices @(1,2,3)
```

In this example, we use the function `New-SPChoiceField` to add the field Pick One to the My Custom List list. We also add the options 1, 2, and 3 using the `-choices` parameter.

The `-choices` parameter accepts an array as input. A simple way to create an array is by placing a comma-separated list of values within the `@()` subexpression, as shown in the previous example.

When creating a `Choice` type field using Windows PowerShell, the display format is set to a drop-down list by default. We can change this to radio buttons, as shown here:

```
PS > $spField = $spList.Fields.GetField("ChoiceField")
PS > $spField.EditFormat = "RadioButtons"
PS > $spField.Update()
```

In this example, we retrieve the ChoiceField field by using the `GetField` method provided by the `SPFieldCollection` class. We then change the `EditFormat` property to `RadioButtons` and call the `Update` method to commit the changes to the content database.

We can also set a default choice using the `DefaultValue` property.

```
PS > $spField = $spList.Fields.GetField("ChoiceField")
PS > $spField.DefaultValue = "Second Choice"
PS > $spField.Update()
```

Adding a Lookup Field

To add a lookup field to a SharePoint list, use the `AddLookup` method of the `SPFieldCollection` class. You need to provide the method with the field's display name and the ID of the list that the lookup field should point to.

In the next example, we get the ID of an existing list named Tasks, store the ID of the list in a variable, and use the variable to create a lookup field.

```
PS > $lookupListId =
>> (Get-SPList -url "http://nimaintra.net/site/Lists/Tasks").Id
PS > $spList.Fields.AddLookup("LookupField",$lookupListId,$false)
```

The following is the same code wrapped in a function.

```
function New-SPLookupField (
  [string]$url,
  [string]$lookupListURL,
  [string]$field,
  [switch]$required
  ) {
  # Use the Get-SPList function to retrieve a list
  $spList = Get-SPList -url $url
  $lookupListId = (Get-SPList -url $lookupListURL).Id
  if($spList -and $lookupListId) {
    $spList.Fields.AddLookup($field, $lookupListId, $required);
  }
}
```

Run the function by typing the following:

```
PS > New-SPLookupField -url "http://nimaintra.net/site/Lists/My Custom List" `
>> -lookupListURL "http://nimaintra.net/site/Lists/Tasks" `
>> -field 'My Lookup'
```

In this example, we create a lookup field named My Lookup. The lookup field points to the Tasks list.

Creating a lookup field that points to a list in a different site requires the list ID and the site ID. In the following example, we retrieve the list ID and the site ID using the `Get-SPWeb` cmdlet, and then use the values with the `AddLookup` method.

```
PS > $lookupListId =
>> (Get-SPList -url "http://nimaintra.net/finance/Lists/Tasks").Id
PS > $lookupWebId = (Get-SPWeb -Identity http://nimaintra.net/finance).Id
PS > $spList.Fields.AddLookup("SubsiteLookup",$lookupListId,$lookupWebId,$false)
```

SharePoint 2010 also supports a dependent lookup field type, which depends on a primary lookup field for its relationship to the list from which it gets its values. In the following example, we store the primary lookup field's ID in a variable and use the variable as input to the AddDependentLookup method of the SPFieldCollection to create a dependent lookup field.

```
PS > $spList = Get-SPList -url "http://nimaintra.net/site/Lists/My Custom List"
PS > $primaryFieldId = $spList.Fields["LookupField"].Id
PS > $spList.Fields.AddDependentLookup("Dependent lookup",$primaryFieldId)
```

A dependent lookup field added using Windows PowerShell points to the Title field by default. We can change this by editing the field's LookupField property, as shown here:

```
PS > $sourceList = Get-SPList -url "http://nimaintra.net/site/Lists/Tasks"
PS > $spList = Get-SPList -url "http://nimaintra.net/site/Lists/My Custom List"
PS > $spList.Fields["Dependent lookup"].LookupField =
>> $sourceList.Fields["Start Date"].InternalName
PS > $spList.Fields["Dependent lookup"].Update()
```

In this example, we point the LookupField property to the Start Date field of the source list.

Managing SharePoint Views

List views in SharePoint 2010 enable you to create customized representations of list data for specific purposes, such as displaying specific fields. When a new list in SharePoint is created, a default view is added. Document Library lists get the All Documents view, Picture Library lists get the All Pictures view, and most of the other list types get the All Items view.

You can manage the views associated with a SharePoint 2010 list using Windows PowerShell. Let's first take a look at how to modify an existing view.

Modifying a View

Before you can edit an existing view in SharePoint 2010, you need to retrieve it. You can use the GetViewFromUrl method of the SPWeb class. Let's get the custom list we created earlier.

```
PS > $spWeb = Get-SPWeb -Identity "http://nimaintra.net/site"
PS > $spWeb.GetViewFromUrl("/Lists/My Custom List/AllItems.aspx")
```

You can also retrieve the view from an SPList object using its indexed Views property.

```
PS > $spList = Get-SPList -url "http://nimaintra.net/site/Lists/My Custom List"
PS > $spView = $spList.Views["All Items"]
```

When you use this approach, all views are loaded into memory, and then a comparison is made to match each view's title with the text in the brackets. If you have a list with a lot of views, it is better to use the `GetViewFromUrl` method.

In this chapter, we have added a few fields to our custom list. When a field is added using Windows PowerShell, it is not automatically added to the default view. Let's add the text field to the view. First, we need to create a reference to the field that we want to add to the view.

```
PS > $spField = $spList.Fields["TextField"]
```

Then we can use the `Add` method provided by the `SPViewFieldCollection` class to add the field to a view.

```
PS > $spView.ViewFields.Add($spField)
PS > $spView.Update()
```

You may also want to change the order in which items are displayed in the list view. The `Query` property of the `SPView` class contains a Collaborative Application Markup Language (CAML) query that defines the subset of list items that is returned when this view is selected.

NOTE   We are only able to briefly look at how we can use CAML queries as it stretches beyond the scope of this book. To learn more about CAML and to be able to create more advanced queries, we recommend looking at the reference found on MSDN at http://msdn.microsoft.com/en-us/library/dd588106(office.11).aspx.

```
PS > $spView.Query
<OrderBy><FieldRef Name="ID" /></OrderBy>
```

In this example, the command returns `<OrderBy><FieldRef Name="ID" /></OrderBy>`, which is the CAML query used by the default view. You can change the query using Windows PowerShell. In the next example, we change the query so that the items appearing in the view are ordered by the value of Title instead of ID.

```
PS > $spView.Query = '<OrderBy><FieldRef Name="Title" /></OrderBy>'
PS > $spView.Update()
```

It is also possible to change the style of a list view using Windows PowerShell. Retrieve the available view styles from the `ViewStyles` property.

```
PS C:\> $spWeb.ViewStyles | Select-Object -Property Title, Id |
>> Format-Table -AutoSize

Title                    ID
-----                    --
Basic Table              0
Picture Library Details  6
                         7
```

```
                              8
                              9
Boxed, no labels             12
Boxed                        13
Document Details             14
Newsletter                   15
Newsletter, no lines         16
Shaded                       17
Issues Boxed                 18
Issues Boxed, no labels 19
Preview Pane                 20
```

Notice that the view styles with the IDs of 7, 8, and 9 are missing a title. These are the Month, Week, and Day View styles used with calendar views.

Let's go ahead and change the view style for a list view. The next example demonstrates how to change the view style of the All Items view.

```
PS > $spView.ApplyStyle($spWeb.ViewStyles.StyleByID(17))
PS > $spView.Update()
```

In this example, we change to the Shaded view style, which has an ID of 17.

Creating a New View

It is also possible to create a completely new list view using the Add method of the SPViewCollection class. When adding a new view, you have the option to specify which fields you want to show in the view. The Add method accepts an object of the type System.Collections.Specialized.StringCollection as a value for the parameter that specifies which fields should be added to the view. The string collection must contain the internal names of the fields. The following is an example of creating such a string collection.

```
PS > $viewFields = New-Object System.Collections.Specialized.StringCollection
PS > $viewFields.Add("Title")
PS > $viewFields.Add("TextField")
PS > $viewFields.Add("ChoiceField")
```

You also have the opportunity to add a custom CAML query to the view. In this example, we add a query that groups items by the value of the ChoiceField field.

```
PS > $query = '<GroupBy Collapse="TRUE" GroupLimit="30">' +
>> '<FieldRef Name="ChoiceField" /></GroupBy>'
```

Finally, we create the new view.

```
PS > $spList.Views.Add("My View",$viewFields, $query, 100, $true, $false)
```

Our new view is named My View. We add the fields Title, TextField, and ChoiceField. We then add the CAML query stored in the `query` variable. The value `100` is the number of items that will be displayed per page. The first Boolean value specifies that the view should display more items page by page, and the last Boolean value specifies if the view should be set as the default view of the list. Since it is set to `False`, the view will not be the default view of the list. The complete `New-SPView` function follows.

```
function New-SPView (
  [string]$url,
  [string]$view,
  [array]$fields,
  [string]$query,
  [int]$itemsDisplayed,
  [switch]$paged,
  [switch]$default
) {
# Use the Get-SPList function to retrieve a list
$spList = Get-SPList -url $url
if($spList) {
  $viewFields = New-Object System.Collections.Specialized.StringCollection
  foreach($field in $fields) {
    $viewFields.Add($field)
  }
  $spList.Views.Add(
    $view, $viewFields, $query, $itemsDisplayed, $paged, $default
  )
  }
}
```

Run the function by typing the following:

```
PS > New-SPView -url "http://nimaintra.net/site/Lists/My Custom List" `
>> -view "New View" -fields @("Title","TextField") -itemsDisplayed 100 -paged
```

In this example, we use the `New-SPView` function to create a new view named New View in the My Custom List list. We add the fields Title and TextField so that the fields will be shown in the view. We also specify that 100 items should be displayed per page and that the view should display more items page by page.

Removing a View

You can remove a view from a SharePoint 2010 list using the `Delete` method provided by the `SPViewCollection` class. The next example shows how to delete the My View view that we created in a previous example.

```
PS > $spList = Get-SPList -url "http://nimaintra.net/site/Lists/My Custom List"
PS > $spView = $spList.Views["My View"]
PS > $spList.Views.Delete($spView.Id)
```

In this example, we store the view that we want to delete in a variable before using the `Delete` method. Notice that we need to use the view's ID as input to the `Delete` method.

Here is a simple function that deletes views from a SharePoint list:

```
function Remove-SPView ([string]$url, [string]$view) {
  # Use the Get-SPList function to retrieve a list
  $spList = Get-SPList -url $url
  if($spList) {
    $spView = $spList.Views[$view]
    $spList.Views.Delete($spView.Id);
  }
}
```

We can remove our new view from our SharePoint 2010 list using our `Remove-SPView` function, as shown here:

```
PS > Remove-SPView -url "http://nimaintra.net/site/Lists/My Custom List" `
>> -view 'New View'
```

Additional Functionality in SharePoint 2010

SharePoint 2010 offers many ways to create and customize lists through the graphical user interface. Lists can be saved as templates both from SharePoint Designer and from the browser-based interface. Figure 14-1 shows an example of the custom list template Nima Project Tasks appearing among the default templates in the list creation dialog box. Custom list templates are stored at the site collection level and can be found in the Galleries section of the Site Settings page.

With the use of content types and site columns, SharePoint 2010 offers a way to manage and control which columns should be available in lists of any given type, such as Calendar or Contacts. By using content types, it is possible to associate Microsoft Office Word or PowerPoint templates with document libraries, so that whenever a user creates a new document in the library, it will be based on the specified template.

Using content types and site columns is good practice when creating and maintaining a content structure in your SharePoint 2010 environment. However, in the real world, it can be very difficult to enforce the use of content types and site columns, especially in larger environments with a lot of independent site owners.

Figure 14-1. Custom list templates are displayed when creating new lists.

Summary

In this chapter, we demonstrated how to create SharePoint lists, fields, and list views using Windows PowerShell. Even though this is an easy task to perform through the graphical user interface, there are situations where scripting SharePoint lists, fields, and views can save you a lot of time.

We also looked at some important concepts around how to optimize scripts by using the GetList and GetField methods to minimize the memory usage. You saw how to use CAML queries when managing list views. In the next chapter, which covers managing content in SharePoint list items, we will look at some other scenarios where CAML queries are useful.

CHAPTER 15 | Managing SharePoint List Items

harePoint 2010 offers the functionality to change the properties of multiple list items at the same time using the Datasheet view. Updating multiple items at the same time is also a viable task for Windows PowerShell and could be very useful when updating items across multiple lists.

In this chapter, we will cover automating the procedures of creating, updating, and deleting list items using Windows PowerShell. The last example demonstrates how to use Windows PowerShell to copy list items from one list to another list. The destination list can be located in a different site, and with modification to the script, it could even be in a different SharePoint farm.

Knowing how to work with list items using Windows PowerShell will come in handy when creating more complex scripts that need to interact with content in SharePoint lists. We presented an example of this usage in Chapter 11, where we created a script that checked for items in the request site list with a specific status, and if found, created a new site collection.

Creating List Items

For the examples in this chapter, we will use a custom list containing a variety of fields, as shown in Figure 15-1. This custom list contains fields of the following types: Text (single line of text), Note (multiple lines of text), Choice, Number, Currency, DateTime, Lookup, Boolean (yes/no), User (person or group), and URL (hyperlink or picture).

We'll begin by creating some new list items using Windows PowerShell. First, we need to retrieve a list object. Here, we use the Get-SPList function presented in Chapter 14.

```
PS > $spList = Get-SPList -url "http://nimaintra.net/Lists/Custom List"
```

The SPList class provides the AddItem method, which is used to create new list items. When you call the AddItem method, an object of the type Microsoft .SharePoint.SPListItem is returned.

Since we want to populate the properties of the new list item, we need to store the object in a variable in order to continue to work with it.

```
PS > $spListItem = $spList.AddItem()
```

Now we can start assigning values to the different fields the corresponding list item inherits from the parent list. The SPListItem class provides a parameterized Item property for accessing the value contained in a particular field. To specify the value of the Title field, we can use the following:

```
PS > $spListItem.Item("Title") = "My new ListItem"
```

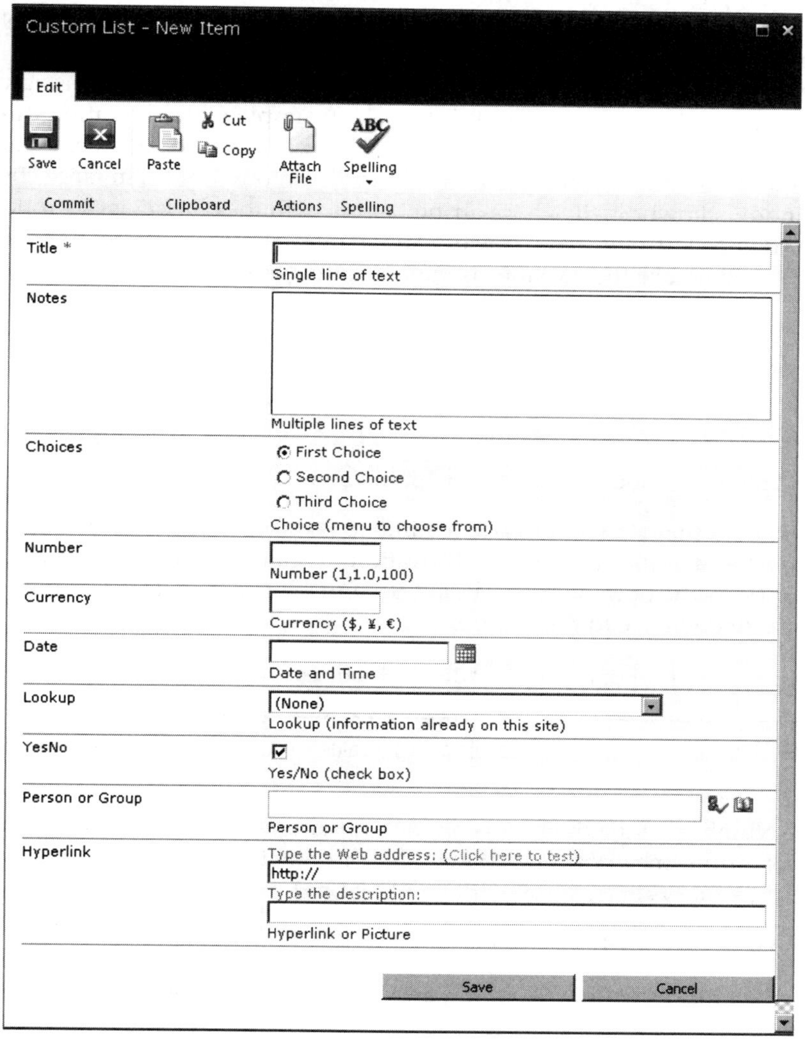

Figure 15-1.   Custom list in SharePoint 2010

Because the `Item` property is also an indexer for this class (more information is available at http://msdn.microsoft.com/en-us/library/microsoft.sharepoint.splistitem .aspx), we can also access field values simply using the indexing notation: placing the field's name within `[" "]`. So, our previous example could also be in this form:

```
PS > $spListItem["Title"] = "My new ListItem"
```

In this example, we assign the value `My new ListItem` to the list item's Title field. Note that the field name is case-sensitive! Since the Title field is a single line of text type, we assign a `System.String` value to it.

The second field in the list is a multiple lines of text type, so we can assign a `System.String` value that spans multiple lines. A simple way of creating this kind of value is by using a here-string. A here-string is typically used for storing text with newlines, quotation marks, and other characters commonly found in large chunks of text. In Windows PowerShell, a here-string begins with the characters `@"` followed by a new line and ends with the `"@` characters. In the next example, we store a here-string in a variable, and then use the variable as value for the Notes field.

```
PS > $multipleLines = @"
>> First Line
>> Second Line
>> Third Line
>> "@
PS > $spListItem["Notes"] = $multipleLines
```

The next field that we want to add a value to is the Choices field. In this type of field, we must add values that match the options available in the field. In this example, the field supports the options First Choice, Second Choice, and Third Choice. We assign a value of Second Choice to the Choices field.

```
PS > $spListItem["Choices"] = "Second Choice"
```

NOTE If a `Choice` type field accepts multiple values, use the `;` character to separate them.

For the Number field, which can contain only numeric values, we can simply type a number as input, since Windows PowerShell automatically interprets numbers as `System.Int32` or `System.Double`, depending on the value.

```
PS > $spListItem["Number"] = 1.8
```

In this example, we use 1.8 as input, and Windows PowerShell will interpret the number as a `System.Double` object.

Like the `Number` type field, a `Currency` type list field accepts numeric values. The next example shows how to add a value to this field.

```
PS > $spListItem["Currency"] = 10
```

The `DateTime` type list field accepts values that can be interpreted as date and time designators. Windows PowerShell includes the `Get-Date` cmdlet, which we can use when working with such fields in SharePoint 2010.

```
PS > $spListItem["Date"] = Get-Date
```

The YesNo field accepts Boolean values. This example shows how to supply a value of `True` as input.

```
PS > $spListItem["YesNo"] = $true
```

The `Lookup` field type differs a little from the previous examples because fields of this type contain just a reference to a list item that exists in a different list. In SharePoint 2007, the value added to a lookup field needed to start with the list item's ID followed by ";#", followed by the list item's title. This also works in SharePoint 2010, as shown in the following example, in which we retrieve a list item from the Announcements list and create a string value that matches the lookup field format.

```
PS > $spAnnouncementsList =
>> Get-SPList -url "http://nimaintra.net/Lists/Announcements"
PS > $spLookupListItem = $spAnnouncementsList.GetItemById(1)
PS > $strLookupListItem =
>> [string]$spLookupListItem.ID + ";#" + $spLookupListItem.Title
```

Here, we store the reference to the Announcements list in a variable and use the `GetItemById` method to retrieve a list item. We then use the `ID` and `Title` properties of the `SPListItem` object to create a string that we can use as value for a lookup field. We also explicitly cast the ID as a `System.String` object; otherwise, Windows PowerShell will attempt to interpret all the values as `System.Int32`, and an error will occur. Here is the resulting string value:

```
PS > $strLookupListItem
1;#Get Started with Microsoft SharePoint Foundation!
```

We can then use our variable as the value for the lookup field.

```
PS > $spListItem["Lookup"] = $strLookupListItem
```

In SharePoint 2010, you can also use a list item object as value to a lookup field directly, instead of creating a string in a specific format.

```
PS > $spListItem["Lookup"] =
>> (Get-SPList "http://nimaintra.net/Lists/Announcements").
GetItemById(1)
```

Person or group type fields are similar to lookup fields in that they support values that follow the `ID;#Title` format, where `Title` is the display name of the user or group to add. In fact, these fields are lookup fields that, behind the scenes, reference the hidden User Info list in each site collection.

In SharePoint 2010, you can use the `Get-SPUser` cmdlet to return a user account from a SharePoint site. Just as with lookup fields, you can either create a string value that follows the `ID;#Title` format or use an `SPUser` object as input. The following example shows how to retrieve the account of user Kenny Bania and use it as the value for the field.

```
PS > $spUser = Get-SPUser -Web http://nimaintra.net `
>> -Identity POWERSHELL\kennybania
PS > $spListItem["Person or Group"] = $spUser
```

The last field in our example is a hyperlink or picture field. The valid format of a value for a field of this type is an address, followed by a comma, followed by a description, as shown here:

```
PS > $spListItem["Hyperlink"] =
>> "http://www.powershell.nu, Windows PowerShell blog"
```

When we have assigned values to all the fields of our new item, we call the `Update` method to commit the changes to the SharePoint 2010 content database.

```
PS > $spListItem.Update()
```

The following is the `New-SPListItem` function, which creates new list items in a SharePoint 2010 list. The function uses the `Get-SPList` function described in Chapter 14.

```
function New-SPListItem ([string]$url) {

  # Use the Get-SPList function to retrieve a list
  $spList = Get-SPList -url $url

  return $spList.AddItem();
}
```

And here is an example of this function in action:

```
PS > $spListItem = New-SPListItem -url "http://nimaintra.net/Lists/Custom List"
PS > $spListItem["Title"] = "My List Item"
PS > $spListItem.Update()
```

Figure 15-2 shows the new item added to the list.

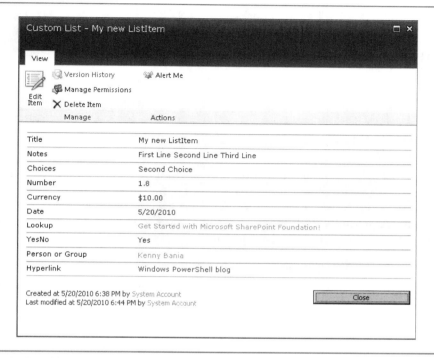

Figure 15-2.   List item created using Windows PowerShell

Updating List Items

The `SPList` class provides a few methods we can use to retrieve an item from a list in SharePoint 2010. The following methods are the most commonly used:

- `GetItemById`, which requires that we know the ID of the particular item
- `GetItems`, which is used to return all list items or a subset of list items as defined by search criteria in a CAML query

First, let's take a look at the `GetItemById` method. The method takes the ID of a list item as input and returns a `SPListItem` object. This example shows how to retrieve the list item with the ID of `1` from a list and store it in a variable.

```
PS > $spList = Get-SPList -url "http://nimaintra.net/Lists/Custom List"
PS > $spListItem = $spList.GetItemById(1)
```

Once we have a list item stored in a variable, we can get or set any of the field values available. In the following example, we retrieve the list item's title.

```
PS > $spListItem["Title"]
My new ListItem
```

We can change the list item's title by assigning a new value and calling the Update method.

```
PS > $spListItem["Title"] = "New Title"
PS > $spListItem.Update()
```

The GetItems method is better suited if you want to retrieve multiple items. You can use the GetItems method without any input, which will return all list items. Alternatively, you can use a CAML query to select specific list items.

To use a CAML query with the GetItems method, we first need to create an object of the type Microsoft.SharePoint.SPQuery.

```
PS > $spQuery = New-Object Microsoft.SharePoint.SPQuery
```

The SPQuery object supports the Query property, which we use to place a CAML query. Here's the CAML query we'll use in our example:

```
PS > $camlQuery =
>> '<Where>
>>    <Eq>
>>      <FieldRef Name="YesNo" />
>>        <Value Type="Text">True</Value>
>>    </Eq>
>> </Where>'
>>
```

We create a new query containing a Where statement using the <Where> tag. Next, we specify an equals expression using the <Eq> tag. For other types of searches, you can replace this tag with the appropriate one, such as <Lt> or <Gt> to search for list items where the value of this field is less than or greater than a value, respectively.

We then specify the field we want to query against using the <FieldRef> tag. In this example, we want to look at the YesNo field in the list.

Finally, we use the <Value> tag to specify that the value type is Text and that the value should equal True.

Once we have created a CAML query and stored it in a variable, we assign it to the Query property of our SPQuery object.

```
PS > $spQuery.Query = $camlQuery
```

Before using the SPQuery with the GetItems method, we should specify the RowLimit property that is used to limit the amount of items returned per page.

If we run the `SPQuery` without setting the row limit, the query will select all items matching the criteria, and might fail on lists with a large number of items.

```
PS > $spQuery.RowLimit = 100
```

Here, we set the `RowLimit` property to `100` so that only 100 list items are returned per page. The `RowLimit` value should be between 1 and 2000.

Finally, we can call the `GetItems` method with the `SPQuery` object instance we created earlier for input.

```
PS > $spListItemCollection = $spList.GetItems($spQuery)
```

In this example, we retrieve list items wrapped up in a `SPListItemCollection` object and store this object in a variable. We can now use the `ForEach-Object` cmdlet to iterate through the items and perform an action. In the next example, we change the text in the Notes field to "Updated using Windows PowerShell."

```
PS > $spListItemCollection | ForEach-Object {
>> $_["Notes"] = "Updated using Windows PowerShell"
>> $_.Update()
>> }
```

The `Get-SPListItem` function uses a CAML query to retrieve list items where the value of a specified field equals the value assigned to the function's `–value` parameter. The following is the complete function.

```
function Get-SPListItem (
  [string]$url,
  [string]$field,
  [string]$value,
  [int]$rowLimit = 100
  ) {

  # Use the Get-SPList function to retrieve a list
  $spList = Get-SPList -url $url

  # Create Query based on field and value
  $camlQuery =
  '<Where><Eq><FieldRef Name="' +
  $field +
  '"/><Value Type="' +
  $spList.Fields[$field].Type +
  '">' +
  $value +
  '</Value></Eq></Where>';

  # SPQuery object
  $spQuery = New-Object Microsoft.SharePoint.SPQuery;
```

```
# Add query
$spQuery.Query = $camlQuery;
# Set rowlimit
$spQuery.RowLimit = $rowLimit;

return $spList.GetItems($spQuery);
}
```

You can use the function by typing the following:

```
PS > $spListItem = Get-SPListItem `
>> -url "http://nimaintra.net/Lists/Custom List" `
>> -field Title -value "My List Item"
```

In this example, we use the `Get-SPListItem` function to retrieve all list items from the Custom List list where the Title field value equals My List Item.

Using the `GetItems` method without a CAML query returns a `SPListItemCollection` containing all items in the list. The following is an example of this.

```
PS > $spListItemCollection = $spList.GetItems()
```

You can use the `Where-Object` cmdlet to retrieve individual list items from the `SPListItemCollection` that match specified criteria. In the following example, we retrieve all list items where the value of the YesNo field equals `True`.

```
PS > $spListItemCollection | Where-Object { $_["YesNo"] -eq "True" }
```

If we want to perform an action on the list items where the value of the YesNo field equals `True`, we can use the `ForEach-Object` cmdlet, as shown here:

```
PS > $spListItemCollection | Where-Object { $_["YesNo"] -eq "True" } |
>> ForEach-Object {
>> $_["Choices"] = "Third Choice"
>> $_.Update()
>>}
```

In this example, we change the value of the Choices field to Third Choice.

NOTE   When using the `GetItems` method without a CAML query, all the items in the list are read into memory; therefore, large lists may consume a lot of memory.

Deleting List Items

To delete items from a list in SharePoint 2010, use the `Delete` method provided by the `SPListItem` class. In the next example, we use the `GetItemById` method to retrieve a list item, and then remove the item.

```
PS > $spList = Get-SPList -url http://nimaintra.net/Lists/Custom List"
PS > $spListItem = $spList.GetItemById(1)
PS > $spListItem.Delete()
```

Using the `Delete` method to remove a large number of list items will take time and consume a lot of memory, since it loads each list item into memory. A better approach to removing many items from a list is to use the `ProcessBatchData` method provided by the `SPWeb` class. First, you need a collection of the list items you want to remove, and then you can use the `Get-SPListItem` function to retrieve a list of items that match a given criteria, as shown in this example:

```
PS > $spListItemCollection =
>> Get-SPListItem -url "http://nimaintra.net/Lists/Custom List" `
>> -field Choices -value "Second Choice"
```

Now that we have a populated list item collection, we can create a CAML command string that we will use to remove all the list items in the list item collection. The first part of the CAML string contains the XML declaration followed by the `<Batch>` tag.

```
PS > $batchRemove = '<?xml version="1.0" encoding="UTF-8"?><Batch>'
```

Next, we need to add a batch string of commands for each list item that we want to delete. The CAML string used in the next example starts with the `<Method>` tag followed by the `<SetList Scope="Request">` tag where we define the scope.

```
PS > $command = '<Method><SetList Scope="Request">' +
>> $spList.ID +
>>'</SetList><SetVar Name="ID">{0}</SetVar>' +
>> '<SetVar Name="Cmd">Delete</SetVar></Method>'
```

In this example, we use the ID from the current list as value. Next, we use the `<SetVar Name="ID">` and set that `{0}` should be the value. Finally, we use the `<SetVar Name="Cmd">` tag and specify `Delete` as the type of command to be executed.

After we have created a CAML string, we will loop through each list item and append the query to the `batchRemove` variable.

```
PS > foreach ($item in $spListItemCollection) {
>> $batchRemove += $command -f $item.Id
>> }
```

Notice how we use the `-f` operator to replace the format string `{0}` with each list item's ID.

Finally, we complete the CAML query by closing the `<Batch>` tag.

```
PS > $batchRemove += "</Batch>"
```

The last step is to execute the command using the `ProcessBatchData` method of the `SPWeb` class.

```
PS > $spList.ParentWeb.ProcessBatchData($batchRemove) | Out-Null
```

The following function, `Remove-SPListItem`, demonstrates how to wrap the code in a reusable function so that we can remove one or more list items with a single line of code.

```
function Remove-SPListItem (
  [string]$url,
  [string]$field,
  [string]$value,
  [int]$rowLimit = 100
  ) {

  # Use the Get-SPList function to retrieve a list
  $spList = Get-SPList -url $url

  # Create Query based on field and value
  $camlQuery =
  '<Where><Eq><FieldRef Name="' +
  $field +
  '"/><Value Type="' +
  $spList.Fields[$field].Type +
  '">' +
  $value +
  '</Value></Eq></Where>';

  $spQuery = New-Object Microsoft.SharePoint.SPQuery;
  $spQuery.Query = $camlQuery;
  $spQuery.RowLimit = $rowLimit;

  $spListItemCollection = $spList.GetItems($spQuery);

  # Create batch remove CAML query
  $batchRemove = '<?xml version="1.0" encoding="UTF-8"?><Batch>';

  # The command is used for each list item retrieved
  $command = '<Method><SetList Scope="Request">' +
   $spList.ID +'</SetList><SetVar Name="ID">{0}</SetVar>' +
   '<SetVar Name="Cmd">Delete</SetVar></Method>';

  foreach ($item in $spListItemCollection) {
    # Loop through each list item and add the string
    # to the batch command
    $batchRemove += $command -f $item.Id;
  }
  $batchRemove += "</Batch>";
```

```
  # Remove the list items using the
  # batch command
  $spList.ParentWeb.ProcessBatchData($batchRemove) | Out-Null
}
```

Run the function by typing the following:

```
PS > Remove-SPListItem -url "http://nimaintra.net/Lists/Custom List" `
>> -field Choices -value "Second Choice"
```

This example removes all list items where the value of the Choices field equals Second Choice. The script removes list items in batches of 100, as it is specified as the default value in the function.

Copying List Items

To copy items from one list in SharePoint 2010 to another list, you can use the `AddItem` method provided by the `SPListItem` class, just as when you create new list items. The difference is that you read the field values from an existing list item and create a new list item in another list based on these values. This requires that both lists contain the same fields.

The first step in copying list items from a list in SharePoint 2010 is retrieving the items from the source list. You can do this by using the `GetItems` method provided by the `SPList` class. In this example, we use the Announcements list.

```
PS > $sourceSPList = Get-SPList -url "http://nimaintra.net/Lists/Announcements"
PS > $sourceSPListItemCollection = $sourceSPList.GetItems()
```

Some fields in either list are marked as read-only, so we cannot copy the values of those fields. We can handle this by looping through each field and checking if it is a read-only field. In this example, we store the available fields in a variable so that we can use it when we loop through the list items.

```
PS > $sourceSPFieldCollection = $sourceSPList.Fields
```

We also need to bind to the destination list. In this example, we retrieve the Announcements list from a different site.

```
PS > $destinationSPList =
>> Get-SPList -url "http://nimaintra.net/Site/Lists/Announcements"
```

Once we have retrieved the source list items and bound to the destination list, we can loop through each item and create it in the destination list. First, we open a `foreach` loop.

```
PS > foreach($spListItem in $sourceSPListItemCollection) {
```

In the `foreach` loop, we start by creating a new list item in the destination list.

```
>> $newSPListItem = $destinationSPList.AddItem()
```

Then we loop through each field stored in the `spFieldCollection` variable to exclude read-only fields and the Attachments field using an `if` statement. Copying the attachments requires a different approach, so we will handle them later in the loop.

```
>> foreach($spField in $sourceSPFieldCollection) {
>> if($spField.ReadOnlyField -ne $True -and `
>> $spField.InternalName -ne "Attachments") {
```

We then assign the values of every other field that is not read-only to the corresponding field of the new list item in the destination list. We also close the `if` statement and the `foreach` loop.

```
>> $newSPListItem[$($spField.InternalName)] =
>> $spListItem[$($spField.InternalName)]
>> }#end if
>> }#end foreach
```

Next, we handle the attachments. When adding attachments to a list item, we use the `Add` method provided by the `SPAttachmentCollection` class. The `Add` method supports the `leafName` parameter, which accepts a string containing the name of the file to be attached, and the `data` parameter, which accepts a byte array containing the actual attachment. First, we loop through the names of the list item's attachments.

```
>> foreach($leafName in $spListItem.Attachments) {
```

Next, we retrieve the actual attached file using the `GetFile` method provided by the `SPWeb` class. The `GetFile` method accepts a URL as input. We build the URL based on the `UrlPrefix` property of the `SPAttachmentCollection` object followed by the current attachment's name.

```
>> $spFile = $sourceSPList.ParentWeb.GetFile(
>> $($spListItem.Attachments.UrlPrefix + $leafName)
>> )
```

Once we have the `SPFile` object stored in a variable, we can use the `OpenBinary` method to retrieve the corresponding byte array and add the attachment to the new list item.

```
>> $newSPListItem.Attachments.Add($leafName, $spFile.OpenBinary())
>> } #end foreach
```

The last step is to commit the changes in the destination list using the `Update` method.

```
>> $newSPListItem.Update()
>> #end foreach
```

The function `Copy-SPListItem`, shown next, wraps up all the code used in this example.

```
function Copy-SPListItem ([string]$source, [string]$destination) {

  # Get source list
  $sourceSPList = Get-SPList -url $source
  $sourceSPFieldCollection = $sourceSPList.Fields;
  $sourceSPListItemCollection = $sourceSPList.GetItems();

  # Get destination list
  $destinationSPList = Get-SPList -url $destination

  # Loop through each list Item and copy to destination list
  foreach($spListItem in $sourceSPListItemCollection) {
    # Create new Item
    $newSPListItem = $destinationSPList.AddItem();
    foreach($spField in $sourceSPFieldCollection) {
      # At first check fields that are not read only and attachments
      if ($spField.ReadOnlyField -ne $True -and `
        $spField.InternalName -ne "Attachments") {
        # Store value in new SPListItem object
        $newSPListItem[$($spField.InternalName)] =
          $spListItem[$($spField.InternalName)];
      }
    }
    # Handle Attachments
    foreach($leafName in $spListItem.Attachments) {
      $spFile = $sourceSPList.ParentWeb.GetFile(
       $($spListItem.Attachments.UrlPrefix + $leafName)
      );

      $newSPListItem.Attachments.Add($leafName, $spFile.OpenBinary());
    }
    # Update Item
    $newSPListItem.Update();
  }
}
```

You can use the function by typing the following:

```
PS > Copy-SPListItem `
>> -source http://nimaintra.net/Lists/Announcements `
>> -destination http://nimaintra.net/Site/Lists/Announcements
```

When we run this example, the script copies all the items stored in http://nimaintra.net/Lists/Announcements to the Announcements list in the subsite `Site`.

Additional Functionality in SharePoint 2010

SharePoint 2010 offers the capability to update the properties of multiple items at the same time through the graphical user interface. This became possible in SharePoint 2010 thanks to the introduction of check boxes and the Ribbon, allowing users to perform actions on more than one item at a time. Users can also use the Datasheet view when updating multiple list items.

Copying items from one list to another is possible only for documents in document libraries, and it is possible to copy only one item at a time using the Send To Other Location feature, as shown in Figure 15-3. This feature enables you to set up a relationship between the source document and the target document so that the author can get a notification in case the document is changed. In SharePoint lists based on other templates—such as calendars, task lists, and custom lists—this option is not available.

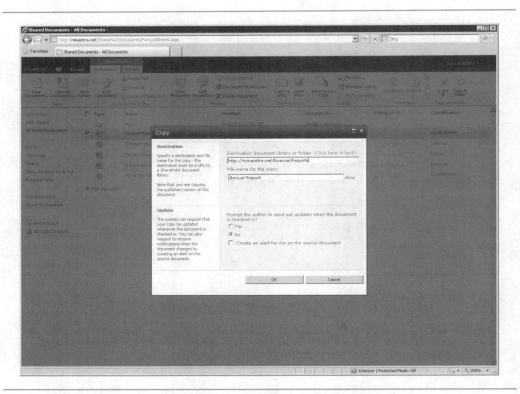

Figure 15-3. Copying a document from one document library to another

Summary

In this chapter, we looked at how to work with list items using Windows PowerShell. We demonstrated creating, updating, and removing list items in SharePoint 2010.

When managing list items, it is important to try to minimize the performance impact by optimizing the queries used, since working with large lists could generate large amount of SQL queries and consume a lot of system resources. A good way to do that is to use CAML queries together with the `GetItems` method supported by `SPList` objects.

In the last scenario, we presented an example of how to copy list items from a source list to a destination list using Windows PowerShell, including how to copy list item attachments.

SharePoint 2010 allows users to update and delete multiple list items through the graphical user interface. However, in some cases, you will want to look for specific values in lists or copy entire lists, which can be done programmatically in scripts.

In document libraries, you can send documents to other locations, which creates a parent-child relationship. This is possible only with document libraries, and not with other types of lists.

CHAPTER 16 | Managing Documents in Document Libraries

Whether SharePoint has been available in your company for years or it has recently been implemented, you might face situations where you need to handle a large amount of documents. For example, you might need to migrate file shares or documents stored outside SharePoint into SharePoint document libraries.

In this chapter, we will look at automating management of documents in document libraries. First, we will explore how to create new libraries and modify the properties of existing ones. Next, we will describe how to upload files to a document library, and then create a PowerShell function that can be used when moving documents, such as from file shares into SharePoint. We will also look at how to copy documents between document libraries and create a script that can be used to automate the process.

As mentioned in the previous chapter, SharePoint 2010 now offers the capability to modify the metadata of multiple files or list items at the same time. In a similar fashion, it is also possible to execute other actions, such as checking in and checking out multiple documents. In document libraries where there are mandatory fields, documents will not become available to end users until the mandatory fields contain data. This can sometimes be a problem if end users upload documents by opening the document library in a Windows Explorer window (accessing it by means of the WebDAV protocol), where they will not be able to fill in the mandatory fields. Here, we will look at how to manage checked-out documents and also create a function for checking in and checking out all documents in a document library.

In our last scenario, we will enable the use of content types in a document library. We will then create a new content type using PowerShell and apply it to our document library.

Working with Document Libraries

Working with document libraries is similar to working with SharePoint lists, as described in the preceding chapters. To demonstrate, we'll create a new document library and then show how to add items to document libraries.

Creating Document Libraries

Creating a new document library using Windows PowerShell is similar to creating any other type of list. You can use the same Add method provided by the SPListCollection class. This example demonstrates how to create a document library using the New-SPList function described in Chapter 14.

```
PS > New-SPList -url http://nimaintra.net/Site -name "My Docs" `
>> -description "My Document Library" -template DocumentLibrary
```

To retrieve a library in SharePoint 2010, use the Get-SPList function, just as when retrieving lists.

```
PS > $spDocumentLibrary = Get-SPList -url "http://nimaintra.net/Site/My Docs"
```

Document libraries in SharePoint 2010 inherit many properties and methods from the SPList class, but also include specific properties and methods available only for document libraries. For instance, to check if a document library is a gallery, such as Site Templates, List Templates, Web Parts, or Master Pages, use the IsCatalog property of the SPDocumentLibrary class.

```
PS > $spDocumentLibrary.IsCatalog
False
```

Here, the property returned False because the document library is not a gallery.

You can use the IsCatalog property if you are looping through a collection of document libraries and want to exclude galleries. In the next example, we use the GetListsOfType method to retrieve a collection of all document libraries in a site, and then we use the Where-Object cmdlet to pick out only the document libraries where the IsCatalog property is not equal to True. Finally, we use the ForEach-Object cmdlet and perform an action on each of the document libraries.

```
PS > $spWeb = Get-SPWeb -Identity http://nimaintra.net/Site
PS > $spWeb.GetListsOfType("DocumentLibrary") |
>> Where-Object { $_.IsCatalog -ne $true } |
>> ForEach-Object { Write-Host $_.Title }
```

There are other useful properties that can be set when creating or updating a document library, such as versioning settings, which we will discuss in the next chapter.

SharePoint document libraries may have folders to better organize the contents of the library. These folders can be created using the same AddItem method used for adding new list items. The difference is that you use another overload definition of this method, which also accepts a value of type Microsoft.SharePoint .SPFileSystemObjectType that instructs it whether the new item is a file or a folder.

```
PS > $spFolder = $spDocumentLibrary.AddItem(
>> "",[Microsoft.SharePoint.SPFileSystemObjectType]::Folder,"My New Folder")

PS > $spFolder.Update()
```

The ability to create folders can be enabled or disabled from the graphical user interface. This setting can also be modified by Windows PowerShell through the EnableFolderCreation property.

```
PS > $spDocumentLibrary.EnableFolderCreation = $false
PS > $spDocumentLibrary.Update()
```

 NOTE   Even if the EnableFolderCreation property is set to False, you can still create folders using the SharePoint object model, such as with Windows PowerShell.

To remove a document library, use the Delete method—again, just as with lists.

```
PS > $spDocumentLibrary.Delete()
```

Uploading and Managing Files

To upload files to a SharePoint document library, use the Add method provided by the Microsoft.SharePoint.SPFileCollection class, which represents a collection of SPFile objects in SharePoint 2010.

Before you can access a file collection in SharePoint 2010, you must create an instance of the Microsoft.SharePoint.SPFolder class using the GetFolder method provided by the Microsoft.SharePoint.SPWeb class. This example demonstrates how to use the GetFolder method on the Shared Documents document library.

```
PS > $spWeb = Get-SPWeb -Identity http://nimaintra.net/Site
PS > $spFolder = $spWeb.GetFolder("Shared Documents")
```

Once you have bound to the document library, you can store the file collection in a new variable, which you can later use to add files, as follows:

```
PS > $spFileCollection = $spFolder.Files
```

The Add method provided by the Microsoft.SharePoint.SPFileCollection class is used to create a file in a file collection. This is very versatile method that has 21 overload definitions. For the one that we will be using in our example, we need to specify the file's relative URL, a byte array containing the file, and a Boolean value that determines whether an existing file with the same name should be overwritten. Let's take a look at the byte array first.

It is possible to expose a sequence of bytes using the System.IO.FileStream class, which we can pass on to the Add method. A simple way of retrieving an object of the type System.IO.FileStream is by using the OpenRead method provided by the System.IO.FileInfo class. When using the Get-ChildItem cmdlet on a file, we get an object of the type System.IO.FileInfo, as shown here:

```
PS > $file = Get-ChildItem C:\Documents\MyDoc.docx
PS > $file.GetType().FullName
System.IO.FileInfo
```

Now we can use the OpenRead method when adding a new file to a SharePoint library.

```
PS > $spFile =
>> $spFileCollection.Add("Shared Documents/MyDoc.docx",$file.OpenRead(),$false)
```

In this example, we store the object returned by the Add method in a variable. This allows us to add more information, such as metadata, to the file in SharePoint 2010. We add metadata using an object of the type Microsoft.SharePoint.SPListItem, which we retrieve using the Item property. In the next example, we store the object in a variable and change the value of the list item's Modified field, and finally use the Update method to commit the changes to the content database.

```
PS > $spListItem = $spFile.Item
PS > $spListItem["Modified"] = (Get-Date 8/2/1987)
PS > $spListItem.Update()
```

The Upload-SPFile function, shown next, wraps up the code described previously in a reusable function.

```
function Upload-SPFile([string]$url, [array]$files, [switch]$overwrite) {

  # Use the Get-SPList function to retrieve a list
  $spList = Get-SPList -url $url
  $spFolder = $SPList.RootFolder
  $spFileCollection = $spFolder.Files

  # Loop through each file in the array
  foreach($file in $files) {
    $docURL = $spList.RootFolder.Name + "/" + (Split-Path $file -Leaf)

    # Check if file already exists
    if(-not($overwrite) -and $spList.ParentWeb.GetFile($docURL).Exists) {
      Write-Host "File $file already exists"
      Continue
    }
    # Split-Path used to return the file name
    $spFileCollection.Add(
      $docURL,
      $((Get-ChildItem $file).OpenRead()),
      $overwrite
    ) | Out-Null
  }
}
```

Run the Upload-SPFile function by typing the following:

```
PS > Upload-SPFile -url "http://nimaintra.net/Shared Documents" `
>> -files C:\Myfile\MyDoc.docx -overwrite
```

You can also use the Upload-SPFile function to add multiple files to a library in SharePoint. In the next example, we use the Get-ChildItem cmdlet and retrieve all items in a specific directory with the docx or pptx file extension, and send those objects through a pipeline to the `Select-Object` cmdlet, retrieving the items' full names with the `ExpandProperty` parameter.

```
PS > Get-ChildItem C:\Documents\* -Include "*.docx","*.pptx" |
>> Select-Object -ExpandProperty FullName
C:\Documents\Annual Report.docx
C:\Documents\Content guidence.pptx
C:\Documents\Document Policy.docx
C:\Documents\Nima Design Principles.pptx
C:\Documents\Projects.xlsx
```

The output from this example could be stored in a variable and then used as input for the `Upload-SPFile` function, like this:

```
PS > $arrFiles = Get-ChildItem C:\Documents\* -Include "*.docx","*.pptx" |
>> Select-Object -ExpandProperty FullName
PS > Upload-SPFile -url "http://nimaintra.net/Shared Documents" `
>> -files $arrFiles -overwrite
```

In this example, we add the –overwrite switch parameter, which is used to overwrite existing files. Note that if a file is checked out, the command will not work. Later in this chapter, we will demonstrate how to handle checked-out documents using Windows PowerShell.

Copying Documents Between Document Libraries

To copy files from one document library to another using Windows PowerShell, you can use the `Add` method supported by the `Microsoft.SharePoint.SPFileCollection` class, just as when uploading a file to a document library.

Let's start with retrieving the document libraries. In this example, we use the `Get-SPList` function described in Chapter 14 to bind to the document libraries and store the destination file collection in a variable.

```
PS > $sourceSPList = Get-SPList -url "http://nimaintra.net/Shared Documents"
PS > $destSPList = Get-SPList -url "http://nimaintra.net/Site/Shared Documents"
PS > $spFileCollection = $destSPList.RootFolder.Files
```

Once we have retrieved the document libraries, we can loop through each file in the source document library and create it in the destination document library using a `foreach` loop.

```
PS > foreach($item in $sourceSPList.Items) {
```

In the `foreach` loop, we start by retrieving the current file using the `GetFile` method.

```
>> $file = $sourceSPList.ParentWeb.GetFile($item.File)
```

Then we store the destination file's relative URL in a variable. In the example, we replace the root folder name so that the destination file's URL corresponds with the destination document library.

```
>> $targetDocUrl = $file.Url -replace $sourceSPList.RootFolder.Name,
>> $destSPList.RootFolder.Name
```

Files stored in a document library may be placed in folders and subfolders, so we need to take this into consideration. A simple way of checking if a folder exists is by using the GetFolder method and checking the Exists property, as demonstrated here:

```
>> if(-not($destSPList.ParentWeb.GetFolder($file.ParentFolder.Url).Exists)) {
```

If the folder doesn't exist, we iterate through each parent folder using a for loop. In the next example, we split the folder's URL, loop through each segment, and create each folder in the destination document library.

```
>> $folderURL = $file.Url.Split("/")
>> $addFolder = $folderURL[0]
>> for($i=1;$i -lt ($folderURL.Count -1);$i++) {
>> $addFolder = $addFolder + "/" + $folderURL[$i]
>> $destSPList.ParentWeb.Folders.Add($addFolder) | Out-Null
>> } # end for loop
>> $addFolder = $null
>> } # end if
```

Next, we check if the file already exists. If it does, we continue with the next object in the pipeline.

```
>> if(-not($overwrite) -and $destSPList.ParentWeb
.GetFile($targetDocUrl).Exists) {
>> Write-Host "File $targetDocUrl already exists"
>> Continue
>> } # end if
```

Finally, we use the Add method to create the file in the destination document library.

```
>> $spFileCollection.Add($targetDocUrl,$file.OpenBinary(),$false) | Out-Null
>> } # end foreach
```

The function Copy-SPDocumentLibrary wraps up all the code used in this example.

```
function Copy-SPDocumentLibrary(
  [string]$source,
  [string]$destination,
  [switch]$overwrite
```

```
) {
# Get source list
$sourceSPList = Get-SPList -url $source
# Get destination list
$destSPList = Get-SPList -url $destination
$spFileCollection = $destSPList.RootFolder.Files
# Loop through each item and copy to destination list
foreach($item in $sourceSPList.Items) {
  $file = $sourceSPList.ParentWeb.GetFile($item.File)
  $targetDocUrl = $file.Url -replace $sourceSPList.RootFolder.Name,
   $destSPList.RootFolder.Name
  # Check if folder exists
  if(-not($destSPList.ParentWeb.GetFolder($file.ParentFolder.Url).Exists)) {
    # Check each subfolder
    $folderURL = $file.Url.Split("/")
    $addFolder = $folderURL[0]
    for($i=1;$i -lt ($folderURL.Count -1);$i++) {
      $addFolder = $addFolder + "/" + $folderURL[$i]
      $destSPList.ParentWeb.Folders.Add($addFolder) | Out-Null
    }
  $addFolder = $null
  }
  # Check if target file exists
  if(-not($overwrite) -and `
   $destSPList.ParentWeb.GetFile($targetDocUrl).Exists) {
    Write-Host "File $targetDocUrl already exists"
    Continue
  }
  $spFileCollection.Add(
    $targetDocUrl,
    $file.OpenBinary(),
    $overwrite
  ) | Out-Null
 }
}
```

You can use the function by typing the following:

```
PS > Copy-SPDocumentLibrary -source "http://nimaintra.net/Shared Documents"
>> -destination "http://nimaintra.net/Site/Shared Documents"
```

This example does not copy files that exist in the destination document library. If you want to overwrite existing files, use the overwrite switch parameter, as follows:

```
PS > Copy-SPDocumentLibrary -source "http://nimaintra.net/Shared Documents"
>> -destination "http://nimaintra.net/Site/Shared Documents" -overwrite
```

Checking Out Files

Checking out files in a document library using Windows PowerShell is done with the `CheckOut` method provided by the `Microsoft.SharePoint.SPFile` class. We will start our example by retrieving an existing file using the `GetFile` method.

```
PS > $spWeb = Get-SPWeb -Identity http://nimaintra.net
PS > $spFile = $spWeb.GetFile("Shared Documents/MyDoc.docx")
```

Here, we store an instance of the `Microsoft.SharePoint.SPFile` object in the `spFile` variable.

Before checking out a file from a document library, it is a good idea to see if the file is already checked out. The `Microsoft.SharePoint.SPFile` class provides the `CheckOutType` property, which indicates how a file is checked out.

```
PS > $spFile.CheckOutType
None
```

The return value of `None` tells us that the file is not checked out. The other values `CheckOutType` can return are `Offline`, which indicates that the file is checked out for editing on the local computer, and `Online`, which indicates that the file is checked out for editing on the server.

Next, we store a check-out type in a variable and use it when checking out a file. The `CheckOut` method also supports the `lastModifiedDate` property, which indicates that the file should not be checked out if it has been modified after a specified date. In this example, we set the value to a null reference.

```
PS > $spCheckOutType = >>
[Microsoft.SharePoint.SPFile+SPCheckOutType]::Online
PS > $spFile.CheckOut($spCheckOutType,$null)
```

The `Microsoft.SharePoint.SPFile` class provides additional properties that you can use to gather information regarding the file. In the following example, we use the `Format-List` cmdlet to display some of the check-out properties supported.

```
PS > $spFile | Format-List -Property CheckOutType, CheckedOutDate, CheckedOutBy
CheckOutType    : Online
CheckedOutDate  : 6/1/2010 1:08:52 PM
CheckedOutBy    : SHAREPOINT\system
```

The following script, Invoke-SPFileCheckout.ps1, checks out one or multiple files in a SharePoint document library.

```
<#
.SYNOPSIS
Checks out files in a SharePoint document library.
```

```
.DESCRIPTION
The script checks out a single file or loops
through a document library and checks out all files.

.PARAMETER url
Site URL.

.PARAMETER folder
Folder/Document library name

.PARAMETER file
File name

.PARAMETER checkOutType
Checkout type Online or Offline

.PARAMETER all
Checks out all files.
#>

param(
  [string]$url,
  [string]$folder,
  [string]$file,
  [string]$checkOutType,
  [switch]$all
)

# Check if Snap-in is loaded
if(-not(
  Get-PSSnapin | Where { $_.Name -eq "Microsoft.SharePoint.PowerShell"})
) {
  Add-PSSnapin Microsoft.SharePoint.PowerShell;
}

$spWeb = Get-SPWeb -Identity $url;

# Check if All files should be checked out
if($all) {

  # Get the folder
  $spFolder = $spWeb.GetFolder($folder);
  # Store file collection in a variable
  $spFileCollection = $spFolder.Files;
```

```
  # Loop through files and check out if
  # file is not already checked out
  $spFileCollection | ForEach-Object {
    # Check if file is not checked out
    if($_.CheckOutType -eq "None") {
      # check out file
      $_.CheckOut($checkOutType,$null);
      Write-Host $_.Name checked out;
    } else {
      Write-Host $_.Name already checked out;
    }
  }
} else {
  # Store file path in a variable
  $fileURL = $folder + "/" + $file;
  $spFile = $spWeb.GetFile($fileURL);
  # Check if file is not checked out
  if($spFile.CheckOutType -eq "None") {
    # Check out file
    $spFile.CheckOut($checkOutType,$null);
    Write-Host $spFile.Name checked out;
  } else {
    Write-Host $spFile.Name already checked out;
  }
}
$spWeb.Dispose()
```

To check out a single file in a document library, run the script as follows:

```
PS > .\Invoke-SPFileCheckout.ps1 -url http://nimaintra.net `
>> -folder "Shared Documents" -file MyDoc.docx -checkOutType Online
```

To check out all files in a document library, use the -all switch parameter.

```
PS > .\Invoke-SPFileCheckout.ps1 -url http://nimaintra.net `
>> -folder "Shared Documents" -checkOutType Online -all
```

Checking In Files

To check in files in a document library, use the CheckIn method provided by the Microsoft.SharePoint.SPFile class. The CheckIn method supports the Comment parameter, which you can use to add a comment to the newly created version of the

document. You can also specify the type of check-in for a file using the `Microsoft`
`.SharePoint.SPCheckinType` enumeration, which contains the following members:

- `MinorCheckIn` represents a minor version.
- `MajorCheckIn` represents a major version.
- `OverwriteCheckIn` causes the method to overwrite the current minor version.

In this example, we specify a comment and check in a file as a minor version.

```
PS > $spWeb = Get-SPWeb -Identity http://nimaintra.net
PS > $spFile = $spWeb.GetFile("Shared Documents/MyDoc.docx")
PS > $spFile.CheckIn("Checked in using PowerShell",
>> [Microsoft.SharePoint.SPCheckinType]::MinorCheckIn)
```

If the currently checked-out file is a major version and you try to overwrite the
existing file when checking in, an error occurs. A simple and effective way of handling
terminating errors, such as the one that occurs when trying to overwrite a major
version of a file when checking in, is to use the `Try`, `Catch`, and `Finally` blocks
supported by Windows PowerShell.

```
PS > Try {
>> $spCheckinType = [Microsoft.SharePoint.SPCheckinType]::OverwriteCheckIn
>> $spFile.CheckIn("Checked in using PowerShell",$spCheckinType)
>> } Catch {
>> "You cannot overwrite a major version file"
>> $check = $true
>> } Finally {
>> if($check -eq $true) {
>> "Error occured"
>> } else {
>> "Success"
>> }
>> $check = $null
>> }
```

We start with a `Try` block containing the code we want to test. If the `CheckIn`
method returns an error, the `Catch` block will handle the error and output "You cannot
overwrite a major version file" before setting the variable `check` to `True`. The `Finally`
block runs every time, even if the `Try` block runs without any errors, so we include
an `if` statement and check the `check` variable used in the `Catch` block. If an error has
occurred, the `check` variable contains a value of `True`, and "Error occurred" will be
written to the output; otherwise "Success" will be reported. Before closing the `Finally`
block, we set the `check` variable to null.

NOTE   The `Try`, `Catch`, and `Finally` blocks must run on the same thread. The code used in the previous example will return an error if it is run interactively in a standard Windows PowerShell console and the `ThreadOption` is not set to `ReuseThread`. However, in the SharePoint 2010 Management shell, each line runs on the same thread, so the code works fine. It is also possible to write the code on the same line. Functions and scripts run on the same thread, so the `Try`, `Catch`, and `Finally` blocks can be written on separate lines when writing scripts or functions including them.

The following `Invoke-SPFileCheckin.ps1` script automates the procedure of checking in files in a document library.

```
<#
.SYNOPSIS
Checks in files in a SharePoint document library.

.DESCRIPTION
The script checks in a single file or loops
through a document library and checks in all files.

.PARAMETER url
Site URL.

.PARAMETER folder
Folder/Document library name

.PARAMETER file
File name

.PARAMETER comment
Version comment

.PARAMETER checkinType
Checkin type, can be: Major,
Minor or Overwrite

.PARAMETER all
Checks out all files.
#>

param(
    [string]$url,
    [string]$folder,
    [string]$file,
    [string]$comment,
    [string]$checkinType,
    [switch]$all
)
```

```
# Check if Snap-in is loaded
if(-not(
  Get-PSSnapin | Where { $_.Name -eq "Microsoft.SharePoint.PowerShell"})
) {
  Add-PSSnapin Microsoft.SharePoint.PowerShell;
}

# Use a switch to get checkin type,
# defaults to minor version if value not within range.

switch($checkinType) {
 {$_ -match "^major" } {
  $spCheckinType = [Microsoft.SharePoint.SPCheckinType]::MajorCheckIn;
 }
 {$_ -match "^minor" } {
  $spCheckinType = [Microsoft.SharePoint.SPCheckinType]::MinorCheckIn;
 }
 {$_ -match "^overwrite" } {
  $spCheckinType = [Microsoft.SharePoint.SPCheckinType]::OverwriteCheckIn;
 }
 Default {
  $spCheckinType = [Microsoft.SharePoint.SPCheckinType]::MinorCheckIn;
 }
}


$spWeb = Get-SPWeb $url

# Check if All files should be checked out
if ($all) {

  # Get the folder
  $spFolder = $spWeb.GetFolder($folder);

  # Store file collection in a variable
  $spFileCollection = $spFolder.Files;

  # Loop through files and check out if
  # file is not already checked out

  $spFileCollection | ForEach-Object {

    # Check if file is not checked in
    if ($_.CheckOutType -ne "None") {

      Try {
        $_.CheckIn($comment,$spCheckinType);
      } Catch {
```

```
          "You cannot overwrite a major version file";
          $check = $true;
        } Finally {
          if ($check -eq $true) {
            Write-Host $_.Name Not Checked in;
          } else {
            Write-Host $_.Name checked in;
          }
          $check = $null;
        }

    } else {
      Write-Host $_.Name already checked in;
    }
  }
} else {

  # Store file URL in a variable
  $fileURL = $folder + "/" + $file;
  $spFile = $spWeb.GetFile($fileURL);

  # Check if file is not checked in
  if ($spFile.CheckOutType -ne "None") {

    Try {
      $spFile.CheckIn($comment,$spCheckinType);
    } Catch {
      "You cannot overwrite a major version file";
      $check = $true;
    } Finally {
      if ($check -eq $true) {
        Write-Host $spFile.Name Not Checked in;
      } else {
        Write-Host $spFile.Name checked in;
      }
      $check = $null;
    }
  } else {
    Write-Host $spFile.Name already checked in;
  }
}
$spWeb.Dispose()
```

To use the `Invoke-SPFileCheckin.ps1` script to check in a single file, type the following:

```
PS > .\Invoke-SPFileCheckin.ps1 -url http://nimaintra.net `
>> -folder "Shared Documents" -file MyDoc.docx -checkinType minor
```

To check in all the files in a document library, use the `-all` switch.

```
PS > .\Invoke-SPFileCheckin.ps1 -url http://nimaintra.net `
>> -folder "Shared Documents" -checkinType minor -all
```

Managing Content Types

A content type is a reusable object in SharePoint that allows you to centrally define different types of content with, for instance, metadata and workflows. For example, you might use a content type to ensure that all Microsoft PowerPoint presentations always use the same template and metadata. By creating a content type and making it available in all document libraries, end users will be able to click the New button in the document library and find the template. Also, the mandatory metadata needs to be filled in before the document can be saved.

Content types can easily be created using Windows PowerShell and the `SPContentType` class. SharePoint comes with a number of content types. Your new content types need to derive from any of the root content types or from any other content type you create. You also need to specify which content type collection it should be added to and its name.

In the next example, we use the `New-Object` cmdlet to create an instance of the `Microsoft.SharePoint.SPContentType` class and store it in a variable. The `New-Object` cmdlet supports the `-ArgumentList` parameter, which we use to pass a list of arguments to the constructor of the `Microsoft.SharePoint.SPContentType` class.

```
PS > $spWeb = Get-SPWeb -Identity http://nimaintra.net
PS > $contentType = New-Object Microsoft.SharePoint.SPContentType -ArgumentList `
>> @($spWeb.ContentTypes["Document"],
>> $spWeb.ContentTypes, "Company Presentation")
```

You can set a number of properties on a content type, including the document template to be used and the set of fields that should be associated with the content type. In this example, we specify a group that a content type should belong to by using the `Group` property. When we have set the group name, we use the `Add` method provided by the `Microsoft.SharePoint.ContentTypeCollection` class. If the group does not exist, SharePoint will create it when adding the new content type.

```
PS > $contentType.Group = "Nima Document Content types"
PS > $spContentTypeCollection = $spWeb.ContentTypes
PS > $spContentTypeCollection.Add($contentType)
```

The content type collection contains all the content types available on a site. To get a list of the content types available, we can pipe the collection to the `Select-Object` cmdlet and retrieve the `Name` property. The list now includes the Company Presentation content type we created in the previous example.

```
PS > $spContentTypeCollection | Select-Object -Property Name
```

Now our new content type is available to all sites within the site collection, but in our scenario, we also want to associate the content type with a specific SharePoint document library. In this case, we need to use the `Microsoft.SharePoint.SPList` object. In the following example, we get the Company Presentation content type by using the `Where-Object` cmdlet and filtering on the content type's name. Then we use the returned content type as input to the `Add` method of the relevant `SPDocumentLibrary` object.

```
PS > $contentType = $spContentTypeCollection |
>> Where-Object {$_.Name -eq "Company Presentation"}
PS > $spDocumentLibrary =
>> Get-SPList -url "http://nimaintra.net/Shared Documents"
PS > $spDocumentLibrary.ContentTypes.Add($contentType)
```

The following `Add-SPContentTypeToList` function can be used to add existing content types to a specific list.

```
function Add-SPContentTypeToList ([string]$url, [string]$contentType) {

  # Use the Get-SPList function to retrieve a list
  $spList = Get-SPList -url $url
  $spWeb = $spList.ParentWeb

  # Get the content type
  $spContentType = $spWeb.ContentTypes |
   Where-Object { $_.Name -eq $contentType }

  # Check if the content type exists
  if (-not([string]::IsNullOrEmpty($spContentType))) {
    # Store the list content types in a collection
    $spContentTypeCollection = $spList.ContentTypes;
    # If content type does not exist in list, add it
    if (-not($spContentTypeCollection | Where { $_.Name -eq $contentType })) {
      $spList.ContentTypes.Add($spContentType);
    } else {
      Write-Host "The content type specified already exists";
    }
  } else {
    Write-Host "The content type specified does not exist";
  }
  $spWeb.Dispose()
}
```

You can use the function to add a new content type to a document library by typing the following:

```
PS > Add-SPContentTypeToList -url "http://nimaintra.net/Shared Documents" `
>> -contentType "Company Presentation"
```

Additional Functionality in SharePoint 2010

If a document library contains documents that do not have a checked-in version due to the absence of metadata in the mandatory fields, users with sufficient permissions can take ownership and check in the documents so that they become available to all users. Figure 16-1 shows the Settings page for taking ownership of the checked-out files.

Content types can be managed by users with sufficient permissions through the Site Content Types gallery, as shown in Figure 16-2. In SharePoint 2010, you can reuse content types between site collections and Web applications as long as they share the same managed metadata service application. This is done by designating a site collection to be the content type hub in the connection properties of the managed metadata service application. The publishing of each content type in the content type hub can then be managed separately. By means of timer jobs, the content types are published on regular basis to the consuming Web applications and site collections.

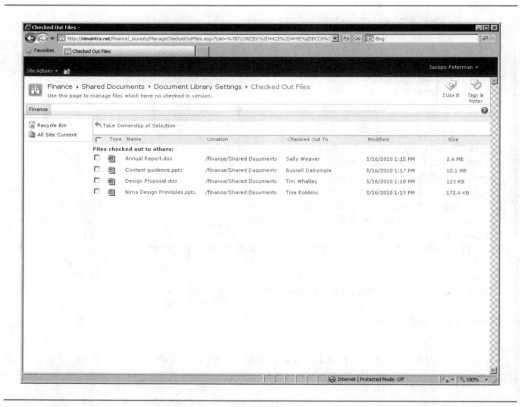

Figure 16-1. Managing files that have no checked-in version

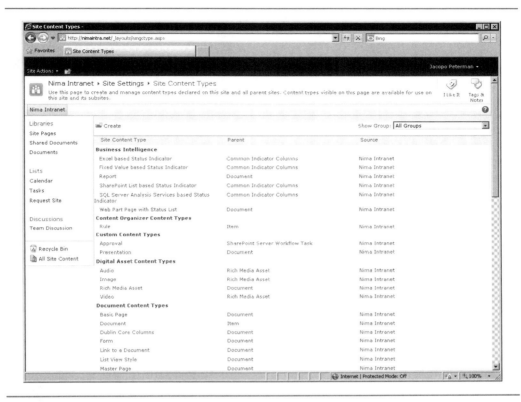

Figure 16-2.   The gallery of site content types

Summary

In this chapter, we looked at how to manage document libraries and their contents using Windows PowerShell. Manipulating document libraries works in much the same way as manipulating SharePoint lists, and in the first scenario we demonstrated this by showing how to connect to and change the properties of a document library. In the next scenario, we looked at how it is possible to upload documents to a document library using the AddItem method, and we created a function that could be used when creating scripts to migrate files from something like a file share into SharePoint.

Next, we created two functions that handle the checking in and checking out of documents to demonstrate how to manage changes to multiple documents. We also looked at the Try, Catch, and Finally blocks, which are useful for handling termination errors.

Finally, we covered how to create content types using Windows PowerShell.

CHAPTER 17 | Managing Versioning

SharePoint 2010 offers a lot of features for enterprise document management. One commonly used feature is versioning, where you have the option to store both major and minor versions of files and list items. Content approval gives you the opportunity to hide minor versions from end users, leaving only published major versions visible.

One downside to versioning is that each version is stored as a full copy of the document or list item in the content database. Suppose that an end user has a 10MB PowerPoint presentation and has saved it ten times, generating ten versions. That will use 100MB of space in the content database. If the document library also allows minor versions, an additional copy will be added for each minor version, which can result in insufficient disk space on the back-end SQL Server.

In this chapter, we will demonstrate how to use Windows PowerShell to set the content approval, version history, draft item security, and check-out settings on lists and document libraries in SharePoint 2010.

Content Approval

Content approval makes it possible to have versions of list items or files in a pending state until the item or file is approved. While the item or file is waiting for approval, it will not be available to end users who do not have sufficient permissions.

Both the SPList and SPDocumentLibrary classes support the EnableModeration property. Setting this property to True enables content approval for a list or document library.

```
PS > $spDocumentLibrary =
>> Get-SPList -url "http://nimaintra.net/site/Shared Documents"
PS > $spDocumentLibrary.EnableModeration = $true
PS > $spDocumentLibrary.Update()
```

The following function, Set-SPContentApproval, enables or disables content approval for a list or a document library.

```
function Set-SPContentApproval (
  [string]$url,
  [switch]$enable,
  [switch]$disable
  ) {

  # Use the Get-SPList function to retrieve a list
  $spList = Get-SPList -url $url
  if ($enable) {
    # Enable content approval
```

```
    $spList.EnableModeration = $true;
  }
  if ($disable) {
    # Disable content approval
    $spList.EnableModeration = $false;
  }
  $spList.Update();
}
```

To use the function to enable content approval for a list or document library, type the following:

```
PS > Set-SPContentApproval -url "http://nimaintra.net/Shared Documents" `
>> -enable
```

To disable content approval, use the –disable parameter.

```
PS > Set-SPContentApproval -url "http://nimaintra.net/Shared Documents" `
>> -disable
```

Version History

By default, version history is not enabled in any new lists or document libraries. When enabling version history in a list, you have the option to create a version each time an item in the list is edited. Document libraries also support major and minor versions, such as 1.0, 1.1, and so on.

The SPList and the SPDocumentLibrary classes include the EnableVersioning property. The following example demonstrates how to enable version history in a list in SharePoint 2010.

```
PS > $spList = Get-SPList -url "http://nimaintra.net/site/Lists/My Custom List"
PS > $spList.EnableVersioning = $true
PS > $spList.Update()
```

The SPDocumentLibrary class also provides the EnableMinorVersions property, which you can use as follows:

```
PS > $spDocumentLibrary =
>> Get-SPList -url "http://nimaintra.net/site/Shared Documents"
PS > $spDocumentLibrary.EnableVersioning = $true
PS > $spDocumentLibrary.EnableMinorVersions = $true
PS > $spDocumentLibrary.Update()
```

You can also specify the number of versions to retain using the MajorVersionLimit property, and the number of major (published and/or approved) versions for which drafts should be kept using the `MajorWithMinorVersionsLimit` property supported by both lists and document libraries. The next example shows how to set the number of major versions to retain and the number of versions for which drafts should be kept in a document library.

```
PS > $spDocumentLibrary.MajorVersionLimit = 10
PS > $spDocumentLibrary.MajorWithMinorVersionsLimit = 5
PS > $spDocumentLibrary.Update()
```

NOTE When setting the `MajorWithMinorVersionsLimit` property on an `SPList`, content approval must be enabled.

The following `Set-SPVersionHistory` function supports both lists and documents.

```
function Set-SPVersionHistory (
  [string]$url,
  [switch]$enable,
  [switch]$enableMinor,
  [switch]$disable,
  [int]$version=0,
  [int]$draft=0
) {

  # Use the Get-SPList function to retrieve a list
  $spList = Get-SPList -url $url

  if ($enable -or $enableMinor) {
    # Enable Versioning
    $spList.EnableVersioning = $true;
    if($enableMinor -and `
     $spList -is [Microsoft.SharePoint.SPDocumentLibrary]) {
      # Enable Major and Minor Version
      $spList.EnableMinorVersions = $true;
    }
    # Set number of versions to keep
    $spList.MajorVersionLimit = $version;

    # Set the number of versions for which drafts should be kept
    if ($spList.EnableModeration -eq $true) {
      $spList.MajorWithMinorVersionsLimit = $draft
    } else {
      Write-Host Enable Content Approval for the list: $splist
    }
```

```
  }
  if ($disable) {
    # Disable Versioning
    $spList.EnableVersioning = $false
    if($spList -is [Microsoft.SharePoint.SPDocumentLibrary]) {
      # Disable versioning on document library
      $spList.EnableMinorVersions = $false;
    }
  }
  $spList.Update()
}
```

You can use the function to enable version history on a list by typing the following:

```
PS > Set-SPVersionHistory -url "http://nimaintra.net/Site/Lists/My Custom List" `
>> -enable -version 10 -draft 5
```

In this example, we enable versioning in the list My Custom List. We also set the maximum number of major versions to 10. On those for which draft versions will be retained, we set the maximum to 5.

If you want to enable versioning in a document library, use an URL to a document library as input to the url parameter.

```
PS > Set-SPVersionHistory -url "http://nimaintra.net/site/Shared Documents `
>> -enableMinor -version 10 -draft 5
```

In this example, we use the enableMinor switch parameter to enable major and minor versions. We also specify that we want to retain 10 major versions, the latest 5 out of which will also retain draft history.

Draft Item Security

With draft item security, we can limit the ability of users to see draft items in a list or document library. With SharePoint 2010 lists, content approval must be enabled for draft item security to be used. With document libraries, you can grant the right to view drafts to users who can read or edit documents, but granting it to those who can approve obviously requires that content approval be enabled.

You can set the draft item security using the DraftVersionVisibility property, which accepts the following values:

- Approver Only the author of the item/document and users with the Approve permissions are able to see the items/documents.
- Author Only the author of the item/document or users with the Edit items permissions can view the items/documents.
- Reader Any user who has access to read the item/document can see the item/document.

The following is an example of how to set the draft version security to allow only users who can approve items to see the draft items in a document library.

```
PS > $spDocumentLibrary =
>> Get-SPList -url "http://nimaintra.net/site/Shared Documents"
PS > $spDocumentLibrary.DraftVersionVisibility = "Approver"
PS > $spDocumentLibrary.Update()
```

The following Set-SPDraftItemSecurity function sets draft item security in a list or document library in SharePoint 2010.

```
function Set-SPDraftItemSecurity(
  [string]$url,
  [switch]$reader,
  [switch]$author,
  [switch]$approver
  ) {
  # Use the Get-SPList function to retrieve a list
  $spList = Get-SPList -url $url
  # Check if Content Approval is enabled
  if ($spList.EnableModeration -eq $true) {
    if ($reader) {
      # Any user who can read items
      $spList.DraftVersionVisibility = "Reader";
    }
    if ($author) {
      # Only the author and users who can edit items
      $spList.DraftVersionVisibility = "Author";
    }
    if ($approver) {
      # Only the author and users who can approve items
      $spList.DraftVersionVisibility = "Approver";
    }
    # Update list settings
    $spList.Update();
  } else {
    Write-Host Enable Content Approval for the list: $spList
  }
}
```

You can use the function's three switch parameters— -reader, -author, and -approver—to specify the desired draft version security level. The following example allows users who can edit items to see the draft items in a document library.

```
PS > Set-SPDraftItemSecurity -url "http://nimaintra.net/site/Shared Documents" `
>> -author
```

Require Check Out

The Require Check Out setting determines whether users must check out a document in a document library before making any changes to it. This setting applies only to document libraries.

You can enable or disable the Require Check Out setting using the `ForceCheckout` property of a document library object.

```
PS > $spDocumentLibrary =
>> Get-SPList -url "http://nimaintra.net/site/Shared Documents"
PS > $spDocumentLibrary.ForceCheckout = $true
PS > $spDocumentLibrary.Update()
```

The following `Set-SPRequireCheckOut` function automates the steps required to configure the Require Check Out setting in a document library in SharePoint 2010.

```
function Set-SPRequireCheckOut(
  [string]$url,
  [switch]$enable,
  [switch]$disable
  ) {

  # Use the Get-SPList function to retrieve a list
  $spList = Get-SPList -url $url
  if($spList -is [Microsoft.SharePoint.SPDocumentLibrary]) {
    if ($enable) {
      # Enable check out requirement
      $spList.ForceCheckout = $true;
    }
    if ($disable) {
      # Disable check out requirement
      $spList.ForceCheckout = $false;
    }
    # Update document library
    $spList.Update();
  }
}
```

The next example shows how to use the `Set-SPRequireCheckOut` function to force the users to check out documents before making any changes to them in a document library.

```
PS > Set-SPRequireCheckOut -url "http://nimaintra.net/site/Shared Documents" `
>> -enable
```

You can also use this function to disable the Require Check Out setting.

```
PS > Set-SPRequireCheckOut -url "http://nimaintra.net/site/Shared Documents" `
>> -disable
```

Additional Functionality in SharePoint 2010

It is possible to manage the versioning settings from the graphical user interface, as shown in Figure 17-1. End users with sufficient permissions in a SharePoint list can limit the number of versions to store. When content approval is enabled, there is an option to have minor versions that could be configured to be visible only to users with sufficient permissions.

The versioning settings are set on each individual SharePoint list. There is no option in the browser-based user interface to apply versioning settings to all lists or document libraries within a site or the entire Web application.

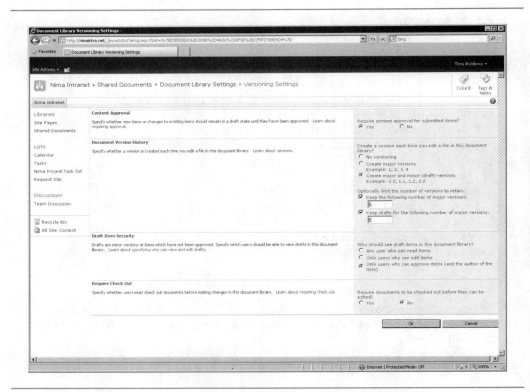

Figure 17-1.   Versioning settings for a SharePoint 2010 document library

Summary

In this chapter, we created several functions to help solve a very common problem in SharePoint environments—an unmanageably large number of list item versions. This included changing the different versioning-related properties that can be applied to lists and libraries.

We also looked at how to configure draft version security using Windows PowerShell. Finally, we demonstrated how to enable and disable the Require Check Out feature on document libraries.

CHAPTER 18 | Managing Service Applications

In Chapter 9, we made a scripted installation of SharePoint 2010 that left us with a "clean" farm, without any Web applications or service applications. In this chapter, we will look at how to create and manage service applications so that their creation can be included in a scripted installation.

In our first scenario, we will create a new managed metadata service application and assign it to the application proxy group Workspaces, which we created in Chapter 10 when we added a new Web application to the farm. We will then look at how to configure an existing service application by adding new service application administrators and changing some of its settings.

Next, we will demonstrate the steps necessary to publish a service application so that the service application data—in this case, the managed metadata—becomes available to another farm. This is very useful in situations where you have different farms for Extranet, Intranet, and Internet access, but want to share, for instance, the same taxonomy structure throughout the whole SharePoint environment.

Working with Service Applications

Windows PowerShell provides many cmdlets for managing service applications. To demonstrate their use, we'll create a service application and then configure some of its properties.

Creating Service Applications

As an example, we will create a managed metadata service application using Windows PowerShell. First, we need to make sure that the service instance corresponding to the managed metadata service application is online.

A *service instance* is the heart of a service application. It is a logical entity that contains information about the service binaries and other components—such as timer jobs and related services—that are required for the service application to function. You can view the service instances available in a farm using the Get-SPServiceInstance cmdlet. If you want to see a specific service instance, you can pipe the objects returned from the Get-SPServiceInstance cmdlet to the Where-Object cmdlet and filter on a specific property. In this example, we display the managed metadata Web service:

```
PS > Get-SPServiceInstance |
>> Where-Object {$_.TypeName -eq "Managed Metadata Web Service"} |
>> Format-Table -Property TypeName, Status -AutoSize

TypeName                      Status
--------                      ------
Managed Metadata Web Service Disabled
```

This example displays the `TypeName` and `Status` properties using the `Format-Table` cmdlet. The status can be either `Online` or `Disabled`. If the status appears as `Disabled`, you can start a service instance using the `Start-SPServiceInstance` cmdlet. Here, we start the managed metadata Web service instance:

```
PS > Get-SPServiceInstance |
>> Where-Object {$_.TypeName -eq "Managed Metadata Web Service"} |
>> Start-SPServiceInstance
```

Some service applications are completely internal to SharePoint 2010, but most expose some of their functionality to developers or other system components as a WCF Web service. These applications run in the context of associated IIS application pools. Application pools are used to consolidate IIS virtual servers or directories that share the same configuration. This means that multiple service applications can share the same application pool. Here's how to discover which application pools the various service applications run within:

```
PS > Get-SPServiceApplication |
>> Select-Object -Property Name,
>> @{Name="AppPool"; Expression={
>> if ($_.ApplicationPool) {$_.ApplicationPool.Name} else {"N/A"}}
>> }
```

When creating a new service application, you can use an existing application pool or create a new one. You can display the available application pools used for service applications using the `Get-SPServiceApplicationPool` cmdlet.

To create a new application pool for a service application, use the `New-SPServiceApplicationPool` cmdlet. The cmdlet requires two input parameters: the new application pool's name and a managed account that will be used as the identity for the application pool process. The following example demonstrates how to create a new application pool.

```
PS > New-SPServiceApplicationPool -Name "Metadata AppPool" `
>> -account (Get-SPManagedAccount "powershell\managedaccount")
```

SharePoint 2010 includes a number of cmdlets to create new service applications of a specific type. You can find out the names of these cmdlets by typing the following:

```
PS > Get-Command -Verb New -Noun *ServiceApplication |
>> Select-Object -Property Name
```

Since we are creating a managed metadata service application, we will use the `New-SPMetadataServiceApplication` cmdlet.

```
PS > New-SPMetadataServiceApplication -Name "MetadataServiceApp" `
>> -ApplicationPool (Get-SPServiceApplicationPool "Metadata AppPool") `
>> -DatabaseName "MetaDataDB01"
```

> *NOTE*   Depending on the type of service application you are creating, other parameters might be required. Use the `Get-Help` cmdlet to find out which parameters a specific cmdlet expects.

A service application also requires a service application proxy. A service application proxy is a logical object used to associate a Web application instance with a service application instance. Without a service application proxy, a Web application will not be able to communicate with a service application. To create a new service application proxy for our metadata service application, we use the `New-SPMetadataServiceApplicationProxy` cmdlet.

```
PS > New-SPMetaDataServiceApplicationProxy -Name "Metadata Service App Proxy" `
>> -ServiceApplication (Get-SPServiceApplication -Name "MetadataServiceApp")
```

Service application proxies are not connected to Web applications directly, but rather through an *application proxy group*. When a new farm is provisioned, a default service application proxy group is created, and all new Web applications are associated with this group by default. You can assign the service application proxy to the default group by adding the `-DefaultProxyGroup` switch parameter to the `New-SPMetaDataServiceApplicationProxy` cmdlet. Alternatively, you can assign it to a specific proxy group later, as demonstrated here:

```
PS > Add-SPServiceApplicationProxyGroupMember -Identity "Workspaces" `
>> -Member (Get-SPServiceApplicationProxy |
>> Where-Object { $_.DisplayName -eq "Metadata Service App Proxy" })
```

Figure 18-1 shows how the configuring of service application associations looks in Central Administration.

Managing Service Applications

Service application settings can be changed using the `Set-ServiceApplication` cmdlet. You can set properties such as the associated application pool and application proxy group. SharePoint 2010 also includes cmdlets that manage specific service applications. Here, we'll use the `Set-SPMetadataServiceApplication` cmdlet to configure properties of our managed metadata service application.

Members of the Farm Administrators group have the rights to manage all service applications in a farm, but you can also grant additional users rights to manage a specific service application in SharePoint 2010. The users will be given limited access to the Central Administration site and will be able to manage settings related only to the specific service application. In the next example, we use the `-AdministratorAccount` parameter supported by the `Set-SPMetadataServiceApplication` cmdlet to grant the user `powershell\sezel` rights to manage our metadata service application.

```
PS > Get-SPServiceApplication -Name "MetadataServiceApp" |
>> Set-SPMetadataServiceApplication -AdministratorAccount powershell\sezel
```

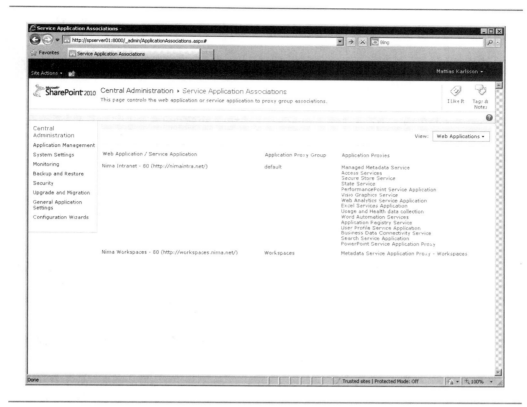

Figure 18-1.   Configuring service application associations in Central Administration

This example replaces the current permissions on the service application with the single value of powershell\sezel. If you want to add a new permission and keep the old permissions, you can use the Add-SPMetadataSAPermission function, as follows:

```
function Add-SPMetadataSAPermission(
  [string]$serviceApplication,
  [string]$administratorAccount,
  [string]$fullAccessAccount,
  [string]$restrictedAccount
) {
# Retrieve metadata service application
$sa = Get-SPMetadataServiceApplication -Identity $serviceApplication
# Store current access rules in variable
$admins = $sa.GetAdministrationAccessControl().AccessRules
$access = $sa.GetAccessControl().AccessRules
```

```
# Set new access rules
$sa | Set-SPMetadataServiceApplication `

-AdministratorAccount $administratorAccount `
-FullAccessAccount $fullAccessAccount `
-RestrictedAccount $restrictedAccount
# Store access control in variable
$adminAccessControl = $sa.GetAdministrationAccessControl()
$accessControl = $sa.GetAccessControl()
# Add old access rules
$admins | ForEach-Object { $adminAccessControl.AddAccessRule($_) }
$access | ForEach-Object { $accessControl.AddAccessRule($_) }
# Set access control
$sa.SetAdministrationAccessControl($adminAccessControl)
$sa.SetAccessControl($accessControl)
}
```

The function stores the service application's current permissions in a variable, and then it uses the `Set-SPMetadataServiceApplication` cmdlet to apply the new permissions. Finally, the function adds the service application's previous permissions.

You can use the function by typing the following:

```
PS > Add-SPMetadataSAPermission -serviceApplication MetadataServiceApp `
>> -administratorAccount "powershell\nigo"
```

The `Set-SPMetadataServiceApplication` cmdlet also allows you to designate a site collection that should act as the content type hub. A *content type hub* is a new feature in SharePoint 2010. It is a central location where you can manage and publish content types. Subscribing to a content type hub allows Web applications to retrieve published or updated content types from a central location. This means that you can easily reuse content types between Web applications or even between farms. The following example demonstrates how to specify the content type hub URL for a managed metadata service application.

```
PS > Get-SPServiceApplication -Name "MetadataServiceApp" |
>> Set-SPMetadataServiceApplication -HubUri "http://nimaintra.net"
```

Configuring a service application to use a content type hub also requires that you modify the corresponding service application proxy. In the next example, we configure the managed metadata service application proxy so that it automatically consumes content types from a content type hub.

```
PS > Get-SPServiceApplicationProxy |
>> Where { $_.DisplayName -eq "Metadata Service App Proxy" } |
>> Set-SPMetadataServiceApplicationProxy -ContentTypeSyndicationEnabled
```

Removing Service Applications

To remove a service application from SharePoint 2010, you can use the `Remove-SPServiceApplication` cmdlet. The cmdlet supports the `-RemoveData` switch parameter, which is used to delete the databases and other data associated with the service application. We remove our metadata service application as follows:

```
PS > Remove-SPServiceApplication `
>> -Identity (Get-SPServiceApplication -Name "MetadataServiceApp") -removedata
```

This command does not remove the application pool used by the service application proxy. You can remove the application pool by using the `Remove-SPServiceApplicationPool` cmdlet. Next, we remove our metadata service application pool.

```
PS > Remove-SPServiceApplicationPool -Identity "Metadata AppPool"
```

Finally, we remove our metadata service application proxy using the `Remove-SPServiceApplicationProxy` cmdlet.

```
PS > Get-SPServiceApplicationProxy |
>> Where-Object { $_.DisplayName -eq "Metadata Service App Proxy" } |
>> Remove-SPServiceApplicationProxy -RemoveData
```

Sharing Service Applications Between Farms

The new service application architecture in SharePoint 2010 enables you to share service applications between farms, thus optimizing your resources by providing enterprise-wide services. The types of service applications that can be published are business data connectivity, managed metadata, user profile, search, secure store, and web analytics.

A couple of actions need to be performed in preparation for publishing service applications between farms. First, you need to determine which farm should act as the publishing farm and which farm or farms will consume data from the published service application on the publishing farm. Next, you need to establish a trust between the publishing farm and the consumer farm. This requires two steps:

- Exchange root certificates between the farms.
- Copy a Security Token Service (STS) certificate from the consuming farm to the publishing farm.

Exchanging Root Certificates

Exchanging root certificates between the publishing farm and the consuming farm enables both farms to trust each other for secure communication (over https). This requires that you export and import the root certificates on the two farms.

To export a root certificate from a farm, you can use the `Get-SPCertificateAuthority` cmdlet. The cmdlet returns an instance of the `Microsoft.SharePoint.Administration.SPCertificateAuthority` class. This class provides the `RootCertificate` property, which returns an object of type `System.Security.Cryptography.X509Certificates.x509Certificate2`. The x509Certificate2 object represents an X.509 certificate. Objects of the type x509Certificate2 support the `Export` method. This method has a `contentType` parameter, which accepts an `X509ContentType` value that describes how the output should be formatted. The supported values are `Cert`, `SerializedCert`, and `Pkcs12`. Passing any other value from the `X509ContentType` enumeration causes an exception.

The `Export` method returns an array of bytes that represent the certificate. Since we want to copy the root certificate to a different farm, we write the output to a file using the `Set-Content` cmdlet. This cmdlet supports the `–Encoding` parameter, which has the default value of `Unicode`. Since the `Export` method returns an array of bytes, we change the encoding to `Byte`, as follows:

```
PS > (Get-SPCertificateAuthority).RootCertificate.Export("Cert") |
>> Set-Content -Path "\\SPServer01\Share\PublishingRootCert.cer" `
>> -Encoding Byte
```

Next, we run the command on the consuming farm.

```
PS > (Get-SPCertificateAuthority).RootCertificate.Export("Cert") |
>> Set-Content -Path "\\SPServer01\Share\ConsumingRootCert.cer" `
>> -Encoding Byte
```

After the root certificates have been exported, you need to create a trusted root authority on both farms using the `New-SPTrustedRootAuthority` cmdlet. This cmdlet supports the `Name` and `Certificate` parameters. The `Name` parameter accepts an object of type `System.String` and is used to specify the name of the trusted root authority to create. The `Certificate` parameter accepts an object of type `X509Certificate2`, which can be obtained from the previously saved copy using the `Get-PfxCertificate` cmdlet. This example demonstrates how to add a trusted root authority to the publishing farm:

```
PS > $rootCert =
>> Get-PfxCertificate -FilePath "\\SPServer01\Share\ConsumingRootCert.cer"
PS > New-SPTrustedRootAuthority -Name "Consumer Farm" -Certificate $rootCert
```

Next, we run the command on the consumer farm.

```
PS > $rootCert =
>> Get-PfxCertificate -FilePath "\\SPServer01\Share\PublishingRootCert.cer"
PS > New-SPTrustedRootAuthority -Name "Publishing Farm" -Certificate $rootCert
```

Copying an STS Certificate

To export the STS certificate, you can use the `Get-SPSecurityTokenServiceConfig` cmdlet. This cmdlet returns an object of type `Microsoft.SharePoint.Administration` `.Claims.SPSecurityTokenServiceManager`, which represents the STS in the farm. This type provides the `LocalLoginProvider` property, which represents the local STS login settings, and the `SigningCertificate` property, which you can use to retrieve the STS X.509 certificate.

 TIP To learn more about Secure Token Services and claims-based authentication, we recommend reading the TechNet article on authentication planning, at http://technet.microsoft.com/en-us/library/cc288475.aspx.

The following example demonstrates how to export an STS certificate on the consumer farm to a file on a shared folder.

```
PS > $c =
>> (Get-SPSecurityTokenServiceConfig).LocalLoginProvider.SigningCertificate
PS > $c.Export("Cert") |
>> Set-Content -Path "\\SPServer01\Share\ConsumingSTSCert.cer" -Encoding byte
```

To copy the STS certificate to the publishing farm, use the `New-SPTrustedServiceTokenIssuer` cmdlet. The cmdlet sets up a trust between the farms using the STS certificate. The following example demonstrates how to add the STS certificate to the publishing farm.

```
PS > $stsCert =
>> Get-PfxCertificate -FilePath "\\SPServer01\Share\ConsumingSTSCert.cer"
PS > New-SPTrustedServiceTokenIssuer -Name "Consumer Farm" `
>> -Certificate $stsCert
```

Once the root certificates are exchanged between the farms and the STS certificate has been copied to the publishing farm, you can go ahead and configure the Application Discovery and Load Balancing Service Application (also known as the Topology Service), which handles the discovery of a farm's service applications.

Configuring the Application Discovery and Load Balancing Service Application

Granting the consumer farm permissions to the Application Discovery and Load Balancing Service Application establishes a relationship between the farms and allows you to set permissions to other service applications as well.

You can manage the security for a service application using the `Set-SPServiceApplicationSecurity` cmdlet. In the next example, we retrieve a claims provider that provides claim information that relates to the server farm.

```
PS > $claimProvider = (Get-SPClaimProvider -Identity System).ClaimProvider
```

Next, we use the `New-SPClaimsPrincipal` cmdlet to create a new claims principal.

```
PS > $claimsPrincipal = New-SPClaimsPrincipal -ClaimType `
>> "http://schemas.microsoft.com/sharepoint/2009/08/claims/farmid" `
>> -ClaimProvider $claimprovider `
>> -ClaimValue "27ea4ca4-9a17-4a3a-b862-75dbe5a0f424"
```

In this example, we use the `-ClaimType` parameter and specify a URI used for the farm identifier claim type. We use the `-ClaimProvider` parameter and specify the claims provider reference stored in the `claimProvider` variable. Finally, we use the `ClaimValue` parameter and specify the consumer farm's GUID.

 NOTE You can find the consumer farm's GUID by running the following command on the consumer farm: `(Get-SPFarm).Id`.

You can add the claims principal to a `SPObjectSecurity` object using the `Grant-SPObjectSecurity` cmdlet. In the following example, we add a new security principal containing a claims principal and grant the principal `Full Control` rights, which is the only permission level supported by the Topology Service Application.

```
PS > $security = Get-SPTopologyServiceApplication |
>> Get-SPServiceApplicationSecurity
PS > Grant-SPObjectSecurity -Identity $security `
>> -Principal $claimsPrincipal -Rights "Full Control"
```

Finally, we update the Topology Service Application with the security principal using the `Set-SPServiceApplicationSecurity` cmdlet.

```
PS > Get-SPTopologyServiceApplication |
>> Set-SPServiceApplicationSecurity -ObjectSecurity $security
```

Once the Application Discovery and Load Balancing Service Application is configured, you can publish a service application.

Publishing a Service Application

You can use the `Publish-SPServiceApplication` cmdlet to publish a service application. In this example, we will publish the metadata service application, which will enable content types and terms to be accessible on the consuming farm.

```
PS > Publish-SPServiceApplication `
>> -Identity (Get-SPServiceApplication -Name "MetadataServiceApp")
```

Next, we need to create a new metadata service application proxy on the consuming farm that connects to the published service application on the publishing farm. Adding a remote connection requires the URI of the published metadata service. First, we retrieve the URL of the Topology Service by typing the following command on the publishing farm:

```
PS > (Get-SPTopologyServiceApplication).LoadBalancerUrl.AbsoluteUri
https://rig8c3:32844/Topology/topology.svc
```

Then we use the `Receive-SPServiceApplicationConnectionInfo` cmdlet on the consumer farm to retrieve the URI of the published managed metadata service applications. This example returns an object of type `System.Uri`.

```
PS > $uri = (Receive-SPServiceApplicationConnectionInfo `
>> -FarmUrl https://rig8c3:32844/Topology/topology.svc |
>> Where-Object {$_.Name -eq "MetadataServiceApp"}).Uri
```

Next, we create a new metadata service application proxy using the `System.Uri` object stored in the `uri` variable as value for the `Uri` parameter and add the new proxy to the default proxy group.

```
PS > New-SPMetadataServiceApplicationProxy -Name "Metadata Service App Proxy" `
>> -URI $uri -DefaultProxyGroup
```

Finally, we grant permissions to the published managed metadata service application to allow the consumer farm to connect to it. The metadata service application supports three different types of permissions: `Read Access to Term Store`, `Read and Restricted Write Access to Term Store`, and `Full Access to Term Store`. The following example demonstrates how to set up the metadata service application permissions.

```
PS > $claimProvider = (Get-SPClaimProvider -Identity System).ClaimProvider
PS > $claimsPrincipal = New-SPClaimsPrincipal -ClaimType `
>> "http://schemas.microsoft.com/sharepoint/2009/08/claims/farmid" `
>> -ClaimProvider $claimprovider `
>> -ClaimValue "27ea4ca4-9a17-4a3a-b862-75dbe5a0f424"
PS > $security =
>> Get-SPMetadataServiceApplication -Identity MetadataServiceApp |
>> Get-SPServiceApplicationSecurity
PS > Grant-SPObjectSecurity -Identity $security `
>> -Principal $claimsPrincipal -Rights "Read Access to Term Store"
PS > Get-SPTopologyServiceApplication |
>> Set-SPServiceApplicationSecurity -ObjectSecurity $security
```

We have now gone through the steps that are necessary to publish a service application from one farm to another, allowing the consuming farm to pull data from the managed metadata service application.

Additional Functionality in SharePoint 2010

Service applications can be managed through the Central Administration site. As discussed in Chapter 2, you have the option to delegate the administration of each service application individually. Creating, modifying, and deleting service applications and their associations are also easily done through Central Administration, as shown in Figure 18-2.

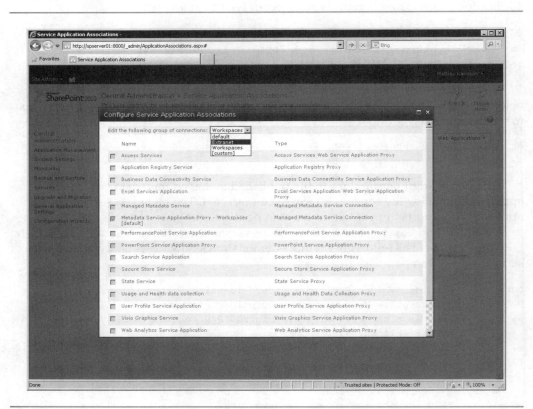

Figure 18-2.   Changing service application associations for a proxy group

Additionally, Central Administration offers an interface for publishing service applications. You can use the Publish button in the Central Administration site to publish a service application, as shown in Figure 18-3.

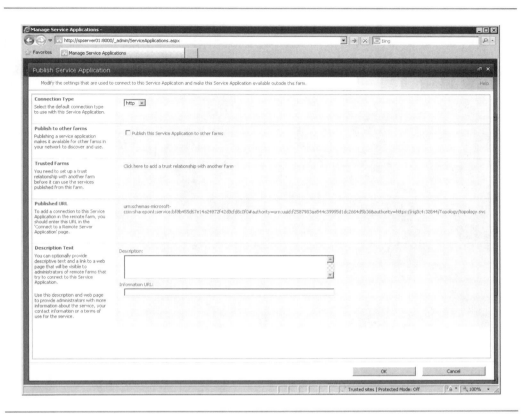

Figure 18-3.   Publishing a service application from Central Administration

Summary

In this chapter, we demonstrated many of the built-in Windows PowerShell cmdlets
for managing service applications in SharePoint 2010. We created a new managed
metadata service application, and then associated it with a new proxy group. We also
briefly looked at how to change the settings of a service application. In our example, we
added a new administrator and specified the site collection to be used as the content
type hub.

We then looked at the steps that need to be taken to publish a service application for
interfarm access. This required setting up a trust between two SharePoint 2010 farms
and exchanging root certificates.

CHAPTER 19 | Managing Users and Groups

A common question when implementing SharePoint is how site permissions should be handled. The short answer is that it depends on how the SharePoint site or sites are used. In some cases, the best way is to add Active Directory groups into SharePoint groups. In scenarios where access rights change often, it might be better to add individual user accounts to SharePoint groups directly. Managing these SharePoint groups and their members could quickly turn into a lot of time-consuming tasks. Another situation arises when you have a number of sites that are inheriting permissions from a single parent, but then at some point need to start using their own unique permissions—thus bringing about the requirement to create new groups for each site.

Along with groups, individual user accounts must be managed. For example, when an employee has left the company, the account is usually disabled or deleted in the Active Directory, but in SharePoint, the user still shows up in the site permissions. Security-wise this is not a problem as long as the account is disabled or removed, but it often generates a lot of questions since the SharePoint users cannot see that the account is disabled.

In this chapter, we will cover how to can manage SharePoint groups and user permissions with Windows PowerShell by implementing simple yet useful functions for creating, modifying, and deleting SharePoint groups. We will also go through populating groups with user accounts, as well as modifying and removing users.

Working with Groups

Groups in a site collection can be retrieved using the `SiteGroups` property of any of the instances of the `Microsoft.SharePoint.SPWeb` class that are members of this site collection. The property returns a collection of objects of type `Microsoft.SharePoint.SPGroup`. The following example demonstrates how to store a collection of groups in a variable and use the `Select-Object` cmdlet to retrieve some basic information about the groups.

```
PS > $spWeb = Get-SPWeb http://nimaintra.net
PS > $spGroupCollection = $spWeb.SiteGroups
PS > $spGroupCollection | Select-Object -Property Name, Owner, Description
```

To retrieve only the groups for a specific site, use the `Groups` property instead of the `SiteGroups` property.

Creating Groups

The `Microsoft.SharePoint.SPGroupCollection` class provides the `Add` method for adding new groups to a site collection. The method has parameters for the name, owner, default user, and description. The name and description parameters are of type `System.String`, so you can simply use string literals as values for them. The owner and default user parameters are of types `Microsoft.SharePoint.SPMember` and

Microsoft.SharePoint.SPUser, respectively. You can use the Get-SPUser cmdlet
to obtain the values to be passed to the method.

The following example demonstrates how to add a new group to a site collection.

```
PS > $owner = Get-SPUser -Web http://nimaintra.net -Identity POWERSHELL\maka
PS > $defaultUser =
>> Get-SPUser -Web http://nimaintra.net -Identity POWERSHELL\nigo
PS > $spGroupCollection.Add("New Group",$owner,$defaultUser,"Group Description")
```

If the users do not exist in the site, the Get-SPUser command will fail. You can
add a user to a site using the New-SPUser cmdlet, as described later in this chapter.
Alternatively, you can use the EnsureUser method to add a user to the sites User Info
list, as demonstrated here:

```
PS > $spWeb.EnsureUser("powershell\nigo")
```

Adding groups as shown in this example works only for Web applications that use
Windows authentication. If the Web application is using claims-based authentication,
you can use the following code instead.

```
PS > $owner = Get-SPUser -Web http://nimaintra.net -Identity `
>> (New-SPClaimsPrincipal POWERSHELL\maka -IdentityType WindowsSamAccountName)
PS > $defaultUser = Get-SPUser -Web http://nimaintra.net -Identity `
>> (New-SPClaimsPrincipal POWERSHELL\nigo -IdentityType WindowsSamAccountName)
PS > $spGroupCollection.Add("New Group",$owner,$defaultUser,"Group Description")
```

The following function, New-SPGroup, automates the task of adding groups.

```
function New-SPGroup(
  [string]$url,
  [string]$group,
  [string]$owner,
  [string]$defaultUser,
  [string]$description
) {
$spWeb = Get-SPWeb $url
# Store groups in collection
$spGroupCollection = $spWeb.SiteGroups;
# Check if group already exists
if ($spGroupCollection[$group]) {
  Write-Host "The group: $group already exists";
} else {
  # Check if Web application uses Claims authentication
  if ($spWeb.Site.WebApplication.UseClaimsAuthentication) {
    $owner = (New-SPClaimsPrincipal $owner `
    -IdentityType WindowsSamAccountName).ToEncodedString();
    $defaultUser = (New-SPClaimsPrincipal $defaultUser `
    -IdentityType WindowsSamAccountName).ToEncodedString();
  }
```

```
  # Ensure user
  if(($spWeb.EnsureUser($owner)) -and ($spWeb.EnsureUser($defaultUser))) {
   $objOwner = Get-SPUser -Web $url -Identity $owner;
   $objdefaultUser = Get-SPUser -Web $url -Identity $defaultUser;
    # Create Group
    $spGroupCollection.Add($group,$objOwner,$objDefaultUser,$description);
  }
 }
 $spWeb.Dispose()
}
```

To use the `New-SPGroup` function to add a new group to a site collection, type the following:

```
PS > New-SPGroup -url http://nimaintra.net -group "New Group" `
>> -owner powershell\maka -defaultUser powershell\nigo -description "My Group"
```

If the group already exists, the function returns "Group already exists." Otherwise, the group is created in the site collection.

Modifying SharePoint Groups

You can also modify existing groups in SharePoint 2010 using Windows PowerShell. First, retrieve an existing group from the group collection, as shown here:

```
PS > $spWeb = Get-SPWeb http://nimaintra.net
PS > $spGroupCollection = $spWeb.SiteGroups
PS > $spGroup = $spGroupCollection["New Group"]
```

Since this is a task that might be repeated many times, we wrap the code up in a function named `Get-SPGroup`.

```
function Get-SPGroup([string]$url, [string]$group) {
  $spWeb = Get-SPWeb $url
  $spGroupCollection = $spWeb.SiteGroups;
  $spWeb.Dispose()
  return $spGroupCollection[$group];
}
```

In this function, we store a group collection in the variable `spGroupCollection` and return a specific group by using the group name as the index value. You can use the function by typing the following:

```
PS > $spGroup = Get-SPGroup -url http://nimaintra.net -group "New Group"
```

With an instance of a `Microsoft.SharePoint.SPGroup` object stored in a variable, we can change the properties of the group. The next example demonstrates how to change the group name.

```
PS > $spGroup.Name = "New Group Name"
```

It's also possible to change the value of the Description property. However, this property does not surface anywhere in the browser-based user interface. What appears in the browser on the groups.aspx page is actually the value of the About Me (with the internal name Notes) field of the corresponding item in the User Info list. This is set to the same value as the group's description once when the group is created, but is not changed later if the value of the Description property changes. And if a user edits a group's description in the browser, this doesn't change the value of the Description property either. The following example demonstrates how to set the value of a group's Description property and set the Notes property of the corresponding item in the User Info list.

```
PS > $spGroup.Description = "New Description"
PS > $spGroupListItem = ($spWeb.Lists["User Information List"].Items |
>> Where-Object {$_["Group"] -eq $spGroup.Name})
PS > $spGroupListItem["Notes"] = $spGroup.Description
PS > $spGroupListItem.Update()
```

To change the owner of the group, you assign to the Owner property an object of type Microsoft.SharePoint.SPUser, which can be retrieved using the Get-SPUser cmdlet.

```
PS > $spGroup.Owner =
>> Get-SPUser -Web http://nimaintra.net -Identity POWERSHELL\maka
```

The final step is to use the Update method to commit the changes to SharePoint.

```
PS > $spGroup.Update()
```

The following Set-SPGroup function wraps up the code to modify groups in a reusable function.

```
function Set-SPGroup(
  [string]$url,
  [string]$group,
  [string]$name,
  [string]$owner,
  [string]$description
  ) {
  $spWeb = Get-SPWeb $url
  # Store groups in collection
  $spGroupCollection = $spWeb.SiteGroups
  # Get group
  $spGroup = $spGroupCollection[$group]
  if($spGroup) {
    # Change group name
    if($name) {
      $oldName = $spGroup.Name
```

```
      $spGroup.Name = $name
    }
    # Change owner
    if($owner) {
      if($spWeb.Site.WebApplication.UseClaimsAuthentication) {
        $owner = (New-SPClaimsPrincipal $owner `
         -IdentityType WindowsSamAccountName).ToEncodedString()
      }
      # Ensure user
      if($spWeb.EnsureUser($owner)) {
        $spUser = Get-SPUser -Web $url -Identity $owner
        $spGroup.Owner = $spUser
      }
    }
    # Change description
    if($description) {
      $spGroup.Description = $description;
      # Update item in User Information List
      $spGroupListItem = ($spWeb.Lists["User Information List"].Items |
      Where-Object {$_["Group"] -eq $oldName})
      $spGroupListItem["Notes"] = $description
      $spGroupListItem.Update()
    }
    # Update group
    $spGroup.Update()
  } else {
    Write-Host "Group: $group not found"
  }
  $spWeb.Dispose()
}
```

Run the function by typing the following:

```
PS > Set-SPGroup -url http://nimaintra.net -group "New Group" `
>> -name "New name" -owner powershell\nigo -description "New group Description"
```

In this example, we use the Set-SPGroup function to change the name, owner, and description of an existing SharePoint group.

Removing Groups

The Microsoft.SharePoint.SPGroupCollection class provides the Remove method for removing a group from a site collection in SharePoint 2010. The Remove method uses the group name as identifier when removing a group. The next example demonstrates how to retrieve a group collection and remove a group from it.

```
PS > $spWeb = Get-SPWeb http://nimaintra.net
PS > $spGroupCollection = $spWeb.SiteGroups
PS > $spGroupCollection.Remove("New Group")
```

The following `Remove-SPGroup` function wraps up the code to remove groups.

```
function Remove-SPGroup([string]$url, [string]$group) {
  $spWeb = Get-SPWeb $url
  $spGroupCollection = $spWeb.SiteGroups
  $spGroupCollection.Remove($group)
  $spWeb.Dispose()
}
```

You can use the function by typing the following:

```
PS > Remove-SPGroup -url http://SPServer01 -group "New Group"
```

Working with Users

Several Windows PowerShell cmdlets are available for managing user accounts. These allow you to add, modify, and remove users.

Adding Users in SharePoint 2010

The SharePoint 2010 Management shell includes the `New-SPUser` cmdlet, which you can use to add a user account to a SharePoint site collection. The cmdlet requires a site collection and a user alias when adding a user to a site collection, as demonstrated here:

```
PS > New-SPUser -UserAlias powershell\seze -web http://nimaintra.net
```

It is also possible to set additional user properties such as display name, e-mail, and mobile number using the corresponding parameters supported by the `New-SPUser` cmdlet.

The `New-SPUser` cmdlet also supports the `PermisssionLevel` parameter to set a permission level for a user, such as `Full`, `Contribute`, `Read`, or `All`. In the next example, we add a new user and set the permission level to `Contribute`.

```
PS > New-SPUser -UserAlias powershell\seze -web http://nimaintra.net `
>> -PermissionLevel Contribute
```

In the following example, we add a new user and add the user to an existing SharePoint group which makes the user inherit the permissions from the group.

```
PS > New-SPUser -UserAlias powershell\seze -web http://nimaintra.net `
>> -Group 'New Group'
```

Finally, here's how to add a new user as a site collection administrator:

```
PS > New-SPUser -UserAlias powershell\seze -web http://nimaintra.net `
>> -SiteCollectionAdmin
```

Modifying Users in SharePoint 2010

You can manage existing users in SharePoint 2010 using the Set-SPUser cmdlet. In the following example, we use the Get-SPUser cmdlet to retrieve a specific user and pipe the object to the Set-SPUser cmdlet to change the user's display name.

```
PS > Get-SPUser -Web http://nimaintra.net -Identity powershell\nigo |
>> Set-SPUser -DisplayName "Goude"
```

This changes the value of both the DisplayName property and the Name property on the object.

It is also possible to synchronize user information from the user directory store using the SyncFromAD switch parameter.

```
PS > Get-SPUser -Web http://nimaintra.net -Identity powershell\nigo |
>> Set-SPUser -SyncFromAD
```

The Set-SPUser cmdlet supports the AddPermissionLevel parameter to add a permission level to a specific user. The permission level must be one of the following types: Contribute, Design, Full Control, Limited Access, or Read. In the next example, we add the Contribute permission level to a user in SharePoint 2010.

```
PS > Set-SPUser -AddPermissionLevel "Contribute" -Web http://nimaintra.net `
>> -Identity powershell\nigo
```

To remove a permission level from a specific user, use the RemovePermissionLevel parameter.

```
PS > Set-SPUser -RemovePermissionLevel "Contribute" -Web http://nimaintra.net `
>> -Identity powershell\nigo
```

To clear all the granted permissions for a user, use the ClearPermissions switch parameter.

You can add a user to a specific group using the Group parameter.

```
PS > Set-SPUser -Web http://nimaintra.net -Identity powershell\nigo `
>> -Group "Home Members"
```

In this example, we add the user powershell\nigo to the Home Members group.

It is also possible to store an instance of the `Microsoft.SharePoint.SPGroup` class in a variable and use the variable as input to the `Group` parameter. The next example demonstrates this.

```
PS > $spGroup = Get-SPGroup -url http://SPServer01 -group "Home Members"
PS > Get-SPUser -Web http://SPServer01 -Identity powershell\nigo |
>> Set-SPUser -Group $spGroup
```

Removing Users in SharePoint 2010

You can remove users from a group or site in SharePoint 2010 using the `Remove-SPUser` cmdlet. To remove a user from a specific group, use the `Group` parameter.

```
PS > Remove-SPUser -Web http://nimaintra.net -Identity powershell\nigo `
>> -Group "Viewers"
```

In this example, we remove the user `powershell\nigo` from the Viewers group.

NOTE   The `Remove-SPUser` cmdlet does not remove the user from the Active Directory Domain Services.

To remove a user from a site, use the `Identity` parameter supported by the `Remove-SPUser` cmdlet,

```
PS > Get-SPWeb -Identity http://nimaintra.net |
>> Remove-SPUser -Identity powershell\nigo
```

Additional Functionality in SharePoint 2010

Managing users and groups from the graphical user interface has become a lot easier in SharePoint 2010, and with the use of the Office Ribbon, it has become much more user-friendlier. As we mentioned in Chapter 1, the Check Permissions feature makes it possible to check which permissions a specific user has on the site, including the permissions obtained through membership in Active Directory groups that are added to the site.

When creating new sites from the user interface, you can specify if the site should inherit permissions from the parent or if it should have unique permissions. If you select unique permissions, you will be presented with a page where you create or select three existing user groups that will be used for hosting viewers, members, and owners of the site, as shown in Figure 19-1. These are known as *associated groups*.

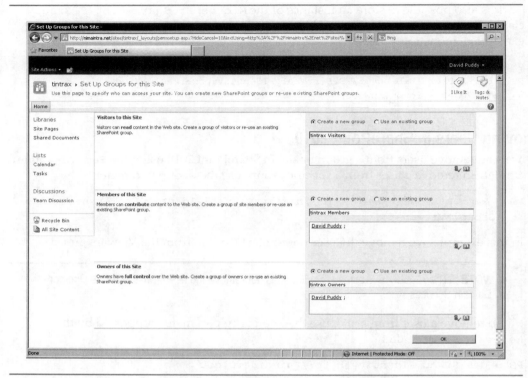

Figure 19-1.   Creating or reusing existing SharePoint groups for a new site

Even though the Viewers, Members, and Owners groups have a default permission level assigned, you can change the permissions, as shown in Figure 19-2. For example, you might choose to prevent contributors from modifying the site using SharePoint Designer or other remote interfaces.

Through the graphical user interface, you can easily remove users from SharePoint groups. For example, when a user has left the company, you can delete the user's

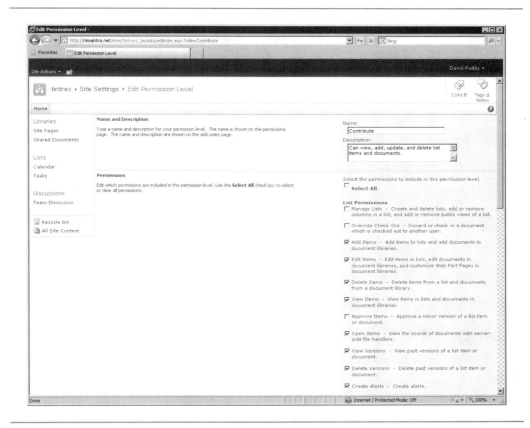

Figure 19-2.   Changing the default permission levels

profile from the User Profile Service application, as shown in Figure 19-3. This
will remove the My Site for the specific user. Then when you click the user's name
somewhere within SharePoint, you will get to the current site's local user information
page instead of the user's My Site. From here, users with sufficient permissions have
the option to remove the user from the site collection, and that user will then be deleted
from all SharePoint groups within the site collection.

NOTE   Users are never completely removed from SharePoint. This is to avoid having content
items with "unknown" authors.

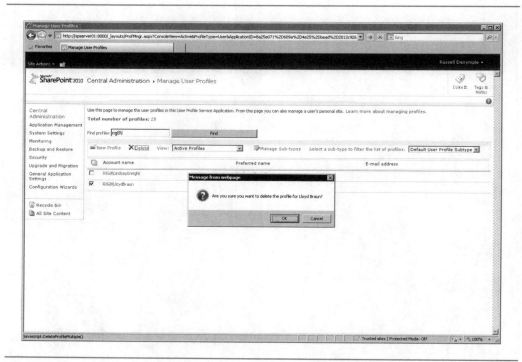

Figure 19-3. Deleting a user profile from the User Profile Service application

Summary

In this chapter, we looked how to use Windows PowerShell to manage SharePoint users and groups by creating several reusable scripts. We used the Add and Delete methods of the SPGroupCollection class to create and delete groups. When modifying groups, we first retrieved the group using the SiteGroups property of the SPWeb class.

We also demonstrated how to work with users using the Get-SPUser, New-SPUser, Set-SPUser, and Remove-SPUser cmdlets.

CHAPTER 20 | Working with Content Databases

As the use of SharePoint increases within the organization, it is very common to see the amount of content stored in SharePoint grow dramatically. This makes it necessary to increase the number of content databases to maintain good performance. Having a large number of content databases is not a problem in itself, since SharePoint 2010 supports hundreds of content databases per Web application. The issue is that it's important to maintain a good naming standard for all those databases. Unfortunately, it is very often the case that there is no naming standard applied at all, causing difficulties in distinguishing which content databases are used by which Web application. This makes troubleshooting more difficult, not to mention the frustration it causes the SQL Server team.

In our first scenario in this chapter, we will address the database-naming problem by creating a Windows PowerShell script that first detaches all content databases from a Web application, renames them on SQL Server using a defined naming standard, and then reattaches the content databases to the Web application. This will create consistent database names on SQL Server and remove database names containing GUIDs and similar elements.

By default, any binary large object (BLOB) in SharePoint 2010, such as the contents of a document in a document library, is stored inside a content database, in a column of type IMAGE. As usage increases, the total amount of BLOB data can easily outgrow the structured data stored in your content databases, thus making database operations less efficient. To address this, SharePoint 2010 offers the ability to use Remote BLOB Storage (RBS) providers, allowing you to configure your Microsoft SQL Server 2008 to store the BLOB data outside the database using more cost-efficient storage solutions.

In our second scenario, we will look at how to configure SharePoint 2010 and Microsoft SQL Server 2008 to use the RBS FILESTREAM provider included in the Microsoft SQL Server 2008 R2 Feature Pack.

Managing Content Database Naming

Our solution involves detaching the content databases from a Web application, renaming those databases, and then reattaching them. Since we want to rename the content databases in the SQL Server instance, and then connect them again with new names but the same values for the Maximum Number of Site Collections and Site Collection Level Warning settings, we need to store the information about these values before we detach the content database.

Storing Content Database Information

The Web application used in this example includes two content databases. For demonstrative purposes, we will start by working with a single content database.

First, we use the Get-SPContentDatabase cmdlet to retrieve information about a specific content database.

```
PS > $cd = Get-SPContentDatabase -WebApplication http://nimaintra.net |
>> Where-Object { $_.Name -eq "WSS_Content" }
```

Since it's very easy to work with XML data in Windows PowerShell, we will store the information from the content database in an object of type System.Xml.XmlDocument. Here, we create the object:

```
PS > [xml]$xml = @"
>> <ContentDatabases>
>>  <ContentDatabase>
>>   <Name>{0}</Name>
>>   <NewName></NewName>
>>   <MaxSiteLevel>{1}</MaxSiteLevel>
>>   <WarningSiteLevel>{2}</WarningSiteLevel>
>>   <DatabaseStatus>{3}</DatabaseStatus>
>>   <Server>{4}</Server>
>>  </ContentDatabase>
>> </ContentDatabases>
>> "@ -f $cd.Name, $cd.MaximumSiteCount, $cd.WarningSiteCount,
>> $cd.Status, $cd.Server
```

When we use the [xml] cast as shown in this example, the input here-string is converted to an object of type System.Xml.XmlDocument. The first tag created in this example defines the top-level node and is followed by elements. The lowest-level elements (the ones that do not have any children) are regarded by Windows PowerShell as object properties.

We also use the format operator to assign values to the properties. We can type the variable's name followed by ContentDatabases.ContentDatabase to display the properties available in the element.

```
PS > $xml.ContentDatabases.ContentDatabase


Name             : WSS_Content
NewName          :
MaxSiteLevel     : 15000
WarningSiteLevel : 9000
DatabaseStatus   : Online
Server           : SQLServer01
```

As we said, our Web application has another content database, so we need to add elements to the XMLDocument object for that database. First, we'll retrieve the additional content database using the Get-SPContentDatabase cmdlet.

```
PS > $cd2 = Get-SPContentDatabase -WebApplication http://nimaintra.net |
>> Where-Object { $_.Name -eq "WSS_Content2" }
```

Next, we use a here-string followed by the format operator to store the information from the content database in an object, which we can use to insert XML code into our existing XMLDocument object.

```
PS > $properties = @"
>> <Name>{0}</Name>
>> <NewName></NewName>
>> <MaxSiteLevel>{1}</MaxSiteLevel>
>> <WarningSiteLevel>{2}</WarningSiteLevel>
>> <DatabaseStatus>{3}</DatabaseStatus>
>> <Server>{4}</Server>
>> "@ -f $cd2.Name, $cd2.MaximumSiteCount, $cd2.WarningSiteCount,
>> $cd2.Status, $cd2.Server
```

Adding the code to the XMLDocument object requires that we create a new element using the CreateElement() method supported by objects of this type.

```
PS > $element = $xml.CreateElement("ContentDatabase")
```

Next, we add the inner structure of the element using the InnerXml property.

```
PS > $element.InnerXml = $properties
```

Finally, we add the element to the XMLDocument object using the AppendChild() method.

```
PS > [void]$xml.ContentDatabases.AppendChild($element)
```

The NewName property does not contain a value, since we haven't decided on a new naming standard for the content databases yet. Let's go ahead and add a value to the property.

```
PS > for ($i=0;
>> $i -lt ([array]$xml.ContentDatabases.ContentDatabase).Count;
>> $i++) {
>> ([array]$xml.ContentDatabases.ContentDatabase)[$i].NewName =
>> "NimaIntra_ContentDB_{0:d2}" -f $($i + 1)
>> }
```

In this example, we use a for loop to iterate through each element and assign a value to the NewName property. When assigning a value, we use the format operator to ensure that the numeric value provided on the right-hand side always includes two digits. When we display the values, we see that the strings end with two digits.

```
PS > $xml.ContentDatabases.ContentDatabase | Format-List Name, NewName

Name    : WSS_Content
NewName : NimaIntra_ContentDB_01
```

```
Name    : WSS_Content2
NewName : NimaIntra_ContentDB_02
```

Finally, we can save the XML document as a file on a local disk.

```
PS > $xml.Save("E:\ContentDatabase.xml")
```

Detaching Content Databases

In Chapter 4, we looked at how to retrieve a list of all content databases connected to the farm or to a specific Web application using the Get-SPContentDatabase cmdlet, as well as how to detach a content database from a Web application using the Dismount-SPContentDatabase cmdlet. By piping the result from the Get-SPContentDatabase cmdlet to the Dismount-SPContentDatabase cmdlet, you can detach all content databases for a specific Web application with a simple command, as follows:

```
PS > Get-SPContentDatabases -WebApplication http://nimaintra.net |
>> Dismount-SPContentDatabase
```

In this example, we will detach a specific content database for demonstrative purposes.

```
PS > $cd | Dismount-SPContentDatabase -Confirm:$false
```

Now let us see how we can change the name of the database in the SQL Server instance.

Renaming Content Databases

Windows PowerShell offers the ability to connect to an instance of the Microsoft SQL Server service using an object of the type System.Data.SQLClient.SQLConnection, which supports execution of queries against a SQL Server database. The following Set-SQL function uses this feature to connect to a database and allow us to alter the name of a database in SQL Server.

```
function Set-SQL([string]$command, [string]$connectionString) {
  $connection = New-Object System.Data.SQLClient.SQLConnection;
  $connection.ConnectionString = $connectionString;
  $connection.Open();
  $sqlCommand = New-Object System.Data.SQLClient.SQLCommand;
  $sqlCommand.Connection = $Connection;
  $sqlCommand.CommandText = $command;
  $sqlCommand.ExecuteNonQuery();
  $connection.Close();
}
```

The function supports two parameters: command and connectionString. It commences by storing an object of type System.Data.SQLClient.SQLConnection in a variable. Next, the connection string provided is used as value for the ConnectionString property. The Open method is used to open a database connection using the information specified in the ConnectionString. Then we create an object of type System.Data.SQLClient.SQLCommand and use the connection variable as the value for the Connection parameter and the command variable as value for the CommandText parameter. When retrieving information from a database using a SELECT statement, the ExecuteReader() method is used, but since we want to actually modify a database, we use the ExecuteNonQuery() method instead. Finally, we close the connection using the Close method.

A connection string includes the target database name and other information needed to establish a connection. Let's take a look at a typical connection string using the value stored in the XML file we created earlier. First, we load the XML file into an object in Windows PowerShell, as shown here:

```
PS > $xml = New-Object System.Xml.XmlDocument
PS > $xml.Load("E:\ContentDatabase.xml")
```

Next, we store the elements in a variable, working with a single content database for this example.

```
PS > $xmlElement = $xml.ContentDatabases.ContentDatabase |
>> Where-Object { $_.Name -eq "WSS_Content" }
```

Now we use the value from the Server property as input to the connection string.

```
PS > $conn = "server=" +
>> $xmlElement.Server +
>> ";database=master;trusted_connection=true;"
```

Here's what the resulting connection string looks like:

```
PS > $conn
server=SQLServer01;database=master;trusted_connection=true;
```

First, we add a server name using the value stored in the Server property, and then we specify the database to use. Since we are going to alter the name of a database, we need to use the master database. Finally we add trusted_connection=true, since the SQL Server instance we are connecting to uses Integrated Windows Authentication.

TIP A good reference for other types of connection strings is available at www.connectionstrings.com.

To make changes to the database, we use the Transact-SQL statement ALTER DATABASE, which allows us to modify a database or the files and filegroups associated with a database. First, we set the Restrict Access setting on the content database to Single_User to get exclusive access, next we rename the database, and finally, we set Restrict Access back to Multi_User. Here is how we build up the command string:

```
PS > $command = "ALTER DATABASE " + $xmlElement.Name +
>> " SET SINGLE_USER WITH ROLLBACK IMMEDIATE; ALTER DATABASE " +
>> $xmlElement.Name + " MODIFY NAME = " +
>> $xmlElement.NewName + "; ALTER DATABASE " +
>> $xmlElement.NewName + " SET MULTI_USER"
```

And here's what the string looks like:

```
PS > $command
ALTER DATABASE WSS_Content set single_user with rollback immediate; ALTER
DATABASE WSS_Content MODIFY NAME = NimaIntra_ContentDB_01; ALTER DATABASE
NimaIntra_ContentDB_01 SET MULTI_USER
```

We can execute this Transact-SQL statement using the `Set-SQL` function.

```
PS > Set-SQL -command $command -connectionString $conn
-1
```

The output from the function is returned from the `ExecuteNonQuery()` method inside the function. When using UPDATE, INSERT, or DELETE statements, the value returned represents the number of rows affected. Other statements, such as ALTER, return –1.

NOTE Changing the database name as shown in this example does not change either the logical or the physical names of any of the database files. It is possible to use the ALTER DATABASE Transact-SQL statement to change these names as well. You can read more about the ALTER DATABASE statement at MSDN: http://msdn.microsoft.com/en-us/library/ms174269.aspx.

Reattaching Content Databases

The last step is to reattach the content database to the Web application using the `Mount-SPContentDatabase` cmdlet. In the following example, we use the information stored in the XML file as input to the cmdlet.

```
PS > Mount-SPContentDatabase $xmlElement.NewName -DatabaseServer `
>> $xmlElement.Server -WebApplication http://nimaintra.net `
>> -MaxSiteCount $xmlElement.MaxSiteLevel `
>> -WarningSiteCount $xmlElement.WarningSiteLevel -Confirm:$false
```

Scripting Content Database Renaming

The following Rename-SPContentDatabase.ps1 script puts together the previously described commands to automate renaming multiple content databases attached to a Web application. The script may need slight modifications to fit your environment.

```
param ([string]$webApplication, [string]$prefix, [string]$file)

function Set-SQL([string]$command, [string]$connectionString) {
  $connection = New-Object System.Data.SQLClient.SQLConnection;
```

```
    $connection.ConnectionString = $connectionString;
    $connection.Open();
    $sqlCommand = New-Object System.Data.SQLClient.SQLCommand;
    $sqlCommand.Connection = $Connection;
    $sqlCommand.CommandText = $command;
    $sqlCommand.ExecuteNonQuery();
    $connection.Close();
}

# Create xml template
[xml]$xml = "<ContentDatabases></ContentDatabases>"

# Store XML code in variable
$properties = @"
<Name>{0}</Name>
<NewName></NewName>
<MaxSiteLevel>{1}</MaxSiteLevel>
<WarningSiteLevel>{2}</WarningSiteLevel>
<DatabaseStatus>{3}</DatabaseStatus>
<Server>{4}</Server>
"@

# Enumerate content databases in Web application
Get-SPContentDatabase -WebApplication $webApplication | ForEach-Object {

    # Create new XML element
    $element = $xml.CreateElement("ContentDatabase");
    $element.InnerXml = $properties -f $_.Name, $_.MaximumSiteCount,
    $_.WarningSiteCount, $_.Status, $_.Server;

    # Append element to the document
    [void]$xml["ContentDatabases"].AppendChild($element);

    # Detach Content Database
    Dismount-SPContentDatabase -Identity $_.ID -Confirm:$false;
} # end ForEach

# Loop through the content databases in the XML file
for ($i=0; $i -lt ([array]$xml.ContentDatabases.ContentDatabase).Count; $i++) {

    # Pick content database to process
    $cd = ([array]$xml.ContentDatabases.ContentDatabase)[$i];

    # Create connection string using Windows integrated authentication
    $connection = "server=" + $cd.Server +
    ";database=master;trusted_connection=true;"

    # Calculate content database's new name
    $newName = $prefix + "_{0:d2}" -f $($i + 1);
```

```
# Update XML document
$cd.NewName = $newName;

# Set the Restrict Access to Single_User
# Rename the database to the new name
# Set the Restrict Access to Multi_User

$command = "ALTER DATABASE " + $cd.Name +
" SET SINGLE_USER WITH ROLLBACK IMMEDIATE; ALTER DATABASE " +
$cd.Name + " MODIFY NAME =" +
$cd.newName+"; ALTER DATABASE " +
$cd.newName+" SET MULTI_USER";

# Apply changes SQL
Set-SQL -command $command -connectionString $connection | Out-Null;
# Attach content database with new name
Mount-SPContentDatabase $cd.NewName -DatabaseServer $cd.Server `
-WebApplication $webApplication -MaxSiteCount $cd.MaxSiteLevel `
-WarningSiteCount $cd.WarningSiteLevel -Confirm:$false;
}

# Save XML to file on disk for reference
if ($file) {
  $xml.Save($file);
}
```

You can use the script to rename multiple content databases in a Web application by typing the following:

```
PS > .\Rename-SPContentDatabases.ps1 `
>> -WebApplication http://workspaces.nima.net `
>> -prefix SharePoint_Workspace_ContentDB -file e:\ContentDatabases.xml
```

This example changes the names of all content databases in a Web application to standardized names and outputs an XML file containing specific content database information.

Setting Up Remote BLOB Storage

RBS is a set of APIs available as an add-on feature pack for the Microsoft SQL Server 2008. It allows storage and retrieval of BLOBs outside SQL database files. By storing BLOBs outside a content database, you can significantly decrease the size of your database, which is key when it comes to successful storage optimization of large SharePoint farms. One of the main benefits of moving BLOBs to a storage solution is the opportunity to reduce the total cost of ownership (TCO) for the SharePoint environment.

SharePoint 2010 supports the RBS FILESTREAM provider, which is included in the SQL Server Remote BLOB Store installation package. The RBS FILESTREAM provider uses the SQL Server FILESTREAM that stores BLOB content on the local file system.

 NOTE The FILESTREAM provider included in Microsoft SQL Server 2008 offers only a small amount of the functionality available within the RBS API. For instance, you can save BLOBs only to the local disk. Other RBS providers allow you to save BLOBs to any type of media. One such provider is the free DocAve Extender from AvePoint (www.avepoint.com), which offers a wide range of functions and allows you to set up rules for how and where BLOBs should be stored.

Configuring the Database to Use RBS

First, you need to enable the FILESTREAM provider on SQL Server. In the SQL Server Configuration Manager console, select the SQL Server Services node (on the left side of the window), right-click the SQL Server service instance for which you want to enable the FILESTREAM provider, and select Properties. In the dialog box, select the FILESTREAM tab, select the Enable FILESTREAM for Transact-SQL access check box, and specify the name of a file share to use, as shown in Figure 20-1.

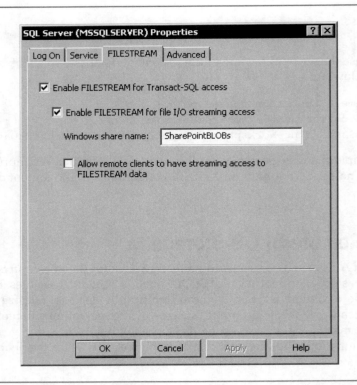

Figure 20-1. Enabling the FILESTREAM provider on a SQL Server instance

Next, you need to set the correct access level. In the following example, we use the Set-SQL function we created earlier in this chapter to set the FILESTREAM access level to 2, which enables Transact-SQL and allows Win32 APIs to work with the files.

```
PS > $conn =
>> "server=SQLServer01;database=NimaIntra_ContentDB_01;trusted_connection=true;"

PS > $command = "EXEC sp_configure filestream_access_level, 2 RECONFIGURE"

PS > Set-SQL -command $command -connectionString $conn
```

After the FILESTREAM provider is enabled and the access level is set to 2, we can provision a BLOB store.

First, we check if a master key exists. If not, we create one with a specific password, as demonstrated here:

```
PS > $command = "IF NOT EXISTS (SELECT * FROM sys.symmetric_keys " +
>> "WHERE name = N'##MS_DatabaseMasterKey##') CREATE master key encryption " +
>> "BY password = N'P@ssw0rd'"
PS > Set-SQL -command $command -connectionString $conn
```

Next, we add a new filegroup, specifying CONTAINS FILESTREAM.

```
PS > $command = "IF NOT EXISTS (SELECT groupname FROM sysfilegroups WHERE " +
>> "groupname=N'RBSFSProvider')ALTER DATABASE [NimaIntra_ContentDB_01] " +
>> "ADD FILEGROUP RBSFSProvider CONTAINS FILESTREAM"
PS > Set-SQL -command $command -connectionString $conn
```

The last step is to add a virtual file to the newly created filegroup and associate it with a directory on the local file system. Note that the lowest level directory specified in the path must not exist. The folder will be created by the Transact-SQL command.

```
PS > $command = "alter database [NimaIntra_ContentDB_01] add file " +
>> "(name = RBSFSFile, filename = 'C:\Blobstore') to filegroup RBSFSProvider"
PS > Set-SQL -command $command -connectionString $conn
```

The database is now configured to use RBS.

Installing the RBS Provider

Now you need to install the RBS provider on all the Web servers in the SharePoint 2010 farm. Download the RBS.msi from the SQL Server 2008 R2 Feature Pack, at http://go.microsoft.com/fwlink/?LinkID=177388.

Next, run the following command on the first Web server to start the installation.

```
PS > msiexec /qn /l*v C:\BLOB\Install_log.txt /i C:\BLOB\RBS.msi
TRUSTSERVERCERTIFICATE=true FILEGROUP=PRIMARY DBNAME="NimaIntra_ContentDB_01"
DBINSTANCE="sqlserver01" FILESTREAMFILEGROUP=RBSFSProvider
FILESTREAMSTORENAME=FILESTREAM_Blob_Store
```

This has the Microsoft Installer program install the RBS provider on the Web server. We use the following parameters in this example:

- We set the UI level using the /qn parameter, so that a silent installation is performed.
- We specify that a log file should be created and that the log file should contain all available information, including verbose output, by using the /l*v parameter followed by the path to the log file.
- We use the /i parameter and specify the path to the package that should be installed.
- We set TRUSTSERVERCERTIFICATE to true so that connecting clients trust the self-signed certificate for encrypted connections initiated by RBS.
- The FILEGROUP parameter sets the filegroup for internal tables.
- The DBNAME parameter indicates which database to use—the NimaIntra_ContentDB_01 database in this example.
- The DBINSTANCE parameter points to the SQL Server instance.
- We specify the FILESTREAM BLOB store filegroup using the FILESTREAMFILEGROUP parameter, pointing it to the FILESTREAM group created in an earlier example.
- We set a new FILESTREAM store name with the FILESTREAMSTORENAME parameter.

The command can take a while to complete. If you want to wait until the command completes, you can use the Get-Process and Wait-Process cmdlets supported by Windows PowerShell, as follows:

```
PS > Get-Process msiexec | Wait-Process
```

The RBS provider also needs to be installed on all additional Web front end servers. Since the connection to the FILESTREAM group already exists, we specify the components to install using the ADDLOCAL parameter.

```
PS > msiexec /qn /l*v C:\BLOB\Install_log.txt /i C:\BLOB\RBS.msi
DBNAME="NimaIntra_ContentDB_01" DBINSTANCE="sqlserver01"
ADDLOCAL="Client,Docs,Maintainer,ServerScript,
FilestreamClient,FilestreamServer"
```

Enabling RBS in SharePoint 2010

The final step is to enable RBS in SharePoint 2010. First, use the Get-SPContentDatabase cmdlet to return a database.

```
PS > $contentDB = Get-SPContentDatabase -Identity NimaIntra_ContentDB_01
```

The BLOB storage settings can be configured using the `RemoteBlobStorageSettings` property. The `SPRemoteBlobStorageSettings` object associated with this property supports the `Installed()` method, which we can use to check if the SQL Server RBS is installed on the content database.

```
PS > $spRBSSettings = $contentDB.RemoteBlobStorageSettings
PS > $spRBSSettings.Installed()
True
```

Before we enable the resources required to use RBS, we set the value of the `ActiveProviderName` property to the SQL Server RBS provider—`FILESTREAM_Blob_Store` in this example.

```
PS > $spRBSSettings.SetActiveProviderName("FILESTREAM_Blob_Store")
```

If you are uncertain of the SQL Server RBS provider name, you can use the `GetProviderNames()` method to display the names of all SQL Server RBS providers registered on the content database.

```
PS > $spRBSSettings.GetProviderNames()
FILESTREAM_Blob_Store
```

Finally, we enable the resources required to use RBS using the `Enable()` method.

```
PS > $spRBSSettings.Enable()
```

It is also possible to set the minimum size of BLOBs stored in the BLOB store using the `MinimumBlobStorageSize` parameter. By default, the value is set to 0, meaning that all BLOBs are stored in the BLOB store. You can change the value so that only BLOBs larger than a specific size are stored in the BLOB store by supplying a new value as number of bytes. In the following example, we set the value to 250KB so that BLOBs larger than 250KB are stored in the BLOB store and BLOBs smaller than 250KB are stored in the content database.

```
PS > $spRBSSettings.MinimumBlobStorageSize = 250KB
```

Note that we use the multiplier suffix KB to represent the value in kilobytes. Other supported multiplier suffixes are MB and GB.

To disable RBS on a content database, simply set the provider name to an empty string using the `SetActiveProviderName()` method, as shown here:

```
PS > $contentDB = Get-SPContentDatabase -Identity NimaIntra_ContentDB_01
PS > $spRBSSettings = $contentDB.RemoteBlobStorageSettings
PS > $spRBSSettings.SetActiveProviderName([string]::Empty)
```

Additional Functionality in SharePoint 2010

You can attach and detach content databases from the Central Administration site, but it does not allow you to rename the databases. To do that, you would need to detach the content databases manually one by one, change their names on the SQL Server instance, and then attach them with the new names.

When adding content databases to SharePoint, SharePoint will first check if a database with the specified name already exists. If the existing database has no user-defined schema (that is, it is empty) or has a SharePoint-compatible schema, SharePoint will try to attach it. If SharePoint does not find the database on the specified SQL Server instance, it will create the database for you.

The only way to control storage from Central Administration is to specify the maximum amount of site collections that should be stored in the content database. This will not limit the size of the content database, unless you are using site quotas on your site collections.

Summary

In this chapter, we first demonstrated how to go outside SharePoint, connect to a SQL Server instance, and used Windows PowerShell to run queries against content databases. We stored the information about the configuration of some content databases in an XML file and used SharePoint cmdlets to detach and reattach the databases. This example really demonstrated the power of Windows PowerShell. It showed that you can work with SQL Server, XML files, and SharePoint within one and the same script.

In the second scenario, we looked at how to enable a content database to use RBS by installing the RBS FILESTREAM provider included in the Microsoft SQL Server 2008 R2 Feature Pack. We then enabled RBS using Windows PowerShell and showed how to change vital RBS settings.

CHAPTER 21 | Backup and Restore

In this last chapter of the book, we will look at the options for backup and restore of SharePoint 2010 data using Windows PowerShell. As we have mentioned earlier, backup and restore operations has been significantly improved in SharePoint 2010, offering administrators much more granularity and better tools to quickly recover from disasters or unintentional deletion of content.

Windows PowerShell cmdlets are available for backup and restore of items such as farm configuration, content databases, and Web applications. The import and export cmdlets offer granular backup and restore options in SharePoint 2010.

The new unattached content database feature of SharePoint 2010 lets you connect a content database to your farm without attaching it to any specific Web application. This makes it possible to export items such as sites or lists for restoration purposes, without interfering with any of the Web applications running on the farm. In SharePoint 2007, you needed a different "stand-by" farm to be able to accomplish these tasks. In the last scenario, we will connect an unattached content database and demonstrate how to export sites and lists using only Windows PowerShell.

Backing Up and Restoring SharePoint Farms

One of the most anticipated features when it comes to backup and restore of data in SharePoint 2010 is the possibility to back up and restore the configuration settings of a farm. This allows you to not only restore the farm configuration in case of a disaster, but it also enables you to create a template with standardized settings to use when installing new farms within the company or when provisioning new staging environments. To perform a configuration-only backup of our farm, use the `Backup-SPConfigurationDatabase` cmdlet.

```
PS> Backup-SPConfigurationDatabase -Directory \\SPServer01\Backup\ `
>> -DatabaseServer SPServer01 -DatabaseName SharePoint_NimaIntra_ConfigDB
```

`Backup-SPConfigurationDatabase` backs up just the configuration settings, not the actual configuration database itself. This also means that items such as content databases, Web applications, and service applications are not backed up.

NOTE   You can also perform a back up of the farm configuration settings using the `Backup-SPFarm` cmdlet with the `ConfigurationOnly` switch. Like `Backup-SPConfigurationDatabase`, this backs up only the configuration settings, not the configuration database.

To restore a farm configuration, use the `Restore-SPFarm` cmdlet with the `ConfigurationOnly` parameter, and then simply point to the location where the backup is stored. If the backup location contains more than one farm configuration, you can point to a specific backup instance using the `BackupId` parameter. If a parameter is omitted, the cmdlet will automatically use the latest backup instance available. In the following example, we restore the configuration settings to the same farm using the `RestoreMethod` parameter with the value `Overwrite`.

```
PS> Restore-SPFarm -Directory \\SPServer01\Backup\ -RestoreMethod Overwrite `
>> -ConfigurationOnly -BackupId 478ecd4b-e519-4c22-bb62-29b4a89d28d8
```

To create a new farm with the same configuration settings, change the `RestoreMethod` value to `New` and add the parameter `NewDatabaseServer` to specify the SQL Server instance to use as the default instance for the new farm.

```
PS> Restore-SPFarm -Directory \\SPServer01\Backup\ -RestoreMethod New `
>> -ConfigurationOnly -NewDatabaseServer SQLServer02
```

The `Backup-SPFarm` cmdlet allows you to back up the entire SharePoint farm. You can also specify a particular Web application or content database. The `Backup-SPFarm` cmdlet has the very useful `ShowTree` parameter, which returns a hierarchical list of all the objects that you could back up individually as an alternative to doing a full farm backup. Using the `Item` parameter, you can then select the object that you want to back up. In the next example, we select the Web applications in the farm, and since we use the `ShowTree` parameter, the cmdlet will display a list of objects that will be backed up if this item is selected.

```
PS> Backup-SPFarm -ShowTree `
>> -Item "Microsoft SharePoint Foundation Web Application"
```

The next example retrieves all the Web applications using the `Get-SPWebApplication` cmdlet and pipes the results to the `ForEach-Object` cmdlet, which executes the `Backup-SPFarm` cmdlet using the current pipeline object as the value for the `Item` parameter. We also specify that we want to use a full backup and set the amount of threads to be used to ten (the default is three, and up to ten threads are supported).

```
PS> Get-SPWebApplication | ForEach-Object {
>> Backup-SPFarm -directory \\SPServer01\Backup\ `
>> -BackupMethod Full -item $_.DisplayName `
>> -BackupThreads 10 }
```

The `Backup-SPFarm` cmdlet also supports creating a backup of a specific content database. The first time you make a backup of a content database, you must choose `full` as backup method. As soon as you have a full backup of a content database, you can perform differential backups by specifying `differential` as the backup method. The next example demonstrates how to back up a specific content database using the `Item` parameter, indicates where to store the backup using the `Directory` parameter, and performs a full backup using the `BackupMethod` parameter.

```
PS > Backup-SPFarm -Directory \\spserver01\Backup\ -BackupMethod full `
>> -Item NimaIntra_ContentDB_01
```

You can view all the backup operations that have been performed using the `Get-SPBackupHistory` cmdlet. In the following example, we indicate the location of the backup files using the `Directory` parameter.

```
PS > Get-SPBackupHistory -Directory \\spserver01\Backup\
```

The cmdlet displays a list of all backups that have been performed. It also displays a GUID of each backup instance, which you can use when restoring the backup, as demonstrated here:

```
PS > Restore-SPFarm -Directory \\spserver01\Backup\ `
>> -RestoreMethod Overwrite -Item NimaIntra_ContentDB_01 `
>> -BackupId 87e466e2-7104-45e4-a6ce-4b1f2a670bc7
```

Creating Database Snapshots

In SharePoint 2010, you can create database snapshots of content databases using Windows PowerShell. A *database snapshot* is a read-only copy of a database as it was at the moment the snapshot was taken. Snapshots are very useful in backup and restore scenarios.

NOTE   Database snapshots are available only in the Enterprise and Developer editions of Microsoft SQL Server.

In the following example, we create a snapshot using the `CreateSnapshot()` method of the `SPContentDatabase` object.

```
PS > $contentDB = Get-SPContentDatabase -Identity NimaIntra_ContentDB_01
PS > $contentDB.Snapshots.CreateSnapshot()
```

Snapshots are always located on the same database server as the source database. Snapshots can also be used when recovering data from unattached content databases, as discussed later in this chapter.

Exporting and Importing Sites, Lists, and List Items

You can export sites, lists, and list items using the `Export-SPWeb` cmdlet. Here's a one-line command that exports a site, including all versions of all lists and libraries:

```
PS> Export-SPWeb http://nimaintra.net/finance -path "e:\backup\finance.cmp" `
>> -IncludeVersions All -IncludeUserSecurity -NoFileCompression
```

This example also exports the security settings (which contain information about when and by whom objects has been created and modified). We use the

-NoFileCompression switch parameter to ignore the default compression. This is mainly for performance improvement and is recommended when exporting larger sites.

Another option that could be useful when exporting large objects is to use the -UseSqlSnapshot parameter, which will create a temporary SQL Server database snapshot when the process starts and perform the export from the snapshot. When the export is finished, the temporary snapshot is deleted.

If you want to perform a backup on each site in a site collection, you can loop through a site collection using the ForEach-Object cmdlet.

```
PS > $folder = "\\SPServer\Backup\"
PS > Get-SPSite -Identity http://SPServer | Get-SPWeb |
>> ForEach-Object {
>> Export-SPWeb -Identity $_ `
>> -Path ($folder + ($_.Url -Replace "^(http|https)://{2}",
>> "" -Replace "/","_")) -Force

>>}
```

In this example, we use the replace operator and test if the value of $_.Url starts with http or https, followed by the : character and two / characters. If a match is made, the pattern is replaced. We also test if the value contains the character / and replace it with the _ character. The Force switch parameter is also used to ensure that existing backup files are overwritten.

The Export-SPWeb cmdlet can also export lists and libraries. To do this, use the ItemUrl parameter and specify the relative URL to the list or library.

```
PS> Export-SPWeb http://nimaintra.net/finance -path "e:\backup\Calendar.cmp" `
>> -ItemUrl /finance/lists/Calendar -IncludeVersions All -IncludeUserSecurity
```

To import objects that have been exported from Central Administration or by using the Export-SPWeb cmdlet, use the Import-SPWeb cmdlet. The following example imports the Finance site we exported in our previous example.

```
PS> Import-SPWeb http://nimaintra.net/finance -Path e:\backup\Finance.cmp `
>> -IncludeUserSecurity -NoFileCompression
```

NOTE When importing sites using the Import-SPWeb cmdlet, the URL you specify needs to be a site based on the same template type as the one you exported. If the site does not exist or if it uses a different template, the import will not work.

When importing lists and libraries, the Import-SPWeb cmdlet creates a new version of each item by default. Suppose that we have a list with thousands of items, and we've accidentally deleted five items that we want to restore. To address this problem, the `Import-SPWeb` cmdlet has an `-UpdateVersions` parameter, which we can set to `Ignore` to import only items that do not exist in the list.

```
PS> Import-SPWeb http://nimaintra.net -Path e:\backup\Documents.cmp `
>> -IncludeUserSecurity -UpdateVersions Ignore
```

The other possible values for the `-UpdateVersions` parameter are `Append` and `Overwrite`.

The `Export-SPWeb` cmdlet has quite a few other parameters. To display all the available parameters, type the following:

```
PS > Get-Help Export-SPWeb -Parameter *
```

Restoring Data from an Unattached Content Database

Unattached content databases make it possible to connect content databases to a farm without affecting any of the Web applications. To add a content database as unattached, use the `Get-SPContentDatabase` cmdlet with the `-ConnectAsUnattachedDatabase` switch.

```
PS> $contentDB = Get-SPContentDatabase -DatabaseServer SQLServer01 `
>> -DatabaseName NimaIntra_ContentDB_01_Backup `
>> -ConnectAsUnattachedDatabase
```

This example will store an instance of a `SPContentDatabase` object in the variable `contentDB`, which will allow us to work with the content inside the corresponding content database. The database could also be a snapshot, as discussed earlier in the chapter.

Windows PowerShell does not include a cmdlet that exports sites, lists, or libraries from an unattached content database or snapshot, but that does not make it impossible to export such items. Here, we'll go through the procedure, and then wrap it up in a function.

First, we create an instance of an `SPExport` object.

```
PS > $spExport = New-Object Microsoft.SharePoint.Deployment.SPExport
```

The `SPExportSettings` class—an instance of which is the value of the `SPExport` object's `Settings` property—has a parameter called `UnattachedContentDatabase`, which enables us to target our unattached content database or snapshot.

```
PS > $spExport.Settings.UnattachedContentDatabase = $contentDB
```

We must set the absolute URL of the site that we want to restore, so we first need to find that information. We can retrieve a specific site collection stored in the unattached content database using the `Sites` property.

```
PS > $spSite = $contentDB.Sites["/"]
```

Next, we use the `AllWebs` property to retrieve a specific site in the site collection and use the site's full URL as input to the `SiteUrl` parameter.

```
PS > $SPExport.Settings.SiteUrl= $spSite.AllWebs["/finance"].Url
```

We also set the file name and the location of the file, and choose to include the security settings.

```
PS > $spExport.Settings.BaseFilename = "Finance.cab"
PS > $spExport.Settings.FileLocation = "e:\backup\"
PS > $spExport.Settings.IncludeSecurity = "All"
```

There are additional properties that you can set to manage the export settings. To display all of the available properties, type the following:

```
PS > $spExport.Settings
```

Finally, we initiate the export operation using the `Run()` method.

```
PS > $spExport.Run()
```

This example generates a file containing a backup of the Finance site. We can import the site using the `Import-SPWeb` cmdlet.

```
PS> Import-SPWeb http://nimaintra.net/finance -Path e:\backup\Finance.cab `
>> -IncludeUserSecurity -NoFileCompression
```

It is also possible to export subsites, lists, and even items. The following function demonstrates how to export a single list from an unattached content database.

```
function Export-SPUnattachedList(
  [string]$contentDatabase,
  [string]$databaseServer,
  [string]$site,
  [string]$web,
  [string]$list,
  [string]$file,
  [switch]$showSite,
  [switch]$showWeb,
  [switch]$showList
) {

  $ContentDB = Get-SPContentDatabase -DatabaseServer $DatabaseServer `
  -DatabaseName $ContentDatabase -ConnectAsUnattachedDatabase

  if($showSite) {
    # Return site collections
    $contentDB.Sites |
      Select-Object -Property `
```

```
        @{Name="RelativeURL";Expression={([uri]$_.Url).AbsolutePath}}
    Break
}
# Get site collection
$spSite = $contentDB.Sites[$site]
if($showWeb) {
  # Return sites
  $spSite.AllWebs |
    Select-Object -Property `
      @{Name="RelativeURL";Expression={([uri]$_.Url).AbsolutePath}}
  Break
}

# Get site
$spWeb = $spSite.OpenWeb($web)
if($showList) {
  $spWeb.Lists |
    Select-Object -Property @{Name="List";Expression={$_.Title}}
  Break
}

# Check folder
if(-not(Test-Path (Split-Path $file))) {
  New-Item -path (Split-Path $file) -type directory | Out-Null
}
# Check if file already exists
if(Test-Path $file) {
  Write-Host "File $file already exists."
  Break
}
$spList = $spWeb.Lists[$list]

$spExportObject = New-Object Microsoft.SharePoint.Deployment.SPExportObject
$spExportObject.ID = $SPList.ID
$spExportObject.Type = "List"

$spExport = New-Object Microsoft.SharePoint.Deployment.SPExport
# Add content database
$spExport.Settings.UnattachedContentDatabase = $ContentDB
# Add object type
$spExport.Settings.ExportObjects.Add($spExportObject)
# Add site collection URL
$spExport.Settings.SiteUrl= $spSite.URL
# Set additional properties
$spExport.Settings.BaseFilename = (Split-Path $file -Leaf)
$spExport.Settings.FileLocation = (Split-Path $file)
$spExport.Settings.LogFilePath = ($file -Replace "\..*","-log.txt")
$spExport.Settings.IncludeSecurity = "All"
```

```
        $spExport.Settings.IncludeVersions = "All"
        # Initiate export operation
        $spExport.Run()

        # Dispose objects
        $spWeb.Dispose()
        $spSite.Dispose()
        $spExport.Dispose()
}
```

You can run the function by typing the following:

```
PS > Export-SPUnattachedList -contentDatabase NimaIntra_ContentDB_01_Backup `
>> -databaseServer SQLServer01 -site "/" -web /finance `
>> -list Announcements -file C:\Backup\finance.cab
```

If you are uncertain of the site collections available, you can use the showSite switch parameter:

```
PS > Export-SPUnattachedList -contentDatabase NimaIntra_ContentDB_01_Backup `
>> -databaseServer SQLServer01 -showSite
```

If you know the site collection but want to find out which sites and subsites are available in the unattached content database, use the showWeb switch parameter.

```
PS > Export-SPUnattachedList -contentDatabase NimaIntra_ContentDB_01_Backup `
>> -databaseServer SQLServer01 -site "/" -showWeb
```

Finally, if you want to find out which lists are available on a site stored in an unattached content database, you can use the showList switch parameter.

```
PS > Export-SPUnattachedList -contentDatabase NimaIntra_ContentDB_01_Backup `
>> -databaseServer SQLServer01 -site "/" -web /finance -showList
```

 NOTE Backup and restore operations might affect the performance of your SharePoint 2010 environment. It is recommended that you perform them outside business hours.

Additional Functionality in SharePoint 2010

The options to manage backup and restore from Central Administration have been significantly improved in SharePoint 2010. The granular backup has its own category in the Central Administration site, and from there it is possible to not only to export sites or lists, but also to recover data from unattached content databases. From the graphical user interface, you are able to browse down to the list level of an unattached content database and export it to a file share, as shown in Figure 21-1. However, importing the

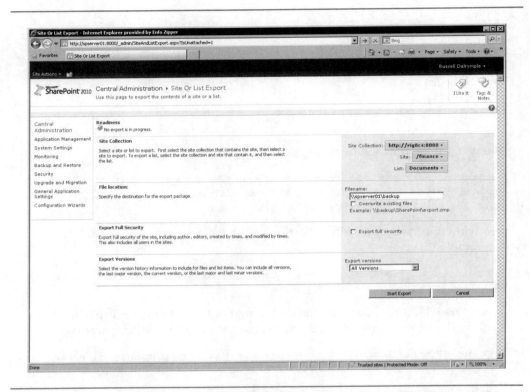

Figure 21-1.   Recovering data from an unattached content database in Central Administration

exported content is not possible from the graphical user interface—that needs to be done using Windows PowerShell.

You can both back up and restore content from the Central Administration site. As shown in Figure 21-2, you can select exactly what you want to back up from a tree view. However, it is still not possible to schedule backups from the Central Administration.

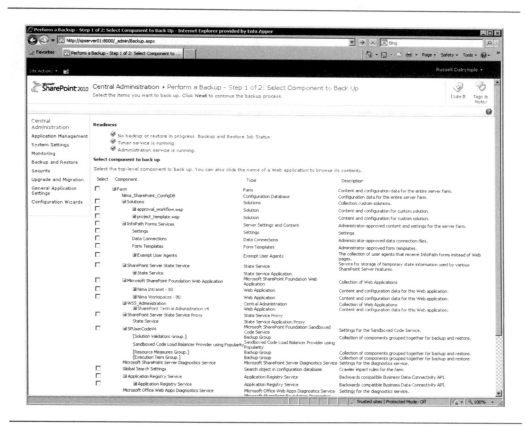

Figure 21-2. Backing up content from Central Administration

Summary

Backup and restore functions have been improved on all levels in SharePoint 2010. In this chapter, we looked at the various cmdlets available for performing backup and restore operations at the farm, Web application, and site collection level. The `Backup-SPConfigurationDatabase` cmdlet makes it possible to back up the farm's configuration settings and restore them either to the same farm or use them as a template for provisioning new farms.

We also covered how to use Windows PowerShell to connect an unattached content database, and then export sites and lists and restore them using the granular restore options available in SharePoint 2010.

Index

Practical Guides for Microsoft SharePoint 2010 Users of Every Level

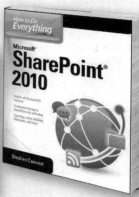
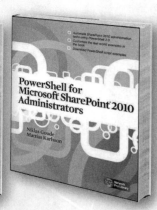